REFUGEE JOURNEYS

HISTORIES OF RESETTLEMENT, REPRESENTATION AND RESISTANCE

REFUGEE JOURNEYS

HISTORIES OF RESETTLEMENT, REPRESENTATION AND RESISTANCE

EDITED BY JORDANA SILVERSTEIN AND RACHEL STEVENS

Australian
National
University

PRESS

ANU PRESS

Published by ANU Press
The Australian National University
Acton ACT 2601, Australia
Email: anupress@anu.edu.au

Available to download for free at press.anu.edu.au

ISBN (print): 9781760464189
ISBN (online): 9781760464196

WorldCat (print): 1232438634
WorldCat (online): 1232438632

DOI: 10.22459/RJ.2021

Cover design and layout by ANU Press. Cover artwork: Zohreh Izadikia, *Freedom*, 2018, Melbourne Artists for Asylum Seekers.

CONTENTS

Part III: Understanding refugee histories and futures

ACKNOWLEDGEMENTS

This volume originated in the Global Histories of Refugees conference organised by Professor Joy Damousi in 2016. We are grateful to her, and her leadership in the Kathleen Fitzpatrick Laureate Research Project in which we worked, as well as to our other colleagues on the project, whose intellectual engagement over the five years enabled this work to be produced: Dr Mary Tomsic, Dr Alexandra Dellios, Dr Niro Kandasamy, Dr Sarah Green and Dr Anh Ngyuen.

Additionally, we want to thank ANU Press and Professor Frank Bongiorno and the Social Sciences Editorial Board for their support of the project, as well as our wonderful copyeditor, Beth Battrick.

Finally, we send a big thanks to our dedicated authors for their efforts to bring this volume together.

Funding to support this edited collection was provided by the Australian Research Council, ARC FL140100049, 'Child Refugees and Australian Internationalism from 1920 to the Present'.

CONTRIBUTORS

Melanie Baak is a research fellow and senior lecturer with University of South Australia Education Futures and co-convenor of the Migration and Refugee Research Network (MARRNet). In recent research projects she has collaborated with refugee background communities to explore areas including belonging, education and employment. She is currently a chief investigator on an Australian Research Council (ARC) Linkage project exploring how schools foster refugee student resilience. Her book *Negotiating Belongings: Stories of Forced Migration of Dinka Women from South Sudan* (Sense, 2016) considers how forced migration shapes experiences of belonging. Melanie was awarded an Endeavour Research Fellowship to the University of Glasgow in 2017 where she researched schools as sites of resettlement for Syrian refugees.

Ann-Kathrin Bartels earned her postgraduate degrees in European history, English and education at the Carl von Ossietzky University Oldenburg, Germany. Her research focuses on the stereotyping of asylum seekers and refugees and its meaning for the concept of national identity. Influenced by having lived and studied in both Germany and Australia, Ann-Kathrin is interested in contrasting both countries' stances towards asylum seekers. Her other research projects have examined the Sino–Soviet border conflict in 1969. Ann-Kathrin currently lives and works in London.

Kathleen Blair has recently completed her PhD at Western Sydney University. Her doctoral work explores the use of anti–asylum seeker talk in Australian election campaigns and the impact this talk has on both the attitudes and voter behaviour of Australians. Kathleen has been a research assistant on the Challenging Racism Project since 2013 and has conducted extensive research on racism and anti-racism, bystander anti-racism and Islamophobia in Australia. Most notably, she was a lead researcher on the 'Face Up to Racism: 2015–2016 National Survey' that investigated the extent and variation of racist attitudes and experiences of racism in Australia.

André Dao is a writer of fiction and non-fiction. He is the co-founder of Behind the Wire, an oral history project documenting people's experience of immigration detention, a producer of *The Messenger* podcast and coeditor of *They Cannot Take the Sky* (Allen & Unwin, 2017).

Jamila Jafari is a Hazara from central Afghanistan. The Hazara people have been fighting for recognition and justice for over a century. A university student, Jamila came to know about Behind the Wire and wanted to share her story to highlight the stark realities of immigration detention in Australia.

Eve Lester is an Australian Research Council DECRA Fellow, ANU College of Law, The Australian National University, and an Associate Member of the Institute for International Law and the Humanities at Melbourne Law School. Her background includes legal practice, policy, research and advocacy in Australia and internationally. She is the author of *Making Migration Law: The Foreigner, Sovereignty and the Case of Australia* (CUP, 2018), and a significant number of book chapters, journal articles, and organisational research and opinion. She is also the Founder of Boniĝi Monitoring and a Myer Innovation Fellow.

Laurel Mackenzie writes and teaches on gender, policy and migration. She has delivered courses investigating the construction of the self in different settings, and wrote her masters' thesis on the self-construction of antebellum women in the 1860s. Her interest in the interrelation of self and policy led to her writing a PhD on the narrative self-construction of post-settlement refugee Hazaras who came to Australia in 2001 and 2010, where she drew on her participants' lived experiences to critique policy. Her current research focuses on the implications of a shifting political care ethic on people with refugee experiences.

Klaus Neumann works for the Hamburg Foundation for the Advancement of Research and Culture. He has written extensively about cultures and pasts in the Pacific Islands, Australia, New Zealand and Germany. His books include, among others, *Refuge Australia*, winner of the 2004 Human Rights Award for non-fiction, and *Across the Seas*, winner of the 2016 CHASS Australia Prize. Klaus has been particularly interested in historical justice, responses to refugees and asylum seekers, and issues of social and public memory. His current research focuses on local public and policy responses to forced migration in Saxony and Hamburg.

Jordana Silverstein is a historian based in Naarm/Melbourne, affiliated with the School of Historical and Philosophical Studies at the University of Melbourne and the Department of Archaeology and History at La Trobe University. The granddaughter of Holocaust survivors and refugees, she researches histories of child refugee policy, as well as of Jewish sexuality and Holocaust memory, in Australia. Jordana is the author of *Anxious Histories: Narrating the Holocaust in Jewish Communities at the Beginning of the Twenty-First Century* (Berghahn, 2015) and coeditor of *In the Shadows of Memory: The Holocaust and the Third Generation* (Vallentine Mitchell, 2016).

Rachel Stevens is a contemporary refugee historian based at the Institute of Humanities and Social Sciences at the Australian Catholic University in Naarm/Melbourne, Australia. She is the author of *Immigration Policy from 1970 to the Present* (Routledge, 2016) and her articles have appeared in *Australian Historical Studies, History Australia, Immigrants and Minorities, Australian Journal of Politics and History* and *Teaching in Higher Education*. She served as guest editor (with Professor Joy Damousi) of the special issue of 'Refugees: Past and Present' in the *Australian Journal of Politics and History* (December 2019).

Savitri Taylor is an associate professor in the Law School at La Trobe University (Melbourne, Australia). She has been researching and publishing on refugee law and asylum policy at the national, regional and international level for over 25 years. Her current major research project (in partnership with Dr Klaus Neumann) is titled 'Protecting Non-Citizens: An Australian legal and political history, 1945–1989'. Dr Taylor is also very involved with the refugee sector in Australia. Most recently (2019), she partnered with the Refugee Council of Australia to publish a research report entitled *The Use of Non-Judicial Accountability Mechanisms by the Refugee Sector in Australia*.

REFUGEE JOURNEYS

Jordana Silverstein and Rachel Stevens[1]

During the Academics for Refugees National Day of Action on 17 October 2018, Behrouz Boochani – 'a Kurdish writer, film maker, scholar and journalist' – issued a statement calling on academics across Australia to act:

> academics have a really important role in researching this policy of exile and exposing it. What I believe from living through this policy and experiencing this prison camp firsthand is that we are only able to understand it in a philosophical and historical way. Definitely Manus and Nauru prison camps are philosophical and political phenomena and we should not view them superficially. The best way to examine them is through deep research into how a human, in this case a refugee, is forced to live between the law and a situation without laws.[2]

In May 2013, Boochani had fled his homeland, Iran, to seek asylum in Australia. As a politically active Kurdish journalist, Boochani faced persecution from the Islamic Revolutionary Guard and likely imprisonment. Once in Indonesia, Boochani embarked on the treacherous sea crossing to northern Australia. His first attempt failed; in his second attempt in July 2013, his boat was intercepted by the Royal Australian Navy and he, along with 60 other asylum seekers, was transported and detained on Christmas Island, a ravaged 135 km² Australian territory in the Indian Ocean that is far closer to Indonesia than mainland Australia.

1   This chapter was written with funding provided by the Australian Research Council Laureate Research Fellowship Project FL140100049, 'Child Refugees and Australian Internationalism from 1920 to the Present'.
2   Behrouz Boochani, 'Statement from Behrouz Boochani in Support of the Academics for Refugees National Day of Action, 17 October 2018', NDA Public Read-Ins, Academics for Refugees, available at: academicsforrefugees.wordpress.com/nda-public-read-ins/?fbclid=IwAR2ZGL1CJIvvGt YKo5vyG-rfVpcQ9_SR61orz6t19I3UMnL3eA-BruEide0.

After one month, in August Boochani was relocated to Manus Island, Papua New Guinea. These precise dates are important. By virtue of Boochani's decision (or forced decision) to seek refuge in Australia in mid-2013, he inadvertently became ensnared in the Machiavellian machinations that characterised the Australian domestic political landscape throughout the 2010s and an increasingly punitive government approach to assessing – or refusing to assess – refugee claims.

How did we get here?

The detention of asylum seekers who arrived by boat has been a feature of Australian Government policy for more than 30 years. When 26 Cambodians arrived in Australia in 1989 without prior authorisation, on a boat codenamed the *Pender Bay*, the Hawke Labor Government invoked the discretionary detention provision under the *Migration Act 1958* (Cth). These asylum seekers would spend the next two-and-a-half years incarcerated at former migrant hostels in suburban Melbourne (Maribyrnong) and Sydney (Villawood) before their refugee claims were rejected and they were forcibly repatriated. In 1991 Gerry Hand, the minister for immigration, local government and ethnic affairs, declared that all subsequent asylum seekers who arrived by boat would be detained in an inhospitable former miners' camp at Port Hedland, in the north-west of the country. The following year, the Labor Government passed with bipartisan support a number of legislative changes to the Migration Act that codified retrospectively the detention of asylum seekers and made mandatory the detention of all people who subsequently came by boat, which came into effect in 1994.[3] In the late 1990s and early 2000s, the conservative Howard Government established more immigration detention centres, often in former military sites and typically in extremely hot and isolated locations, far removed from the assistance of their communities, immigration lawyers, human rights activists and journalists. These detention centres, although distant from population hubs, were on the mainland of Australia. This, however, would change in 2001.

As Kathleen Blair explores in Chapter 6 of this volume, the arrival of the MV *Tampa* off the coast of Australia in August 2001 served as a lightning rod for an incumbent government unpopular with voters in an election

---

3   Rachel Stevens, *Immigration Policy from 1970 to the Present* (New York: Routledge, 2016), 121–22.

year. When a boat carrying 438 asylum seekers began to sink en route to Australia, the nearby Norwegian freighter, the MV *Tampa*, rescued the stranded passengers, and in doing so, prevented a likely catastrophe. The Howard Government threatened the Norwegians with prosecution if they tried to land on Australian territory, specifically the neighbouring Christmas Island, and they were ordered to dock in Indonesia. The mostly Afghan and Hazara asylum seekers resisted the rerouting to Indonesia, which is not a signatory to the *1951 Refugee Convention*, leading to a diplomatic deadlock between the Norwegian, Australian and Indonesian governments. After days drifting at sea, the impasse ended when the New Zealand Government agreed to resettle 150 asylum seekers, while the Micronesian island-state of Nauru detained the remaining 288 individuals at a processing centre in exchange for Australian foreign aid.[4]

The opportunistic Howard Government used the *Tampa* incident to legislate a suite of reforms with the intention of transferring asylum seeker processing to countries outside Australia, which is meticulously documented by Savitri Taylor in Chapter 9 of this volume. In September 2001, the Howard Government introduced the 'Pacific Solution', which excised Christmas Island and Ashmore Reef from the Australian Migration Zone. This migration excision would be extended in 2005 to include all Australian territories except the mainland and Tasmania, while the mainland and Tasmania were excised in 2013.[5] The excision of territories from the migration zone in 2001 marked the beginning of the Australian Government refusing asylum seekers the 'state of having arrived'.[6] This legal exclusion is important as it denied asylum seekers protections under Australian law and, later, access to legal challenges in the courts.

In addition to territory excision, the Australian Government delegated the detention of asylum seekers to two of its client states, both of which are recipients of Australian foreign aid.[7] Immigration detention centres were established on Manus Island, Papua New Guinea and Nauru. Although asylum seekers were physically detained offshore, the management of the

---

4   Kathleen Blair, Chapter 6, this volume.
5   Karen Barlow and staff, 'Parliament Excises Mainland from Migration Zone', *ABC News*, 17 May 2013, available at: www.abc.net.au/news/2013-05-16/parliament-excises-mainland-from-migration-zone/4693940.
6   Stevens, *Immigration Policy*, 132.
7   In the late 2010s, the Australian Government provided over AU$500 million in ODA (official development assistance) to Papua New Guinea; during the same time period, Nauru received approximately AU$25 million per year. Though this figure may seem small, it is equivalent to 25 per cent of Nauruan GDP. See: www.dfat.gov.au/aid/where-we-give-aid/Pages/where-we-give-aid.

centres and the adjudication of the asylum claims remained under the control of the Australian state. Since 2001, so-called offshore processing and the long-term incarceration of asylum seekers has for the most part been the modus operandi of the Australian Government. There was a brief (in relative terms) respite between early 2008 and mid-2012, which Savitri Taylor dubs 'the false spring'.[8] The incoming Rudd Labor Government swept to power in December 2007 with an 18-seat majority and an election pledge to replace offshore processing with onshore mandatory detention of asylum seekers, albeit on the remote Christmas Island.

Arguably, the suspension of offshore processing was contingent on two transient contextual factors: first, the small number of asylum seekers arriving by boat in 2007–08. According to government sources, only 21 individuals arrived by boat seeking asylum in 2007–08; in 2006–07, there were 23 applicants. These figures were a fraction of the 2,222 asylum seekers who arrived by boat in 2001–02 when the Pacific Solution was introduced. With few boat arrivals and resulting media coverage, the issue of asylum seeker policy faded into the background and lost its political salience.[9] Consequently, the Rudd Government was in a secure political position to reform asylum seeker policy with little practical impact. Second, after nearly 12 years in power, there was discontent with the incumbent government and a general desire for generational change at the top. The Rudd Government came to power with a moderate reform agenda on a range of issues, including industrial relations, climate change, education and internet infrastructure. There was therefore an electoral appetite for change, even if the reforms only moderated the excesses of the Howard years. This public desire for change, once satisfied, proved fickle. Coupled with a marked increase in the number of asylum seeker arrivals – 4,597 individuals arrived in 2009–10 – Rudd felt that his position against offshore processing, as well as his leadership of the Labor Party, became untenable.

8   Savitri Taylor, Chapter 9, this volume.
9   Unfortunately, the Australian Election Study did not include a question on the importance of refugees and asylum seekers as an election issue in 2007, perhaps indicative of a lack of interest in the issue at the time. Furthermore, there was no mention of refugees and only a passing reference to asylum seekers in Paul D Williams's reflective commentary on the 2007 election, see 'The 2007 Australian Federal Election: The Story of Labor's Return from the Electoral Wilderness', *Australian Journal of Politics and History* 54, no. 1 (2008): 104–25. doi.org/10.1111/j.1467-8497.2008.00487.x. John Wanna similarly omitted any reference to asylum seeker policy in his summary of the 2007 election, see 'Political Chronicles. Commonwealth of Australia. July to December 2007', *Australian Journal of Politics and History* 54, no. 2 (2008): 289–341. These collective silences in political commentary and analysis suggest that the issue of asylum seeker policies simply did not register with voters or political scientists.

Since 2008–09, the number of asylum seekers arriving by boat steadily increased, peaking in 2012–13 with 18,365 arrivals. Furthermore, in 2011–12 the number of asylum seekers arriving by boat eclipsed the number of asylum seekers arriving by air for the first time.[10] Although both boat and air arrivals requested onshore asylum (as distinct from applying for refugee status offshore, typically in a third country), air arrivals have never triggered a public frenzy simply by virtue of their successful passage through immigration and customs at their port of entry. Conversely, since the first boats of Vietnamese asylum seekers reached the shores of northern Australia in 1976, these migrants have been the subject of hostility, politicking and incarceration, predicated on racist fears of contagion, imaginary threats to security and alleged criminality.[11]

Compounding matters further, between 2010 and 2013 there were a series of high-profile tragedies in which asylum seekers drowned at sea and many more had to be rescued during their journey to Australia. For example, on 15 December 2010, a boat carrying 90 asylum seekers from Iraq and Iran crashed into rocky cliffs at Christmas Island during a monsoonal storm. Fifty people – 35 adults and 15 children – died, the most significant asylum seeker disaster (in terms of lives lost) to occur on Australian territory at that time. Images of distressed bodies and rickety boats floating in choppy waters blanketed TV and print news coverage. Sensational reporting dominated tabloid newspapers and articles were mostly written from the perspectives of local Christmas Islanders, not the surviving asylum seekers. For instance, *The Daily Telegraph* reported anecdotes from locals: 'We witnessed people actually drowning. To see people die and not to be able to do a darn thing is one of the worst things you can possibly do'.[12] The next day, Melbourne tabloid *The Herald Sun* similarly reported on the experiences of helpless witnesses. One local

---

10 This data is sourced from the Parliament of Australia research paper, 'Asylum Seekers and Refugees: What are the Facts?', *Research Paper Series 2014–15*, last updated 2 March 2015, available at: www. aph.gov.au/about_parliament/parliamentary_departments/parliamentary_library/pubs/rp/rp1415/ asylumfacts#_Toc413067443.

11 For further discussion, see Rachel Stevens, 'Political Debates on Asylum Seekers during the Fraser Government, 1977–1982', *Australian Journal of Politics and History* 58, no. 4 (2012): 526–41. doi.org/10.1111/j.1467-8497.2012.01651.x; Katrina Stats, 'Welcome to Australia? A Reappraisal of the Fraser Government's Approach to Refugees, 1975–1983', *Australian Journal of International Affairs* 69, no. 1 (2015): 68–87. doi.org/10.1080/10357718.2014.952707.

12 Alison Rehn, 'Now 50 Feared Dead After Asylum Boat Crashes off Christmas Island', *Daily Telegraph* (Sydney), 15 December 2010.

woman described the scene of the accident: 'It was horrible. They were screaming and yelling for help and falling into the ocean. We just felt so hopeless, there wasn't anything we could do'.[13]

Within a month, there was another tragedy at sea in which 17 asylum seekers drowned off the coast of Java, Indonesia, en route to Australia. In December 2011, an overcrowded vessel sank, resulting in the deaths of at least 160 mostly Afghan and Iranian asylum seekers. Between June and October 2012, there were five separate incidents in which collectively 287 people perished.[14] The Opposition, then led by conservative hardliner Tony Abbott, seized the opportunity to capitalise politically on the asylum seeker tragedies. The conservatives reframed the debate over onshore versus offshore processing, arguing illogically that interdiction and offshore processing saved the lives of asylum seekers. Thus, the Abbott Opposition cloaked their anti-asylum seeker policies in the language of humanitarianism. The hollowness of the conservatives' rhetoric was plain to see; however, by late 2010, the Labor Government had a new leader, Julia Gillard, and was clinging onto power in a hung parliament. Insecure and reactive in leadership, and long holding less sympathetic views about refugees, Gillard sought to quash debate around asylum seekers by reversing Rudd's reforms and reinstating offshore processing in Nauru and Manus Island in late 2012.

Over the last 20 years, politicians of both major parties have used the arrival of asylum seekers to try to gain a political advantage in some way. As a divisive issue, polling data indicates there are sizeable minorities on both sides who are sufficiently galvanised, making a major policy change unlikely in the present environment. The Australian Election Study (AES) has been measuring political attitudes among a nationally representative sample of voters since 1987. Questions about asylum seekers and refugees began in 2001 and have continued in every election year except 2007. The longitudinal nature of this survey, as well as the use of exact question wording, enable comparisons over time, and the data presents a very muddled picture.

---

13   Staff writers, 'Christmas Island Tragedy: Screams, Yells and then they Drowned', *Herald Sun* (Melbourne), 16 December 2010.

14   These figures are drawn from *SBS News*, 'Timeline: Asylum Seeker Boat Tragedies', available at: www.sbs.com.au/news/timeline-asylum-seeker-boat-tragedies.

In the AES surveys, there are three questions that address political attitudes towards asylum seekers and refugees. One, what is the most important non-economic election issue for you? Two, which is your preferred political party policy on refugees and asylum seekers? Three, should boats carrying asylum seekers be turned back or not turned back? The results from the survey are compiled in Table 1.

Table 1. Compilation of AES survey questions that relate to asylum seekers (in percentages)

Year of survey	2001	2004	2010	2013	2016	2019
Most important non-economic issue						
Refugees and asylum seekers	13	3	6	10	6	3
Preferred party policy						
Coalition	46	36	38	41	34	35
ALP	15	22	21	19	19	25
No preference	27	22	27	27	34	22
Attitudes towards asylum seekers						
Boats should be turned back	52	54	51	49	48	50
Boats should not be turned back	20	28	29	34	33	28
No response/undecided	28	18	20	17	19	22

Source: Data compiled by authors from data in Sarah Cameron and Ian McAllister, *Trends in Australian political opinion: Results from the Australian Election Study, 1987–2019* (Canberra: Australian National University, 2019). Downloaded from australianelectionstudy.org.

From the data in Table 1, it is evident that public attitudes are divided on the mandatory detention of asylum seekers. Since 2001 there has been a consistent majority or near majority of respondents who support the turning back of boats containing asylum seekers, despite it constituting refoulement and thus being illegal, as well as immoral and deeply violent. But there has also remained a steady group of opponents, ranging from one in five to one in three respondents. Furthermore, when asked whether boats should be turned back, between 17 and 28 per cent of respondents did not provide a response or were undecided. The presence of so many undecideds speaks to the intractability of a pernicious and long-lasting debate within Australian politics, which has left many unwilling to engage or care about refugees. On the question of preferred political party policy, no political party has received a majority, although the policies of the Coalition parties (generally viewed as more restrictive than the Labor Party), have been the most popular among respondents. Importantly, on average, approximately one-third of respondents had no party preference on asylum seeker policy, which reinforces the argument that a substantial minority of voters are disengaged.

Voter apathy on asylum seeker policy is also evident when respondents were asked to select the most important non-economic issue. In the full AES report, results showed that respondents consistently selected health as the most important non-economic issue, closely followed by environmental/global warming. The data in Table 1 reveals voter volatility on the proportion who nominated asylum seekers/refugees as the most important non-economic issue, with response rates ranging from 3 to 13 per cent. Heightened attention to asylum seekers typically coincided with high-profile events, such as the *Tampa* incident in 2001 and the drownings of asylum seekers from December 2010 through to 2013. As of 2019, asylum seeker policy has once again been relegated to the background, with only 3 per cent declaring the issue as their most important. In conclusion, the data from the AES provides compelling evidence that Australian voters are deeply divided on how to respond to the arrival of asylum seekers by boat, and that this issue will not influence voting behaviour for the vast majority of Australians. These findings have been replicated over the past 12 years in the annual Scanlon Foundation Survey on Mapping Social Cohesion. These reports – which can be viewed online – consistently show that, while a small minority believe asylum seekers are poorly treated under current policies, only 2 per cent of respondents identified asylum seekers as the most important issue facing Australia.[15]

The decision of the Labor Government to reinstall offshore mandatory processing was more than a retreat to the policies of the Howard years; it signalled the beginning of an increasingly aggressive and militarised approach to asylum seekers. When Kevin Rudd seized the leadership of the Labor Party, thus beginning his brief second term as prime minister, his approach to asylum seekers had no resemblance to his 2007 commitment to end offshore processing. In July 2013, Rudd announced that any asylum seeker who arrived without a visa – that is, by boat – would not be eligible for asylum in Australia. Instead, intercepted asylum seekers would be taken to Manus Island and have their refugee claims adjudicated by the Papua New Guinean (PNG) Government. Should they be successful,

---

15   Andrew Markus, *Mapping Social Cohesion: The Scanlon Foundation Surveys, 2019* (Melbourne: Monash University, 2019), 37, available at: scanloninstitute.org.au/research/surveys.

asylum seekers could resettle in PNG but never make a claim for asylum against the Australian Government. In return for their cooperation, the Australian Government offered the PNG Government financial aid. The blanket refusal of the Rudd Government to consider claims for refugee status among asylum seekers marked yet another turning point in the Australian Government's increasingly hostile approach to asylum seekers: from onshore mandatory detention in cities, then in remote desert towns, to the Pacific Solution and, finally, forced resettlement in a poor neighbouring nation.

It is at this time in July 2013 that Behrouz Boochani arrived in Australia, albeit on Christmas Island. Boochani was one of the first to be subject to the Rudd Government's new policy, and, in August 2013, he was relocated to Manus Island processing centre. In effect, Boochani was imprisoned indefinitely, languishing on an impoverished island with no prospect of resettlement in Australia. During his incarceration, the Coalition (conservative) parties came to power in September 2013. For the most part, the incoming government continued the policies of their predecessor, but also added a mix of hysterical rhetoric under their new strategy, Operation Sovereign Borders, along with tightened media access to government information on this policy. Boochani remained incarcerated at Manus Island processing centre until October 2017, at which point the centre officially closed. He, along with the other male asylum seekers imprisoned there, was forcibly moved to 'another prison camp' on the island, living a precarious existence among violence, hunger and protests.[16] At the time of writing, Boochani is living in New Zealand having been granted refugee status, while hundreds of other refugees and asylum seekers remain living precarious and unsupported lives in Port Moresby (PNG), Nauru, and Australia awaiting medical treatment, unable to either leave or re-establish themselves in the manner that they would choose.

Amidst government secrecy on the execution of a brutal government policy, incarcerated asylum seekers filled the vacuum, providing firsthand accounts of life on Manus Island and Nauru. Boochani is perhaps the most well-known asylum seeker-cum-activist in Australia, and has published

---

16 'A Message from Behrouz Boochani – Kurdish Refugee and Independent Journalist', Asylum Seeker Resource Centre, 28 November 2017, available at: web.archive.org/web/20190203095505/www.asrc.org.au/2017/11/28/message-behrouz-boochani-kurdish-refugee-independent-journalist/.

widely in a variety of media, including his award-winning memoir, *No Friend but the Mountains*.[17] During the October 2018 Academics for Refugees National Day of Action, Boochani urged academics:

> to do research that unpacks where these [asylum seeker] policies stem from, why they are maintained and how they can be undone. It's the duty of academics to understand and challenge this dark historical period, and teach the new generations to prevent this kind of policy in future.[18]

This book in part is a response to Boochani's call. Academics, activists and refugees have a duty to dissect the history and current state of affairs on refugees and asylum seekers. In the context of tight government control of information and, at present, minimal media coverage, the edited collection makes an intervention into academic and public discourses, opening a new space to think about the histories, presents and possible futures for refugees and asylum seekers. These are important public and political discussions to have and will have relevance well beyond Australia's borders, as Western countries around the world continue to tighten their borders and institute ever more violent controls over people seeking asylum.

Aims

At its heart, *Refugee Journeys: Histories of Resettlement, Representation and Resistance* understands refugee policy and asylum-seeking movements as a process: refugees undertake physical journeys between countries, and then face the journey of settling and integrating – whether permanently or temporarily, with full or partial social support – in a new place. Those journeys are shaped by a multitude of personal, governmental, social and political forces. What then are those forces? This book provides an exploration of some of them. It presents stories of how governments, the public and the media have responded to the arrival of people seeking asylum, and how these responses have impacted refugees and their lives. The chapters within mostly cover the period from 1970 to the present, providing readers with an understanding of the political, social

---

17 Behrouz Boochani, *No Friend but the Mountains: Writing from Manus Prison*, trans. Omid Tofighian (Sydney: Picador, 2018).
18 Boochani, 'Statement', available at: academicsforrefugees.wordpress.com/nda-public-read-ins/?f bclid=IwAR2ZGL1CJIvvGtYKo5vyG-rfVpcQ9_SR61orz6t19I3UMnL3eA-BruEide0.

and historical contexts that have brought us to the current day. *Refugee Journeys* also considers possible ways to break existing policy deadlocks, encouraging readers to imagine a future where we carry vastly different ideas about refugees, government policies and national identities.

With contributions from academics and activists from a diverse range of backgrounds, *Refugee Journeys* is unique as it provides space for multiple perspectives. Where public discourse often prioritises flattened and simplistic stories and solutions – such as the idea that all boats must be stopped, or that there is a queue that some jump, or that newly resettled refugees do not deserve financial and material support – this book encourages readers to think outside the box. By offering an edited collection, rather than a single-authored monograph – many of which exist and make important contributions to public discussion – we hope to present readers with a much-needed cacophony of different approaches, with multiple speakers and writers jutting up against each other, creating the space for new ideas to thrive. Against singular narratives, there is an urgent need in the Australian landscape for diverse interpretations. Other recent texts have focused on particular questions, such as detention systems, or temporariness, or refugee testimonies. *Refugee Journeys* is able to span a broader range, thereby offering readers the opportunity to understand the fuller social, political, cultural and historical contexts in which refugees and asylum seekers navigate their journeys and the repressive governments with which they interact.

Themes of the book

One of the central methods, or approaches, of this book involves the exploration of some of the different ways that histories and stories are, and have been, used by refugees and asylum seekers, researchers, writers, social workers, community workers and policymakers. Some chapters explore personal histories, whether narrated by refugees and asylum seekers themselves, or refracted through the words of social workers, anthropologists, community workers or historians. Other chapters explore national or community histories, thinking about how they have been understood by newspapers, politicians and historians. Many chapters demonstrate the interplay between individual and communal, private and public, stories. This volume thus responds to anthropologist Miriam Ticktin's recent call for scholars, and the public, to pay attention to the histories that people carry, and to do so in a way that evades the stereotypical discourses of vulnerability and loss that are often understood to be carried by refugees and asylum seekers. Rather than producing a reductive humanitarianism that sees rich nation-states in the role of 'saviour' to vulnerable and crisis-laden refugees and asylum seekers, the histories and stories that people write need to contain greater subtlety and complexity. As she writes:

> humanitarianism provides little room to feel and recognize the value of particular lives (versus life in general), or to mourn particular deaths (versus suffering in general); and little impetus to animate political change.[19]

Instead, this humanitarianism buttresses a binary of racialised rescuer and rescued, of asylum seekers as incapable of determining their own futures, and of the white nation-state as the subject who must always be in control. As Melanie Baak highlights in her chapter in this book, it is necessary to write histories, and create understandings, that avoid the 'deficit model', representing the place of refugees and asylum seekers in the world not as loss or crisis or impossibility.

Similarly, anthropologist Liisa Malkki writes of the ways in which refugees have been too often understood by Western authorities and actors as 'speechless emissaries', incapable of speaking for themselves, or determining their own futures. 'Such forms of representation', she argues, 'deny the very particulars that make of people something other than anonymous bodies, merely human beings'.[20] In this book, successive chapters write against such forms of representation, presenting explorations of, and critical engagements with, the histories that refugees carry in all their multiplicity, individuality and communality. This collection of essays is concerned with thinking about how people label and understand themselves, how they are understood by others and the impacts these labels have.

This deliberately interdisciplinary book seeks to write new histories of Australia and the world's relationships with refugees and asylum seekers, and of refugees and asylum seekers' relationships with Australia and the world. We seek to write new histories of ideas and practices of generosity

---

19   Miriam Ticktin, 'Thinking Beyond Humanitarian Borders', *Social Research: An International Quarterly* 83, no. 2 (2016): 256.
20   Liisa H Malkki, 'Speechless Emissaries: Refugees, Humanitarianism, and Dehistoricization', *Cultural Anthropology* 11, no. 3 (1996): 388. doi.org/10.1525/can.1996.11.3.02a00050.

and humanitarianism, interrogating the often-triumphalist popular histories of Australia's past that currently exist.[21] There is not one past but many being narrated in this book: these are temporally and spatially different pasts, but they also differ depending on who is the author and their positionality and relationality to the pasts that are being described, analysed and critiqued. This volume, then, seeks to make accessible and approachable the complexity of what is at stake in the possibilities of researching, writing and narrating these histories.

State of current research

As Klaus Neumann, Sandra M. Gifford, Annika Lems and Stefanie Scherr made clear in a 2014 article that explored trends and approaches in research on refugees in Australia from 1952 to 2013, there has been an 'exponential' increase in the publication of research on this topic since the end of the 1970s.[22] This trend has continued, as demonstrated in Ruth Balint and Zora Simic's 2018 State of the Field review essay. Their review explores the large body of literature on histories of migrants and refugees in Australia and notes that, 'for those of us who work in the field, there has always been enough scholarship to sustain and inspire us', with many 'exciting' publications coming from researchers at all levels of academia and from across the country.[23] As Neumann et al. note, the sheer number of research institutes, grants, and workshops and conferences around the country in the 2010s further testifies to this large and growing body of research and writing.

There are, however, numerous gaps in the scholarship, which they identify: intersections between histories of the border and settlement processes, and between categories of refugee, asylum seeker and permanent resident, as well as histories of humanitarianism.[24] They conclude their survey by noting:

---

21   Klaus Neumann, Chapter 10, this volume.
22   Klaus Neumann et al. 'Refugee Settlement in Australia: Policy, Scholarship and the Production of Knowledge, 1952–2013', *Journal of Intercultural Studies* 35, no. 1 (2014): 2. doi.org/10.1080/072 56868.2013.864629.
23   Ruth Balint and Zora Simic, 'Histories of Migrants and Refugees in Australia', *Australian Historical Studies* 49, no. 3 (2018): 378. doi.org/10.1080/1031461X.2018.1479438.
24   Neumann, Gifford, Lems and Scherr, 'Refugee Settlement in Australia', 12–13.

Australian scholarship on refugee settlement needs to reinvent itself by taking stock of its past, and firmly situating new inquiry within the broader contexts of migration, humanitarianism and globalisation, to ensure that it does not uncritically endorse current thinking and practice but contributes to charting new approaches to responding to and understanding refugees in Australia and elsewhere.[25]

The large increase in scholarship examining refugees and asylum seekers in and around Australia and the world makes a full exploration of this literature impossible. However, there are four key areas of recent scholarship with which we are engaging here. Firstly, we are engaging with texts that think about the broad historical contexts in which current refugees and asylum seekers today live. Following on from the path set by texts such as Klaus Neumann's *Across the Seas: Australia's Response to Refugees: A History*, Madeleine Gleeson's *Offshore: Behind the Wire on Manus and Nauru*, Claire Higgins's *Asylum by Boat*, William Maley's *What is a Refugee?* and Jane McAdam and Fiona Chong's *Refugee Rights and Policy Wrongs*, various chapters in this volume explore the policy settings, influence of politicians and roles of officials in controlling refugee and asylum seeker journeys to Australia and through the labyrinthine processes that determine how they will live.[26] In both their individual work and their collective work with others on the Deathscapes project, Suvendrini Perera and Joseph Pugliese outline the racial and colonial histories and presents in which refugee and asylum seeker controls are instituted.[27] As these books and projects collectively make clear, there are a wide variety of bureaucratic, social, cultural and political histories that combine to determine how

---

25   Ibid., 13.

26   Klaus Neumann, *Across the Seas: Australia's Response to Refugees: A History* (Melbourne: Black Inc., 2015); Madeleine Gleeson, *Offshore: Behind the Wire on Manus and Nauru* (Sydney: NewSouth Publishing, 2016); Claire Higgins, *Asylum by Boat: Origins of Australia's Refugee Policy* (Sydney: NewSouth Publishing, 2017); William Maley, *What is a Refugee?* (Brunswick: Scribe Publications, 2016); Jane McAdam and Fiona Chong, *Refugee Rights and Policy Wrongs* (Sydney: NewSouth Publishing, 2019).

27   Suvendrini Perera, *Australia and the Insular Imagination: Beaches, Borders, Boats, and Bodies* (New York: Palgrave Macmillan, 2009), doi.org/10.1057/9780230103122; Suvendrini Perera, 'White Shores of Longing: "Impossible Subjects" and the Frontiers of Citizenship', *Continuum* 23, no. 5 (2009): 647–62. doi.org/10.1080/10304310903154693; Suvendrini Perera and Joseph Pugliese, 'White Law of the Biopolitical', *Journal of the European Association of Studies on Australia* 3, no. 1 (2012): 87–100; Joseph Pugliese, 'Migrant Heritage in an Indigenous Context: For a Decolonising Migrant Historiography', *Journal of Intercultural Studies* 23, no. 1 (April 1, 2002): 5–18. doi.org/10.1080/07256860220122368; Joseph Pugliese, 'The Incommensurability of Law to Justice: Refugees and Australia's Temporary Protection Visa', *Law and Literature* 16, no. 3 (Fall 2004): 285–311. doi.org/10.1525/lal.2004.16.3.285; Suvendrini Perera and Joseph Pugliese, 'Deathscapes: Mapping Race and Violence in Settler States', 2016–2020, available at: www.deathscapes.org/.

refugees will be thought of, and affected by, national and international systems of regulation. They also make clear that the refugees themselves play an important role in determining their own histories, pushing back and resisting the controls placed on them where necessary, narrating and enforcing their own self-determination where desired.

Secondly, there is a growing and important body of research that addresses Australia's broader refugee and migrant community histories. We have recently seen the production of Jayne Persian's *Beautiful Balts: From Displaced Persons to New Australians*, Albrecht Dümling and Diana K. Weekes's *The Vanished Musicians: Jewish Refugees in Australia*, Alexandra Dellios's *Histories of Controversy: The Bonegilla Migrant Centre*, and Joy Damousi's *Memory and Migration in the Shadow of War: Australia's Greek Immigrants after World War II and the Greek Civil War*.[28] These accounts, like many of the chapters in the current volume, explore smaller communities, examining their experiences of migration and settlement, the histories that brought them to Australia and the larger Australian histories into which they were thrust. This literature points us to the importance of thinking beyond the level of the nation-state, reminding us of the everyday ways in which lives are lived and journeys are negotiated. Individual people and their histories – as Miriam Ticktin and Liisa Malkki argue – need to be narrated in order for their full humanity to be recognised.

As such, biographical accounts and memoirs of refugee journeys and resettlement in Australia are a third area of scholarship with which this volume engages. Partly as a result of the Australian practice of mandatorily detaining asylum seekers who either attempted to, or successfully came to, Australia, from the late 1980s – a practice that, coupled with other punitive regimes, continues to exist – as well as the practice of autobiographical and memoir writing in Australia and internationally, among other factors, there has been a growth in publications written by people who identify as being, or having been, refugees. These publications tell individual stories, but they also tell broader, larger stories of refugee journeys. Books such as a Teresa Ke's *Cries of Hunger*, Carina Hoang's *Boat People: Personal*

---

28   Jayne Persian, *Beautiful Balts: From Displaced Persons to New Australians* (Sydney: NewSouth Publishing, 2017); Albrecht Dümling, *The Vanished Musicians: Jewish Refugees in Australia*, trans. by Diana K. Weekes (Bern: Peter Lang AG, 2016); Alexandra Dellios, *Histories of Controversy: The Bonegilla Migrant Centre* (Melbourne: Melbourne University Press, 2017); Joy Damousi, *Memory and Migration in the Shadow of War: Australia's Greek Immigrants after World War II and the Greek Civil War* (Cambridge: Cambridge University Press, 2015), doi.org/10.1017/cbo9781316336847.

Stories from the Vietnamese Exodus, 1975–1996 and the reissue of Colin McPhedran's *White Butterflies*, among others, have opened these stories and these modes of narration up to new audiences.[29]

Additionally, and perhaps most importantly, there is an increasing emphasis in the Australian scholarly and public sphere on highlighting refugees writing and speaking in new formations. There are a range of projects, often co-produced by refugees and asylum seekers and Australian citizens, that have influenced this volume. Indeed, as the chapter here by André Dao and Jamila Jafari explores, projects like Behind the Wire – through which people who have been imprisoned by Australia as part of its mandatory detention regime share their experiences – provide an important new method of narrating histories and exploring refugee journeys. Similarly, Behrouz Boochani's *No Friend but the Mountains*, the Facebook page Free the Children NAURU and *The Messenger*, a podcast by Abdul Aziz Muhamat and Michael Green, provide spaces for speaking out in the midst of these journeys through Australian carceral and bureaucratic regimes.[30] All of these books and projects provide important background to the present volume, and we seek to build on the ideas and knowledge that these others have produced.

Outline of the book

This collection is divided into three sections, with each section containing a series of chapters that provide snapshot explorations of the histories of different aspects of the journeys that refugees take, and the settlement processes and modes of control – juridical, narratorial, cultural and political – that governments, states, bureaucracies and others have exerted over refugee and asylum seeker peoples' journeys. From 'Labelling refugees' to 'Flashpoints in Australian refugee history' to 'Understanding refugee histories and futures', each section of this book contributes to exploring the argument that 'refugees' are made in part through strict controls on the movement of populations and the delineation of borders and construction of identities, but also through self-description and

---

29   Teresa Ke, *Cries of Hunger* (Fremantle: Vivid Publishing, 2017); Carina Hoang, *Boat People: Personal Stories from the Vietnamese Exodus, 1975–1996* (Fremantle: Beaufort Books, 2013); Colin McPhedran, *White Butterflies*, updated edition (Sydney: NewSouth Books, 2017).
30   Boochani, *No Friend but the Mountains*; Free the Children NAURU available at: www.facebook. com/childrennauru/; Behind the Wire and the Wheeler Centre, *The Messenger*, available at: www. wheelercentre.com/broadcasts/podcasts/the-messenger?show_all=true.

self-determination. This book offers reflections on the very nature of this storytelling, arguing that the histories that are told, and those that are forgotten, fundamentally shape how people and journeys will be understood and made known by those witnessing them.

Beginning with the notion of 'labelling', this volume will introduce readers to histories of the ways that governments, settlement procedures and bureaucracies have worked to name, control and, at times, demonise displaced people. In the first chapter, an overview of the state of Australian and international legal and governmental approaches from World War II to the present is provided by legal scholar Eve Lester. Lester demonstrates that there have been various shifts and turns in how the national and international community labels and understands refugees and asylum seekers. In the next chapter, Melanie Baak, a refugee education researcher, comments: 'the question becomes, when, if ever do people who have been refugees, stop being refugees (with all of the frames of recognition this entails)?' That is, what is the temporal, emotive and descriptive quality of these labels? Baak explores how Dinka women from South Sudan, among others, narrate themselves and their histories in the face of such labelling. In the following chapter, historian Jordana Silverstein offers an exploration of labelling from another side, exploring the ways that those social workers and government employees who controlled the lives of refugee children in the late 1970s and early 1980s labelled, described and thus imagined unaccompanied Vietnamese and Timorese refugee children. While Baak and Silverstein explore the international coming to the national – refugees coming to Australia – historian Ann-Kathrin Bartels examines the resonances in Germany of the Australian context, providing further evidence of the idea that what happens in Australia is not merely contained within our national borders. Bartels explores newspaper instantiations of public discourses of asylum seekers as 'bogus' or 'economic refugees' that denigrate them for being criminals and focus on their 'cultural differences'. These histories from outside Australia thus shed light on the ways that similar projects of the construction of national identity, and the labelling of refugees as Other, are promulgated within Australia.

In the second section of this volume – 'Flashpoints in Australian refugee history' – three snapshot histories are provided that offer readers an excursion through the different ways that refugees and asylum seekers have been understood within Australian history, thus providing a greater sense of the national context. In her chapter, historian Rachel Stevens shows the ways in which Australians responded to the 10 million refugees who emerged from the Bangladesh Liberation War against West Pakistan in 1971. This chapter thus provides an opportunity to reflect on the gap between government refugee policy and community attitudes in 1971, with many in the community supporting refugees in ways that the government did not. This issue of public and governmental approaches is further developed by social scientist Kathleen Blair in her exploration of the media messaging around the 2013 federal election campaign in Australia. Blair's chapter responds to Bartels', providing the Australian experience of such narratives of demonisation. Finally, in writers André Dao and Jamila Jafari's chapter, Dao interviews Jafari as they work together to understand what it was like for her to share her story through the Behind the Wire project. Through this interview we are able to get a more complex understanding of the ways that stories can be told and people can make a claim to narrating their own pasts. This chapter speaks to many of the other chapters in the book, pointing out the necessity of people controlling their own stories and modes of narration, determining how they themselves will be represented.

The third and final section of this volume is called 'Understanding refugee histories and futures', and it moves readers towards grasping the ways that histories of this past can be, and are being, written, prompting a consideration of how refugee pasts shape future possibilities from the perspective of both refugees and policymakers. What are the stories being told? What narratives do they put forward? It is these questions that animate this section. Sociologist Laurel Mackenzie's chapter opens the section, as she documents the various impacts – both practical and emotional – of Australian Government policy at the grassroots level, focusing on the transition experiences of a group of Afghan Hazaras in Australia. Through her fieldwork, Mackenzie works to understand how these Hazara refugees understand themselves and their journeys. With this new understanding of the ways that individuals narrate their lives and histories, this section then turns to a chapter by legal scholar Savitri Taylor, who examines the 'incremental steps' taken on the journey to Australia's current asylum seeker policy settings and considers the implications of that history for the next 25 years. Taylor argues for the central role that the White Australia policy has played in shaping all future immigration policies, and explores this through a focus on two key features of contemporary asylum seeker policy – mandatory detention, introduced in 1992, and offshore processing, initially introduced in 2001.

This racial history is, indeed, a thread that runs throughout the chapters in this volume. Finally, this section concludes with an exploration of the histories that have been told by Klaus Neumann, a historian. Neumann argues against certain orthodoxies in Australian refugee and asylum seeker historiography, suggesting that, by examining little-known stories and bringing them into prominence, and by considering new 'genealogies of current policies and practices', we can imagine new ways of understanding the past and present, as well as conceptualising viable possible futures.

Together, this book highlights the role of individual, communal and governmental stories. Woven throughout the volume is a series of new explorations of the different aspects of the journey across land or water or by air, through bureaucracy and imprisonment and settlement processes, and into representation in government, public and media discourse, that refugees and asylum seekers have taken and continue to take. Through these chapters, we gain a sense of the vital role that history-writing, and thinking historically, can play in discussions about the place of refugees and asylum seekers in Australia and internationally. At this moment, when Australia's borders are hardened and support services are being retracted – as in many other places around the world – it becomes ever more crucial to understand these histories anew and reconceptualise how new thinking, storytelling and activism could happen from here.

PART I
Labelling refugees

1

AUSTRALIAN RESPONSES TO REFUGEE JOURNEYS

Matters of perspective and context

Eve Lester[1]

Since 1945, more than 9 million people have migrated to Australia.[2] Of these, some 1 million were refugees and displaced people,[3] although in the 1950s and 1960s institutional distinctions were not drawn between refugees and migrants.[4] In 1954, Australia provided the signature that brought the *1951 Convention Relating to the Status of Refugees* ('*Refugee Convention*') into force.[5] To some, whether supporters or opponents of refugee policy, these figures and the decision to accede to the *Refugee Convention* tell the story of refugee resettlement to Australia as a proud and generous history of leadership and humanitarianism dating back to

---

1   The author would like to thank Gabriel Smith for very helpful research assistance for this chapter.
2   Department of Home Affairs ('DHA'), *Fact Sheet: Key Facts About Immigration* (undated), archived webpage available at: webarchive.nla.gov.au/awa/20181010074801/www.homeaffairs.gov. au/about/corporate/information/fact-sheets/02key; DHA, Visa Statistics, relating to the migration, asylum and humanitarian programs available at: homeaffairs.gov.au/research-and-statistics/statistics/ visa-statistics.
3   DHA, *Fact Sheet*; DHA, Visa Statistics. Figures vary, even on the DHA website. By one account, the resettlement figure now stands at 880,000 people; see: immi.homeaffairs.gov.au/what-we-do/ refugee-and-humanitarian-program/about-the-program/about-the-program; Klaus Neumann, *Across the Seas: Australia's Response to Refugees: A History* (Melbourne: Black Inc., 2015), 141.
4   Neumann, *Across the Seas*, 141; see also Senate Standing Committee on Foreign Affairs and Defence, Parliament of Australia, *Australia and the Refugee Problem* (1976), 47.
5   *Convention Relating to the Status of Refugees*, opened for signature 28 July 1951, 189 UNTS 150 (entered into force 22 April 1954), art 31 ('*Refugee Convention*').

the postwar period.[6] To others, the utilitarian undertones of the story complicate the narrative of generosity and humanitarianism, not least in the context of post-arrival treatment.[7]

There is no doubt that there is good in this story. After all, thousands upon thousands of refugees have been resettled to Australia and have seized the chance to rebuild their lives. Yet, when seen in context, the reality is more nuanced and it becomes clear that the narrative of generosity that accompanies this story is a fulsome one with some significant blind spots.[8] And, as we will see, it is one in which the refugee appears to be a secondary consideration, regarded as merely incidental or instrumental in fulfilling geopolitical interests and priorities.[9] It is as a result of this that there is a need to ensure that Australian histories of the refugee journey are both told and understood in global perspective and context, legally, politically and statistically.

With this in mind, this chapter gives an overview of this very context, showing how politico-legal interests and traditions of much longer standing have informed the development of the modern refugee protection framework. There are several important points to note here. First, while the *Refugee Convention* is commonly presented as a global instrument giving protection to refugees, when it was drafted, geographical and temporal restrictions were included in order to exclude major groups of refugees from outside Europe. Second, there was an underlying assumption driven by geopolitical dynamics of the Cold War period that Convention refugees[10] would be provided with permanent settlement outside their country of origin. This assumption gave rise to the 'exilic bias' that characterised

---

6   Barry York, 'Australia and Refugees, 1901–2002: An Annotated Chronology Based on Official Sources' (Information and Research Services, Parliamentary Library, Parliament of Australia, Chronology No 2, 2002–2003), 1.

7   Alexandra Dellios, *Histories of Controversy: The Bonegilla Migrant Centre* (Melbourne: Melbourne University Press, 2017).

8   For two insightful studies of postwar refugee resettlement that describe a more complicated history than the popular narrative of humanitarianism, see Dellios, *Histories of Controversy*; Jayne Persian, *Beautiful Balts: From Displaced Persons to New Australians* (Sydney: NewSouth Publishing, 2017).

9   Guy S Goodwin-Gill, 'The Politics of Refugee Protection', *Refugee Survey Quarterly* 27, no. 1 (2008): 8–23, 9, doi.org/10.1093/rsq/hdn003.

10   A refugee is defined as a person who, 'owing to well-founded fear of being persecuted for reasons of race, religion, nationality, membership of a particular social group or political opinion, is outside his country of nationality [or former habitual residence] and is unable, or owing to such fear, is unwilling to avail himself of the protection of that country': *Refugee Convention* art 1A(2).

postwar approaches to refugee protection.[11] Third, the decolonisation movement of the 1960s and the emergent *1967 Protocol Relating to the Status of Refugees* ('*1967 Protocol*'), which removed the geographical and temporal limitations, opened up the possibility for significantly increased refugee numbers, many of whom were non-European. Their permanent presence in countries of the liberal West was, however, not necessarily perceived to be of economic benefit or strategic interest. This dynamic and, later, the end of the Cold War would therefore produce several major policy effects. In the first instance, it would produce a shift in policy (and discursive) focus from *permanent* solutions with the aforementioned 'exilic bias'[12] to a *durable* solutions discourse and an accompanying state-centric preference for voluntary return.[13] In the second, it led to a lifting of barriers to exit by refugee-producing countries that had hitherto served as the main point of resistance to refugee-hood. This in turn led to new and increasingly elaborate and strident regulatory barriers to *entry* into countries of asylum (or *non-entrée* policies). Finally, it led to a new politicisation of the policy (and discourse) of refugee resettlement. This background frames Australia's evolving response to the refugee and her journey, and at once explains the genesis of Australia's current claims that its refugee resettlement policy positions it as a global leader in refugee protection at the same time as it undermines the credibility of those claims.

Part I of this chapter, 'A prehistory', looks at responses to refugee movements in early international law and selected responses through to the interwar period that are illustrative of a situation-specific approach to refugee protection. Part II, 'The *Refugee Convention*', analyses key geopolitical drivers behind the drafting of the *Refugee Convention* following World War II and the context for Australia's accession to it in 1954. Part III, 'The *1967 Protocol*', examines the shifts in international law and policy in the context of decolonisation and other developments during the Cold War. Part IV, 'The Cold War et seq.', considers approaches to refugee protection and effects on the international legal and policy framework of

---

11   Gervase J L Coles, 'The Human Rights Approach to the Solution of the Refugee Problem: A Theoretical and Practical Enquiry', in *Human Rights and the Protection of Refugees Under International Law*, ed. by Alan E Nash (Conference Proceedings, Montreal, 29 November – 2 December 1987), 195, 209.

12   That is, local integration in the country of asylum and resettlement to a third country.

13   Dennis Gallagher, 'Durable Solutions in a New Political Era', *Journal of International Affairs* 47, no. 2 (1994): 429–50.

the Cold War and the events that marked its end. Part V, 'Charting a way forward in the twenty-first century', looks briefly at present-day responses to the so-called global migration crisis.

Part I: A prehistory

At its heart, the refugee's journey is integral to the story of humanity, whether as a product of conflict or internecine struggles, poverty or natural disaster, persecution or expulsion. Flight and requests for hospitality and asylum are concepts as old as life itself. This flight–hospitality dynamic long predates the emergence of the nation-state as the dominant governing structure. In turn, the manifestation of this dynamic in international society in the person of the 'refugee' is as old as the state system, and it will remain for as long as the state system remains.[14] So, while the focus of this volume is on a particular place (Australia) and a particular period (1970 to the present), we need to situate the refugee and her journey within a much longer historical trajectory and in global context.

The refugee journey in early international law

From its earliest conceptions, European international legal theory contemplated and legitimised the refugee journey as a right of mobility consequential to an *individual* right of self-preservation.[15] By the same token, the nation-state has also recognised that there is potential for the encounter between the foreigner and the sovereign to be hostile and therefore a threat, triggering exclusion measures. So, a tension arises in this border encounter, represented by competing acts and interests of self-preservation.

Early international legal writers such as Vattel resolved this tension by recognising that there would always be situations where the duties of humanity should prevail over the sovereign power of exclusion; situations in which peaceful entry, passage and stay (including the possibility of a permanent asylum) should be permitted to 'those whom

---

14   Emma Haddad, *The Refugee in International Society: Between Sovereigns* (Cambridge: Cambridge University Press, 2008), 209.
15   Eve Lester, *Making Migration Law: The Foreigner, Sovereignty and the Case of Australia* (Cambridge: Cambridge University Press, 2018), 68, 70–73, discussing the work of Samuel Pufendorf.

tempest or necessity obliged to approach their frontiers'.[16] In other words, while exclusion measures may also reflect the claim *of the state* to a right to self-preservation, early international law understood such measures as permissible only to the extent necessary for the purposes of self-defence.[17] As I have argued elsewhere, we know that early (European) international law's refugee was conceptualised as a European *insider*, rather than a non-European *outsider*.[18] In other words, notwithstanding the racial and imperialist power interests and dynamics that shaped the making of international law and ideas about who should benefit from its protections,[19] we can still educe from early treatises recognition that refugees flee out of necessity and that the duties of humanity give rise to concomitant obligations of hospitality.[20]

Situation-specific responses to refugee movements

As we have seen, the concepts of asylum and exile and the corresponding obligation to respect the duties of humanity are longstanding.[21] Nevertheless, historically, responses to refugee movements have tended to be ad hoc and situation specific. So, for example, there were situation-specific responses to the plight of the Huguenots (seventeenth century)[22] – the displaced population to whom the term 'refugee' was first ascribed[23] – as well as a range of ad hoc responses to the Jewish pogroms in Russia

---

16   Emmerich de Vattel, *The Law of Nations; or, Principles of the Law of Nature, Applied to the Conduct of Affairs of Nations and of Sovereigns*, trans. and ed. Joseph Chitty (Lawbook Exchange, first published 1854, 2005 ed.) [trans of: Le Droit des gens; ou Principes de la loi naturelle, appliqués à la conduit et aux affaires des Nations et des Souverains (first published 1758)], bk II ch VII § 94, bk II ch VIII § 100, bk I ch XIX § 231.

17   See Lester, *Making Migration Law*, 99–101, discussing the interpretation of 'self-preservation' in the treatises of Vattel and Sir Robert Phillimore.

18   Ibid., ch 2.

19   On the inextricable relation between imperialism and the making of international law, including in the 'post-colonial' era, see, generally, Antony Anghie, *Imperialism, Sovereignty and the Making of International Law* (New York: Cambridge University Press, 2005); and Sundhya Pahuja, *Decolonising International Law: Development, Economic Growth and the Politics of Universality* (New York: Cambridge University Press, 2011), doi.org/10.1017/cbo9781139048200.

20   Lester, *Making Migration Law*, 76–77.

21   Vattel, *The Law of Nations*, bk II ch VIII § 100; Ibid., 76.

22   The Edict of Potsdam (1685), for example, provided for the safe passage of French Protestants (Huguenots) to Brandenburg-Prussia and accorded them religious freedom denied through the revocation of the Edict of Nantes (Edict of Fontainebleau, 1684) by Louis XIV: John Stoye, *Europe Unfolding: 1648–1688*, 2nd ed. (Oxford: Blackwell, 2000), 272; Lester, *Making Migration Law*, 69–70.

23   Haddad, *The Refugee in International Society*, 51–52.

(nineteenth century).[24] In the early twentieth century and in the wake of World War I, pressure to protect large numbers of Russian[25] and Armenian refugees[26] also produced situation-specific responses, whether through national governments or coordinated international responses in the interwar period under the auspices of the League of Nations.[27]

After World War II, the emergence of an international protection regime might suggest that situation-specific responses would become a thing of the past. However, as we will see in the next section, even with the emergence of an international protection framework, situation-specific responses continued to characterise the way in which the 'international community' responded to many refugee crises. Indeed, even as it was framed as an international instrument, we will see that the *Refugee Convention* itself was a situation-specific response to the absence of protection for the vast numbers of displaced people in Europe.[28] In contrast, the issue of mass displacement of *non*-Europeans in the early postwar years was sidelined by the 'international' protection framework as it was considered to be both strategically marginal and overwhelming in its enormity.

Part II: The *Refugee Convention*

In the wake of World War II, the *Refugee Convention* secured the commitment and cooperation of states parties to accord protection to refugees, not least on account of the international scope and nature of refugee movements. Other international instruments were also crucial, notably the *Charter of the United Nations*[29] and the *Universal Declaration of Human*

---

24   John Doyle Klier, *Russians, Jews, and the Pogroms of 1881–1882* (Cambridge: Cambridge University Press, 2011), 269.

25   Peter Gatrell, *A Whole Empire Walking: Refugees in Russia During World War I* (Bloomington: Indiana University Press, 1999).

26   Peter Balakian, *The Burning Tigris: The Armenian Genocide and America's Response* (New York: HarperCollins, 2003); Stefanie Kappler et al. (eds), *Mass Media and the Genocide of the Armenians: One Hundred Years of Uncertain Representation* (Basingstoke: Palgrave Macmillan, 2016), doi.org/10.1007/978-1-137-56402-3.

27   Gilbert Jaeger, 'On the History of the International Protection of Refugees', *International Review of the Red Cross* 83, no. 843 (2001): 727; Haddad, *The Refugee in International Society,* 31.

28   Pia Oberoi, *Exile and Belonging: Refugees and State Policy in South Asia* (Oxford: Oxford University Press, 2006), 22 n. 26.

29   United Nations, *Charter of the United Nations,* adopted 26 June 1945 1 UNTS XVI, entered into force 24 October 1945 ('*UN Charter*'); Annemarie Devereux, *Australia and the Birth of the International Bill of Human Rights 1946–1966* (Sydney: Federation Press 2005); Eve Lester, 'Internationalising Constitutional Law: An Inward-Looking Outlook', *Australian Feminist Law Journal* 42, no. 2 (2016): 321–49, 335–40, doi.org/10.1080/13200968.2016.1273066.

Rights,[30] which recognised, respectively, the imperative of cooperation between states to maintain international peace and security[31] and the universality of the right to seek and enjoy asylum.[32] The underpinning of international cooperation, intended to embrace a number of postwar issues including finding permanent solutions for refugees, was a critical dimension to these commitments.[33] The characterisation of asylum as an inherently peaceful and humanitarian (and therefore supposedly non-political) act was politically important at the time and endures in theory if not in practice. Nevertheless, it is now more widely recognised that it is unrealistic to imagine that either the 'refugee problem' or humanitarian responses to it can ever be entirely apolitical.[34] So, while international legal discourse on refugee protection between 1950 and 1989 (marking the end of the Cold War) might have been relatively depoliticised, the Western agenda that this depoliticised discourse encouraged and legitimised positioned refugee law as neutral and apolitical – indeed innocent.[35] However, this depoliticised discourse was itself political, because of, rather than in spite of, the discernible geopolitical interests and Cold War dynamics at work. These interests and dynamics deployed law's innocence to determine who would be protected under the *Refugee Convention* and, equally as importantly, who would be neglected.[36]

An 'international' protection framework emerges

It is well recognised that it was large-scale displacement in Europe that prompted the negotiation and adoption of the *Refugee Convention* and the grant by the General Assembly of a (temporary) mandate to the Office

---

30 *Universal Declaration of Human Rights,* GA Res 217A (III), UN GAOR, 3rd sess, 183rd plen mtg, UN Doc A/810 (10 December 1948) ('*UDHR*'). Devereux, *Australia and the Birth of the International Bill of Human Rights 1946–1966*; and specifically on the right to asylum and the issue of free movement, see Lester, 'Internationalising Constitutional Law', 340–44.

31 *UN Charter,* arts 1(3), 55, 56; Volker Türk and Madeline Garlick, 'From Burdens and Responsibilities to Opportunities: The Comprehensive Refugee Response Framework and a Global Compact on Refugees', *International Journal of Refugee Law* 28, no. 4 (2016): 656–78, 658, doi.org/10.1093/ijrl/eew043.

32 See *UDHR*, art 14. For discussions, Devereux, *Australia and the Birth of the International Bill of Human Rights 1946–1966*, and Lester, 'Internationalising Constitutional Law', 328–35.

33 Türk and Garlick, 'From Burdens and Responsibilities to Opportunities', 658–65.

34 Goodwin-Gill, 'The Politics of Refugee Protection', 21; Haddad, *The Refugee in International Society*, 214.

35 For a critical analysis of law's claim to equality, universality and indeed innocence, see Peter Fitzpatrick, 'Racism and the Innocence of Law', *Journal of Law and Society* 14, no. 1 (1987): 119–32.

36 B S Chimni, 'The Geopolitics of Refugee Studies: A View from the South', *Journal of Refugee Studies* 11, no. 4 (1998): 350–74.

of the United Nations High Commissioner for Refugees (UNHCR).[37] At the time of its drafting, the scope of the *Refugee Convention* was temporally limited to 'events occurring before 1 January 1951'.[38] It also included a geographical limitation that enabled states to apply its terms only to pre-1951 events that took place *in Europe*.[39] In addition to this, the Convention's application was confined to the type of refugee who was of political and ideological interest to the West; a person whose fear of persecution had to be for reasons of civil or political status.[40]

The refugee as defined under the *Refugee Convention* was a person whose grant of asylum would, in Cold War terms, serve to weaken the hand of the Eastern Bloc as it strengthened that of the West. Narrowly defined, a person fleeing generalised violence or conflict- or state-induced poverty did not come within its purview unless he[41] could sustain an individualised claim to persecution for one of the five Convention grounds.[42] This constructed what Chimni has described as 'an image of a "normal" refugee' as 'white, male and anti-communist'.[43] The distinction thereby created produced what he has since described as a 'myth of difference'; that is, the idea that refugees fleeing Europe did so for radically different reasons – and indeed had radically different needs – to those fleeing the Third World.[44] Yet, there was large-scale displacement in the Third World at the time of

---

37 Oberoi, *Exile and Belonging*, 20.

38 *Refugee Convention*, art 1A(2).

39 *Refugee Convention*, art 1B. Although textually the most obvious example is the inclusion of art 1D concerning the Palestinians, see also, e.g., Oberoi, *Exile and Belonging*, 17–25, and Laura Madokoro, *Elusive Refuge: Chinese Migrants in the Cold War* (Cambridge, MA: Harvard University Press, 2016), 32.

40 It is a fairly recent development that the possibility of social and economic rights violations grounding a claim to refugee status has been recognised: see, most notably, Michelle Foster, *International Refugee Law and Socio-Economic Rights: Refuge from Deprivation* (Cambridge: Cambridge University Press, 2007), doi.org/10.1017/cbo9780511493980.009.

41 Although from time to time, as here, I intentionally use the male pronoun, I use the female pronoun generically in my writing. Although I acknowledge that dispensing with gendered pronouns in favour of using 'they/them' is a valid and inclusive approach that properly resists the gender binary, my purpose in differentially using the male and female pronouns is part of a broader objective of engaging critically with law and history and highlighting shifting power dynamics over time. In other words, 'she/her' is a form of resistance that is conscious and critical, with transformative possibilities. In making this choice, I am persuaded by Haddad's thinking, recognising that the habitual use of the male pronoun can allow the identity of the subject to go unnoticed by the reader: Haddad, *The Refugee in International Society*, 39–41; see also Wendy Martyna, 'What Does "He" Mean? Use of the Generic Masculine', *Journal of Communication* 28, no. 1 (1978): 131–38, doi.org/10.1111/j.1460-2466.1978.tb01576.x; Lester, *Making Migration Law*, 15–16 n. 49.

42 *Refugee Convention*, art 1A(2).

43 Chimni, 'The Geopolitics of Refugee Studies', 351; cf. Chinese fleeing the victorious Chinese Communist Party during the Chinese Civil War: see Madokoro, *Elusive Refuge*, 2–3, 37.

44 Chimni, 'The Geopolitics of Refugee Studies', 355–63.

drafting and, despite the superficial universality of the *Refugee Convention*, protection of refugees and displaced persons in strategically marginal contexts were not included in its terms.

Sites of non-European displacement on a massive scale included the 1948 Arab–Israeli conflict,[45] the Indian subcontinent in the context of Partition,[46] the Chinese Civil War and the second Sino–Japanese War.[47] Despite their size and significance, none of these situations was contemplated in the Convention's terms. That said, they were central – not marginal – to the thinking of the framers of the *Refugee Convention*. Displacement figures for these situations were in the order of tens of millions. As Oberoi has noted, in the context of decolonisation of India and Pakistan alone, upwards of 30 million people were displaced,[48] representing one of the greatest forced movements of people in contemporary history.[49] Of these, some 14.5 million were 'refugees' in the Convention's sense of being outside their country of origin, in some cases as a result of newly demarcated international borders.[50] Likewise, the Sino–Japanese War (1937–1945), which displaced as many as 95 million people by one account,[51] did not feature in the refugee protection calculus. As Madokoro has noted, the drafting of the Convention similarly disregarded the movement of people out of the Chinese mainland following the victory of the Chinese Communist Party in the Chinese Civil War.[52]

In the text of the Convention, these exclusions would be reflected most tellingly through the incorporation of the geographical and temporal limitations on its reach as well as art 1D, which explicitly excluded from the Convention's embrace refugees receiving assistance from another UN agency. This provision was specifically intended to cover Palestine

---

45   For a detailed discussion of the legal complexities of the situation, see Lex Takkenberg, *The Status of Palestinian Refugees in International Law* (Oxford: Clarendon Press, 1998).

46   Oberoi, *Exile and Belonging*, 11–43.

47   Madokoro, *Elusive Refuge*, 103.

48   Oberoi, *Exile and Belonging*, 1.

49   Ibid.

50   Madokoro, *Elusive Refuge*, 23.

51   Keith A Crawford and Stuart J Foster, *War, Nation, Memory: International Perspectives on World War II in School History Textbooks* (IAP Publishing, 2008), 90. Schoppa describes numbers as being in the tens of millions: R Keith Schoppa, *In a Sea of Bitterness: Refugees During the Sino-Japanese War* (Cambridge MA: Harvard University Press, 2011), 6, doi.org/10.4159/harvard.9780674062986.

52   Madokoro, *Elusive Refuge*, 23.

refugees assisted by the UN Relief and Works Agency ('UNRWA').[53] Notwithstanding their exclusion, the aforementioned non-European situations were the subject of debate during the drafting process. In each instance, arguments were constructed as to why these groups of non-European refugees should be excluded from protection under the *Refugee Convention*. In this connection, the focus of the drafters was on the definition of a refugee set out in art 1A(2) and the issue of legal rights and protection rather than framing an agreement for the provision of material assistance and relief. So, while India and Pakistan positioned themselves in the course of debate as providing international protection and assistance to refugees, this impelled them to concede that their refugees had the protection of a state.[54] In response, therefore, other delegations could assert that Partition refugees did not require international legal protection because they did not lack the protection of a government, and therefore would not need to be covered by the Convention's terms.[55] Similarly, the central argument for excluding Chinese refugees from the People's Republic of China ('PRC') was that they had, at least in theory, a place of refuge in the Republic of China (Taiwan), which still had a seat in the United Nations. Robinson, the Israeli delegate, argued that this meant that Chinese refugees 'had a government of their own … able to provide refuge … to those who sought asylum there'.[56] In Robinson's words, therefore, for 'the purposes of the Convention, there were practically no refugees in the world other than those coming from Europe'.[57] Of course, if that were the case, the geographical and temporal limitations that were incorporated into the Convention would have been moot. Robinson knew also that there were some 750,000 Palestine refugees, but, as noted above,

---

53   Exclusion of Palestinian refugees receiving assistance from UNRWA under art 1D contrasts with arts 2–34 of the *Refugee Convention*, which outline a rights framework for (European) refugees: see, generally, Takkenberg, *The Status of Palestinian Refugees in International Law*.

54   UN General Assembly, Provisional Summary Record of the Two Hundred and Sixty-Third Meeting Held at Lake Success New York on Tuesday, 15 November 1949, at 10.45 am, 15 November 1949, A/C.3/SR.263, [59], available at: www.refworld.org/docid/3ae68bec18.html.

55   UN General Assembly, Fourth Session, Joint Third and Fifth Committees, 264th Plenary Meeting, 2 December 1949, para 73 (Eleanor Roosevelt), cited in Oberoi, *Exile and Belonging*, 21.

56   Although attempts to argue that refugees of Jewish background should avail themselves of Israel's Law of Return, enacted in 1950, have been described as imbued with 'an exquisite irony' given the very raison d'être of the *Refugee Convention*, it is nevertheless striking that this argument should have been raised by the Israeli delegate: see *NAEN v Minister for Immigration and Multicultural and Indigenous Affairs* (2003) 130 FCR 46, 60 (per Sackville J).

57   UN Conference of Plenipotentiaries on the Status of Refugees and Stateless Persons, *Conference of Plenipotentiaries on the Status of Refugees and Stateless Persons: Summary Record of the Twenty-second Meeting*, 26 November 1951, A/CONF.2/SR.22 (Mr Robinson, Israel), available at: www.refworld.org/docid/3ae68cde10.html; Madokoro, *Elusive Refuge*, 30.

they were expressly excluded. Implicitly, therefore, material assistance and relief for non-European refugee populations (even absent legal protection) was considered to suffice.

During the drafting process, there was even resistance to representations that Palestine refugees should be covered by the Convention's terms should UNRWA cease to exist. One delegate suggested that such an approach would not be necessary because a protocol or separate convention that was 'perfectly suited' to the requirements of Palestine refugees could 'easily' be arranged.[58] History of course tells us otherwise, and with Palestine refugees registered by UNRWA numbering 5.6 million in 2019,[59] we are also reminded that refugee populations expand exponentially if their situations are allowed to become protracted and the conditions that produce them remain unresolved.

In the course of debate, the Indian delegate described the *Refugee Convention* as a 'partial remedy involving discrimination', stating that 'the UN should try to help not only special sections of the world's population, but all afflicted people everywhere'. As she said, '[s]uffering knew no racial or political boundaries; it was the same for all'.[60] So, although the geographical and temporal limitations in the Convention had been opposed by a majority of representatives from the emerging Third World states,[61] as well as the UK and (for a time) France, this universalist position was ultimately unsuccessful.[62] Oberoi describes India and Pakistan as being left with a sense of exclusion on the grounds of political expediency.[63]

---

58   UN Conference of Plenipotentiaries on the Status of Refugees and Stateless Persons, *Conference of Plenipotentiaries on the Status of Refugees and Stateless Persons: Summary Record of the Twenty-ninth Meeting*, 28 November 1951, A/CONF.2/SR.29 (Mr Rochefort, France), available at: www.refworld.org/docid/3ae68cdf4.html.

59   'Figures at a Glance', UNHCR.org, as at 18 June 2020, available at: www.unhcr.org/en-au/figures-at-a-glance.html.

60   UN, Fifth Session, Third Committee, 332nd Meeting, 1 December 1950, paras 26–27, cited in Oberoi, *Exile and Belonging*, 24.

61   Oberoi, *Exile and Belonging*, 19–20, and, at 24, referring to the position of the Chilean delegation as well as the position of India and Pakistan. As she notes, the Chilean delegate argued that 'it was the duty of the UN to extend international protection to every person who, for reasons beyond his control, could no longer live in the country of his birth': UN, Fifth Session, Third Committee, 324th Meeting, 22 November 1950, para 36.

62   Oberoi, *Exile and Belonging*, 20; Madokoro, *Elusive Refuge*, 31. This is so, even though the majority of states (including Australia) ultimately opted for a broader geographical reach as provided in *Refugee Convention* art 1B(1)(b).

63   Oberoi, *Exile and Belonging*, 22 n. 26.

The participation of China in the drafting process – as the Republic of China (Taiwan) *not* the PRC – is notable for two reasons. First, Taiwan was invited into negotiations on account of China's history of providing shelter to some 200,000 white Russian and 18,000 Jewish refugees in the 1920s and 1930s rather than out of concern for Chinese refugees.[64] Second, because the General Assembly gave its China seat to Taiwan not the PRC, the Soviet and Polish delegations withdrew from the meetings. This, as Madokoro has noted, gave 'ample room for Western nations to advance their Cold War interests in discussions'.[65]

The geopolitical dynamics at play in the drafting of the *Refugee Convention* make it hard to resist the conclusion that writing the Palestinian, Partition and Chinese refugee crises out of the *Refugee Convention* as unworthy of international protection and permanent rights-based solutions not only reflected Cold War politics and ideology, but was also racialised.[66] Certainly, there is evidence to suggest that an international instrument underwriting both legal protection and material assistance to many millions of non-European refugees was seen by powerful states to be a problem too enormous to manage in the first instance and as strategically unnecessary in the second.[67] It also suggests that the global estimate that 151 million people were forcibly displaced as a result of persecution, conflict, decolonisation and wars of independence between 1940 and 2015 is, at best, conservative.[68]

So, notwithstanding that the *Refugee Convention* presented as an *international* instrument in seemingly benign or neutral terms, it is clear that the debate around its geographical and temporal limitations reveals an informed neglect and deliberate exclusion of large populations of non-European refugees. Although the emergent international framework recognised the importance of legal protection and envisaged permanent solutions, its situation-specific focus was on European refugees and

---

64   Madokoro, *Elusive Refuge*, 26.
65   Ibid.
66   Fitzpatrick, 'Racism and the Innocence of Law'; Madokoro, *Elusive Refuge*, 20, who underscores that refugees fleeing the Chinese Communist Party's victory in the Civil War were a political and ideological fit for the *Refugee Convention* but not a racial one.
67   Oberoi, *Exile and Belonging*, 22.
68   Lydia DePillis, Kulwant Saluja and Denise Lu, 'A Visual Guide to 75 years of Major Refugee Crises Around the World', *Washington Post*, 21 December 2015, available at: www.washingtonpost.com/graphics/world/historical-migrant-crisis/?noredirect=on. However, note that the graphics provide limited information about displacement figures in the context of, for example, the Chinese Civil War and the second Sino–Japanese War.

displaced persons. In contrast, the 'international community' did not see fit to respond to non-European displacement and to deliver to affected refugees the permanent solutions envisaged for European refugees and displaced persons.[69] Instead, assistance (not rights or solutions) was deemed sufficient for the rest. Thus, both the text of the *Refugee Convention* and its *travaux préparatoires* remind us of the way in which non-European refugee situations shaped, and indeed narrowed, its scope. And, as the next section demonstrates, this suited Australia well.

White Australia and the *Refugee Convention*

During World War II, Australia hosted more than 6,000 non-European wartime refugees fleeing the Japanese conquest of South-East Asia.[70] Like many of the ad hoc responses to refugee movements discussed above, this too was a situation-specific response. Importantly, it was only ever intended to be a temporary one and special exemptions to members of this population under Australia's restrictive and racialised immigration legislation were only granted on condition that they return to their own countries once hostilities ceased. Most returned after the war, and Australia took tough legislative measures to ensure that the remaining 1,000 or so who resisted return – because they had settled, married, had children and/or found jobs – could nevertheless be deported.[71]

As we have seen, this differentiated approach to refugee protection was reflected in Australia's position on negotiation of the aforementioned instruments, and in relation to which it played a pivotal role. An examination of Australia's role affirms the view that its diplomatic engagement was always characterised by an 'anxious parochialism' that viewed immigration – including by refugees – as a matter entirely within the domestic purview of the state.[72] There is no doubt that this differentiated approach was driven in particular by the perceived political-economic imperatives of the White Australia immigration policy. So, although

69   Johan Cells, 'Responses of European States to de facto Refugees', in *Refugees and International Relations*, ed. Gil Loescher and Laila Monahan (Oxford: Clarendon Press, 1989), 187, 189.

70   Kevin Blackburn, 'Disguised Anti-Colonialism: Protest Against the White Australia Policy in Malaya and Singapore, 1947–1962', *Australian Journal of International Affairs* 55, no. 1 (2001): 101–17, 103, doi.org/10.1080/10357710120055102.

71   Ibid., 103. For a discussion of the *War-Time Refugees Removal Act 1949* (Cth), see Lester, *Making Migration Law,* 142–51.

72   Lester, 'Internationalising Constitutional Law', 328; see, generally, Devereux, *Australia and the Birth of the International Bill of Human Rights 1946–1966.*

Australia had already received non-European wartime refugees from the region, it had no enduring interest in providing them with the permanent protection contemplated in the *Refugee Convention*. As the secretary of the immigration department, Tasman Heyes, observed in 1950:

> There are thousands of non-European refugees, and acceptance by Australia of a convention which provides that such a class of persons should not be discriminated against and should not be subjected to any penalty for illegal entry, would be a direct negation of the immigration policy followed by all Australian Governments since Federation.[73]

As Neumann has said, this was an understatement.[74] What we can see here is that Australia's participation in the drafting of the *Refugee Convention* and its subsequent accession, as well as the negotiation of other relevant international instruments, were viewed through the lens of a discriminatory immigration policy that sought to exercise absolute and unqualified control. This is consistent with Australia's determination to ensure that non-European wartime refugees could be excluded while young, white, able-bodied refugee labour was welcomed.[75] What we can see, therefore, is that although the White Australia immigration policy would have its day, there is no doubt that it was a policy that not only helped shape the differentiated terms of the *Refugee Convention* but was also enabled by them.

So, how did Australia respond? In November 1954, five years after passing the *Wartime Refugees Removal Act* to enable removal from Australia of non-European refugees and long before it abolished the White Australia immigration policy, Australia became one of the first states to accede to the *Refugee Convention*. As we have seen, there was no pushback in the Convention against Australia's immigration policy and the commitment Australia made to receive postwar refugees as migrants. Indeed, it was entirely consistent with Australia's political-economic (and highly racialised) desire to 'populate or perish' – that 'catchy alliterative'

---

73 Heyes to Secretary, Department of External Affairs, 22 May 1950, NAA: A445, 194/2/3, cited in Neumann, *Across the Seas,* 137.
74 Neumann, *Across the Seas*, 137.
75 See, generally, Persian, *Beautiful Balts*.

nation-building slogan[76] that etched European immigration in the popular imagination as a strategic imperative in the face of unexpectedly low numbers of postwar British settlement.[77] Minister for Immigration Arthur Calwell's 'Beautiful Balts' – blond, attractive, middle-class refugees – were a saleable European substitute.[78] They were, as Persian has noted, 'the elite of the refugee problem'.[79]

Part III: The *1967 Protocol*

Of course, displacement since the early postwar years continued to occur in many places outside Europe. For example, it arose as a consequence of the decolonisation process and associated wars of independence, and in the context of ongoing and new proxy wars of the Cold War superpowers. Decolonisation and wars of independence not only generated large numbers of refugees who needed protection, but they also provided a catalyst for the adoption of further instruments, some international, others regional.[80] Of great significance was the *1967 Protocol*, which removed the geographic and temporal limitations in the *Refugee Convention*.

Decolonisation and the Cold War

The negotiation and adoption of the *1967 Protocol* reflected the realisation that the geographical and temporal limitations to the *Refugee Convention* could no longer be sustained. Whether the reasons for this were primarily legal, political or operational is a matter of debate. As Einarsen has noted, however, it was the non-universality of the refugee definition in the 1951 *Convention* that meant there was little incentive for states that were affected by the process of decolonisation rather than pre-1951 events in

---

76   The term 'populate or perish' was first coined by Billy Hughes as a call for motherhood to serve defence imperatives: see 'Hughes, William Morris (Billy) (1862–1952)', *Australian Dictionary of Biography*, available at: adb.anu.edu.au/biography/hughes-william-morris-billy-6761. It was later co-opted by Australia's first immigration minister as a rallying cry for immigration: James Jupp, *From White Australia to Woomera: The Story of Australian Immigration,* 2nd ed. (Melbourne: Cambridge University Press, 2007), 159, doi.org/10.1017/cbo9780511720222; Catriona Elder, *Being Australian: Narratives of National Identity* (Sydney: Allen & Unwin, 2007), 83–84, 93–114.

77   Judith Brett, 'Fair Share: Country and City in Australia', *Quarterly Essay* 42, (2011), 1–67, 29; Persian, *Beautiful Balts*, 6.

78   Persian, *Beautiful Balts*, 6–7.

79   Ibid., 45.

80   The earliest regional example of a refugee-specific instrument was in Africa: Organization of African Unity (OAU), *Convention Governing the Specific Aspects of Refugee Problems in Africa* ('OAU Convention'), 10 September 1969, 1001 UNTS 45.

Europe to ratify the *Refugee Convention*. In the absence of a duty on the part of those states to cooperate with UNHCR[81] – which was becoming increasingly operational in its delivery of humanitarian assistance and protection – it was difficult for UNHCR to engage them in its work for refugee protection in Africa.[82] This appears to have been a key driver behind the adoption of the *1967 Protocol.*

The transition to a protection regime that was no longer temporally and geographically limited certainly appeared to signal a step towards universalisation. However, while there may be some truth to this, it also coincided with a perceptible shift from the 'exilic bias' of refugee protection to the emergence and consolidation of a range of policies of containment.[83] These policies took different forms. Broadly, however, they can be described as state-centric tools and policies intended to keep the refugees of the Third World at arm's length. As we will see, this led to institutional declarations that voluntary repatriation of refugees was now the 'preferred' solution as well as, with time, the proliferation of laws and policies of exclusion by the liberal West. Although the process of decolonisation presented as a political opportunity for Cold War rivals and the emergent newly independent states as sites for proxy wars, refugees were still regarded as politically and ideologically interesting and continued to serve as pawns in Cold War geopolitical brinksmanship. This suggests that any claim that the *1967 Protocol* tells a progress story needs to be treated with caution. The reality is clearly more complex and nuanced.

Australia and the Indochinese refugee crisis

In the postwar period up to 1975, Australia received some 297,000 refugees, most of whom arrived not as refugees, but as assisted or unassisted migrants.[84] As we have seen, these figures notwithstanding, any

---

81   *Refugee Convention*, art 35.

82   Terje Einarsen, 'Drafting History of the 1951 Convention and the 1967 Protocol', *The 1951 Convention Relating to the Status of Refugees and Its 1967 Protocol: A Commentary*, ed. Andreas Zimmermann (Oxford: Oxford University Press, 2011) 37–73, 69, doi.org/10.1093/actrade/9780 199542512.003.0002.

83   Chimni, 'The Geopolitics of Refugee Studies', 355, 367, 369; see also T Alexander Aleinikoff, 'State-centered Refugee Law: From Resettlement to Containment', *Michigan Journal of International Law* 14, no. 1 (1992): 120–38.

84   Janet Phillips, 'Australia's Humanitarian Program: A Quick Guide to the Statistics Since 1947' (Research Paper Series 2016–17, Parliamentary Library, Parliament of Australia, updated 17 January 2017), 2 (Table 1).

claim to humanitarianism was unquestionably secondary to the enduring political-economic desire to 'populate or perish'. And of course, as we have also seen, the figures pale in comparison to the scale of European displacement, much less global displacement.

Australia did not accede to the *1967 Protocol* until December 1973 and it was not until 1977, more than 20 years after its accession to the *Refugee Convention,* that Australia developed its first clear refugee policy.[85] Even then, in a post-Protocol environment, with the inking of its first refugee policy and the institutional demise of the White Australia immigration policy, Cold War dynamics continued to govern the order of things. The refugee crisis of greatest significance to Australia at this time was the Indochinese refugee crisis of the late 1970s and 1980s.

The departure of some 3 million Indochinese followed the fall of Saigon and other proxy wars in Indochina. As Madokoro has noted, virulent racism accounted at least in part for the international community having frozen out the possibility of refugee protection for Chinese refugees fleeing communism in mainland China in the 1950s.[86] But in the case of the Indochinese, Cold War politics and ideology became the enabler in negotiating multilateral agreements for protection and resettlement of refugees on a large scale.[87] For the most part, refugees were resettled to Australia, Canada, France and the US. For Australia, it was the first real test of Australia's mettle following both its decision to abolish the White Australia policy and its accession to the *1967 Protocol*, which together signalled a willingness to protect post-1951 non-European refugees.

To quell the exodus from Vietnam in a way that would still deliver protection, a memorandum of understanding between the Vietnamese government and UNHCR was negotiated and signed in 1979. Under this Orderly Departure Program (ODP), the Vietnamese government agreed to authorise exit for the purposes of 'family reunion and other humanitarian cases' where other countries were willing to receive them.[88] This meant that at least some people could leave Vietnam without having

---

85   The formulation of a refugee resettlement policy was a major recommendation of a Senate inquiry in 1976: Senate Standing Committee on Foreign Affairs and Defence, *Australia and the Refugee Problem*, 89; Claire Higgins, *Asylum by Boat: Origins of Australia's Refugee Policy* (Sydney: NewSouth Publishing, 2017), 17.
86   Madokoro, *Elusive Refuge*, 27–30.
87   Judith Kumin, 'Orderly Departure from Vietnam: Cold War Anomaly or Humanitarian Innovation?', *Refugee Survey Quarterly* 27, no. 1 (2008): 104–17, 105, doi.org/10.1093/rsq/hdn009.
88   Ibid., 111–12.

to take up the dangerous alternative of a boat journey. As Kumin has noted, the ODP is the only time UNHCR has provided large-scale assistance to people seeking to leave their country of origin, attributing it as much to a fortuitous confluence of events, interests and personalities as from a rational decision to provide would-be refugees with a viable alternative.[89] She has also wondered whether such a model could only work in a Cold War context.[90]

Over the next 10 years, in refugee camps across South-East Asia, the protection tables would start to turn. States were less ready presumptively to accord prima facie recognition to refugees. Over time, and alongside the commitment to resettle, the Comprehensive Plan of Action on Indochinese Refugees (CPA) was negotiated. Adopted in June 1989, it conditioned temporary protection of certain Indochinese refugees by South-East Asian nations on an international commitment to screen asylum claims, to resettle those screened in to third countries, to return those screened out to their countries of origin and to continue processing departures under the ODP. The CPA coincided with the unravelling of the Cold War stand-off that had shaped both international relations and refugee protection in the postwar era and represents a critical moment that would shape state practice in at least two unexpected ways. First, this period marked the diminishing importance of the exit permit by refugee-producing countries that had hitherto served as the main point of resistance to refugee-hood. Second was the decisive emergence of temporary protection as part of a recalibration and reprioritisation of durable solutions. The impact that these developments had on international protection dynamics and the changing political landscape of durable solutions are considered in the following part.

Part IV: The Cold War et seq.

Even before the Berlin wall came down, flight from communism had already begun to lose its ideological cachet. Nevertheless, there were high hopes for a new and enlightened era in refugee protection. They would be short-lived. Instead, and despite a burgeoning refugee law jurisprudence and literature, the *Refugee Convention* and its *Protocol* and their limitations

---

89   Ibid., 105.
90   Ibid., 117.

as instruments of international protection would be brought into sharp relief.[91] As this part explores, geopolitical interests (re)calibrated and (re)prioritised the commitment to protect refugees through measures that restricted access to protection procedures and reshaped the way in which durable solutions were used and understood.

From barriers to exit to barriers to entry

When the Cold War dynamics of the post–World War II period took hold, the single greatest obstacle to protection from persecution that a would-be refugee faced was finding a way out – to exit his[92] country of persecution and the clutches of communism. Exit permits or exit visas – markers of a state-centred politico-legal resistance to the refugee journey – were prized and rare, and of course often fraudulently obtained. People smugglers were celebrated as heroes of the liberal West because they risked their lives to facilitate the escape of others who were refused or could not secure exit permits. Importantly, they were assisting the sort of people the liberal West wanted to protect. So here we see that the refugee fleeing communism was privileged in the sense of being wanted and welcomed, and his clandestine departure celebrated instead of criminalised.

These days, since the wall of communism has crumbled both figuratively and literally, the visa to exit a state of persecution has been replaced by something equally prized and rare, the visa to enter a safe haven. In other words, in the post–Cold War era a pattern of politico-legal resistance to the refugee journey now manifests as resistance to reception. As a result of this shift from barriers to exit to the construction of barriers to entry, refugees are cast adrift into a protection-less space where they lead a 'provisional' or 'bare life' existence in a state of perpetual exception – 'in orbit' or 'in limbo'.[93] These protection-less spaces are created through physical tools of exclusion (such as interdiction on the high seas, biometrics and other border control measures in the international zones of airports,

---

91   Chimni, 'The Geopolitics of Refugee Studies', 360, 362–65; Goodwin-Gill, 'The Politics of Refugee Protection', 18.
92   On the image of the 'normal' refugee as 'white, male and anti-communist', see Chimni, 'The Geopolitics of Refugee Studies', 351.
93   Chan Kwok Bun, 'Getting Through Suffering: Indochinese Refugees in Limbo 15 Years Later', *Southeast Asian Journal of Social Science* 18, no. 1 (1990): 1–18, 6, doi.org/10.1163/080382490x00015; Fiona Jenkins, 'Bare Life: Asylum-Seekers, Australian Politics and Agamben's Critique of Violence', *Australian Journal of Human Rights* 10, no. 1 (2004): 79–95, doi.org/10.1080/132323 8x.2004.11910771; Giorgio Agamben, *Homo Sacer: Sovereign Power and Bare Life*, trans. Daniel Heller-Roazen (Stanford: Stanford University Press, 1998).

or territorial or extraterritorial detention) or tools that exclude refugees from social and economic participation and engagement, leaving them to eke out an existence on society's margins – maybe on the streets, in train stations or in underground passageways. The shift has been perfected in its brutality.

This pattern highlights a central and enduring problem in the global mobility dynamic, namely that the right of a person to leave any country including her own, enshrined in post–World War II international law, has no right of entry counterpart for non-citizens.[94] The lack of a right of entry reflects a Cold War dynamic that problematised barriers to exit as barriers to freedom and therefore positioned the right to leave as imperative, but at the same time retained entry as a choice (of the state) permissibly limited by the immigration laws of the receiving country.[95] The practical effect of this at the end of the Cold War was that once exit permits were no longer needed and a person could leave the putative refugee-producing country with comparative ease, she now risked being stuck in a precarious limbo. In the result, the arbitrariness of exit permit schemes was superseded by a new arbitrariness in which the most pervasive obstacles to protection were now at points of entry. This development has generated a vast and complex state machinery that obstructs access to both territory and procedures, and positions refugee protection as 'by invitation only'.[96] In parallel, as the next section explores, a recalibration of durable solutions has changed the political landscape of protection.

The changing political landscape of durable solutions

As we know from the foregoing, Cold War refugee protection, most notably in the liberal West, was dominated by an 'exilic bias' that privileged European refugees from the Eastern Bloc and prioritised resettlement and local integration over voluntary repatriation to the country of origin. Over time, the relationship between the three durable solutions has been recalibrated and reprioritised. This has happened in ways that have curtailed access to the 'asylum space' and now, alongside voluntary repatriation, includes a growing institutional preference for

---

94 For more detailed discussion, see Lester, *Making Migration Law*, 51 n. 4, 59, 65.
95 Lester, 'Internationalising Constitutional Law', 342 n. 145.
96 Human Rights Watch, '"By Invitation Only"—Australian Asylum Policy', *Human Rights Watch* 14, no. 10 (2002), available at: www.hrw.org/reports/2002/australia/.

temporary protection. Although, of course, not itself a durable solution, temporary protection has come to serve instead as a technique for staving off access to local integration and resettlement, and for channelling the institutional preference for voluntary repatriation. This has had two key effects. First, some states have deployed temporary protection policies as a substitute for local integration. Second, there has been an accompanying politicisation of resettlement. I turn first to temporary protection.

Although not the first time temporary protection policies were activated,[97] it was in the context of the Indochinese refugee crisis that temporary protection secured its place in international protection discourse. Part of the problem since has been the absence of clear content, boundaries and legal foundation for the concept.[98] There has also been an increasing and state-centric tendency for host countries to couple temporary protection with their preference for voluntary repatriation; that is, to qualify the grant of temporary protection with an expectation (or requirement) of voluntary return. So, not only has temporary protection served as an (effective) emergency response technique in situations of mass influx,[99] but it has also become a tool whose use has undermined international protection obligations. For example, legislation granting temporary protection to 4,000 Kosovar and 1,800 East Timorese refugees following their humanitarian evacuation to Australia in 1999 assumed voluntary return would ensue and specifically prohibited both cohorts from applying for asylum. The legislation also provided that decisions to extend, shorten or cancel temporary safe haven visas were a matter of ministerial discretion.[100] In the last few months of 1999, when some Kosovars signalled their resistance to return, the immigration minister threatened them with withdrawal of basic necessities, detention and removal, and told them that it was not a matter of 'if' but 'when' they would return to Kosovo.[101] Policies such as these come and go. Current policy is to

---

97   UNHCR, 'Discussion Paper' (UNHCR Roundtable on Temporary Protection, San Remo, 19–20 July 2012), 3 n. 12.

98   UNHCR, 'Summary Conclusions on Temporary Protection' (UNHCR Roundtable on Temporary Protection, San Remo, 19–20 July 2012), 1 ('Summary Conclusions').

99   Council of the European Union, Council Directive 2001/55/EC of 20 July 2001 on Minimum Standards for Giving Temporary Protection in the Event of a Mass Influx of Displaced Persons and on Measures Promoting a Balance of Efforts Between Member States in Receiving such Persons and Bearing the Consequences Thereof, 7 August 2001, OJ L 212-223, 2001/55/EC, available at: www.unhcr.org/refworld/docid/3ddcee2e4.html.

100   For a discussion, see Michael Head, 'Australia's 1999 "Safe Haven" Refugee Act: Is it Humanitarian?', *Australian International Law Journal* (1999): 224–32.

101   Ibid., 225.

grant Temporary Protection Visas to refugees arriving in Australia without a visa – such as those arriving by boat – and to prohibit them from ever applying for a permanent visa. Quite apart from the perpetual cycle of temporariness and uncertainty that this creates it also, crushingly, denies any possibility of family reunion.[102] Such measures, which are blatantly punitive,[103] form part of a narrative that also politicises resettlement.

In recent years, a contemporary resettlement narrative has emerged that maximises the rhetorical power of resettlement at the same time as it denigrates those who seek protection through other avenues and justifies harsh policies of exclusion. It becomes the basis on which binaries are constructed; binaries that 'split'[104] refugees into the 'good' ones languishing in camps who come 'by invitation only',[105] and the 'bad' ones whose arrival in Australia, whether by boat or by plane, is unsolicited and therefore unwelcome. It is a narrative that eschews (at worst) and cherry-picks (at best) broader perspective and context, whether historical or global, as well as the living realities of the refugee. A 1996 change in government policy, which linked Australia's onshore (asylum) and offshore (resettlement) program, was an important step in cementing the binary that is integral to this emergent resettlement narrative. Under the policy, a cap was placed on the number of refugees given protection, such that increases in the number of onshore refugees would result in a corresponding decrease in access to the resettlement program. Although it has been suggested that Cabinet papers reveal that the reasons for the policy change were to obscure planned cuts in the offshore program,[106] the decision meant that onshore refugees could be blamed for those

---

102 For a summary, see Refugee Advice & Casework Service (RACS), 'Fact Sheet: Temporary Protection Visas (TPV), Safe Haven Enterprise Visas (SHEV)' (RACS, December 2020), available at: www.racs.org.au/fact-sheets.

103 *Refugee Convention*, art 31; An expert roundtable convened by UNHCR concluded that temporary protection should not exceed three years, after which refugees should transition (voluntarily) into more permanent solutions: UNHCR, 'Summary Conclusions', 4–5 [21].

104 Splitting is a discursive device that fends off the accusation of racism or other prejudice by conceding that some members of an out group are good: see Raymond G Nairn and Timothy N McCreanor, 'Race Talk and Common Sense: Patterns in Pakeha Discourse on Maori/Pakeha Relations in New Zealand', *Journal of Language and Social Psychology* 10, no. 4 (1991): 245–62, 251, doi.org/10.1177/0261927x91104002; Martha Agoustinos and Danielle Every, 'The Language of "Race" and Prejudice: A Discourse of Denial, Reason, and Liberal-Practical Politics', *Journal of Language and Social Psychology* 26, no. 2 (2007): 123–41, 132, doi.org/10.1177/0261927x07300075.

105 Human Rights Watch, 'By Invitation Only'.

106 Cameron Stewart, 'Boats Sinking Our Refugee Program', *The Australian*, 21 July 2012, available at: www.theaustralian.com.au/national-affairs/opinion/boats-sinking-our-refugee-program/news-story/55755621cfa91cdb881f592249db0a50.

cuts – cast as 'stealing' places from offshore refugees.[107] The coupling of the onshore and offshore programs not only fuelled populist migration discourses, but also deflected responsibility for the limited number of resettlement places away from policymakers, projecting responsibility instead onto the onshore refugees it deemed to be unworthy. Because of the demographic differences between offshore (resettled) and onshore (asylum) refugee populations, the decision had the further deleterious effect of pitting different cultural communities against one another.

At the same time as the resettlement narrative denigrates the spontaneously arriving refugee as a thief, it frames an image of Australia as one of the most generous refugee receiving countries in the world, and by some accounts the most generous.[108] The power of this 'generosity narrative' lies in its capacity at once to feed and to exploit public perceptions that Australia's refugee *resettlement* program is not just an adequate response to the global protection crisis, but proof that Australia is pulling its weight internationally. However, while compared to other countries Australia is a leading resettlement country, global resettlement numbers represent less than 1 per cent of the world's refugee population. So, in staking its generosity claim, Australia is overlooking the plight of the remaining 99 per cent of the world's refugees.[109] In case these are hard figures to fathom, here is another way of thinking about the numbers. According to figures published by UNHCR, every day in 2019, some 30,137 people were newly displaced globally.[110] That works out to be almost twice as many people as the 18,200 Australia resettled across the whole year.[111] Viewed in this way, Australia's 2019 resettlement program protected little more than a morning's worth of the world's newly uprooted people.

---

107 Robert Manne and David Corlett, 'Sending Them Home: Refugees and the New Politics of Indifference', *Quarterly Essay* 13 (2003).

108 Amanda Vanstone, 'Think We're Tough on Refugees? That's Fake News', *Sydney Morning Herald*, 22 April 2018, available at: www.smh.com.au/politics/federal/think-we-re-tough-on-refugees-that-s-fake-news-20180420-p4zatw.html.

109 Australia's resettlement program accounts for 0.09 per cent of the global refugee population. Resettlement figures have long represented less than 1 per cent of the world's refugee population. However, recent figures suggest a decline to 0.5 per cent, which UNHCR attributes to a decline in resettlement quotas rather than need. The present percentage calculations are based on the following figures published by UNHCR for 2019: 20.4 million refugees under UNHCR's mandate; 4.2 million asylum seekers; and 107,800 refugees admitted for resettlement. See UNHCR, *Global Trends: Forced Displacement in 2019* (UNHCR, 2020), 2–3, 48. Note, if this figure were to include the 5.6 million Palestinian refugees under UNRWA's mandate and without a durable solution, the resettlement percentage would drop to 0.41 per cent.

110 UNHCR, *Global Trends 2019*, 2.

111 Ibid., 52.

For states, it is clear that discourses of humanitarianism, accurate or otherwise, are politically important, domestically and internationally. As Dauvergne has observed, the humanitarianism of the contemporary resettlement narrative seeks to 'mark the nation as good, prosperous, and generous'.[112] However, as she notes, this kind of humanitarianism is 'an impoverished stand-in for justice'.[113] In part, this is because global resettlement figures are so small. Tellingly, the discourse barely conceals the utilitarian nature of this kind of humanitarianism – a functional approach to protection that has a hard core of self-interest coated with a thin veneer of altruism and generosity.

So, how is it possible for states to take this approach? Under international law, there is no binding obligation to resettle refugees.[114] In contrast, states *are* legally obliged not to *refoule* a refugee[115] and, by extension, to grant her protection if she arrives spontaneously and seeks protection. This is what sets resettlement apart as an attractive policy option. Thus, not only is the protection of a refugee who has not directly engaged the protection obligations of the state optional, but also decisions about the size and composition of the program are policy-based.

Part V: Charting a way forward in the twenty-first century

In the twenty-first century, we find an already fractured protection landscape further damaged by state responses to the so-called global migration crisis; a crisis of political will that has arisen in the context and aftermath of the so-called War on Terror and a resurgence in 'neo-' forms of liberalist and colonialist ideologies.

Conflict in the Middle East has had an immeasurable impact on displacement and state responses to the emergent 'global migration crisis', most notably in the context of wars in Iraq and Syria. A key feature of

---

112 Catherine Dauvergne, *Humanitarianism, Identity and Nation: Migration Laws of Australia and Canada* (Vancouver: University of British Columbia Press, 2005), 7.

113 Ibid.

114 Naoko Hashimoto, 'Refugee Resettlement as an Alternative to Asylum', *Refugee Survey Quarterly* 37, no. 2 (2018): 162–86, 163, doi.org/10.1093/rsq/hdy004.

115 *Refoulement* is the forcible return of a person to a place where her life or freedom would be threatened. It is prohibited under *Refugee Convention* art 33 and is also a principle of customary international law.

this time has been the numbers of refugees who have spontaneously sought protection – often by sea – in Europe and other countries of the global North, as it is now known. In Australia, increased numbers seeking asylum reignited debate and reinvigorated controversial policies such as its scheme of extraterritorial detention and processing, dubbed Pacific Solution Mark II, and triggered a further campaign known as Operation Sovereign Borders, an equally controversial policy designed to prevent boat arrivals through pushbacks.

Another dimension to early twenty-first century developments has been the way in which the so-called War on Terror and radicalisation and extremism have enabled security discourse to permeate and complicate the refugee protection debate and state responses to it. These factors have often clouded the reality that the vast majority of refugees are in flight from, rather than causes of, insecurity. As early as 2001, treatment of the *Tampa* refugees rescued off the coast of Australia just days before the 9/11 attacks in the US and their relocation were justified – but later dismissed – as being security related.[116]

Resettlement in the context of the Syrian refugee crisis has been important for individuals and communities, but the numbers have been small in real terms. Australia only agreed to resettle 12,000 Syrian refugees in the face of considerable international pressure. In 2015, the suggestion of resettling some of the 8,000 Rohingya refugees stranded at sea in South-East Asia in flight from genocidal policies in Myanmar was dismissed with a resounding 'Nope, nope, nope' from an Australian prime minister.[117] And in 2018, Australia's minister for home affairs singled out white South African farmers as a community particularly worthy of Australia's concern.[118] All this suggests that state responses continue to be both selective and situation specific.

---

116 Irene Khan, 'Trading in Human Misery: A Human Rights Perspective on the Tampa Incident', *Washington International Law Journal* 12, no. 1 (2003): 9–22, 11.

117 Lisa Cox, '"Nope, Nope, Nope": Tony Abbott Says Australia Will Not Resettle Refugees in Migrant Crisis', *Sydney Morning Herald*, 21 May 2015, available at: www.smh.com.au/politics/federal/nope-nope-nope-tony-abbott-says-australia-will-not-resettle-refugees-in-migrant-crisis-20150521-gh6eew.html; Penny Green, Thomas MacManus and Alicia de la Cour Venning, *Countdown to Annihilation: Genocide in Myanmar* (London: International State Crime Initiative, 2015), available at: statecrime.org/data/2015/10/ISCI-Rohingya-Report-PUBLISHED-VERSION.pdf.

118 Paul Karp, 'Australia Considers Fast-Track Visas for White South African Farmers', *Guardian*, 14 March 2018, available at: www.theguardian.com/australia-news/2018/mar/14/dutton-considers-fast-track-visas-for-white-south-african-farmers.

Institutional responses to the 'global migration crisis'

In September 2016, the UN General Assembly unanimously adopted the *New York Declaration for Refugees and Migrants* ('New York Declaration').[119] The New York Declaration came out of a summit that sought to recognise all refugees and migrants as rights holders and to condemn acts and manifestations of racism, xenophobia and other forms of intolerance. The declaration reaffirmed the importance of the international refugee regime and contains a wide range of commitments by member states to strengthen and enhance mechanisms to protect people on the move, both refugees and migrants. It paved the way for the negotiation of two new global compacts in 2018: one on refugees and the other for safe, orderly and regular migration.

States have since negotiated the text of the *Global Compact for Safe, Orderly and Regular Migration* (GCM), adopted in Marrakech in December 2018. In parallel, states also participated in consultations led by UNHCR on the text of the *Global Compact on Refugees* (GCR). Although the names of the compacts suggest a focus in the first instance on migrants and in the second on refugees, there is not a clear line between the two. In particular, the text of the GCM includes a number of issues that are directly relevant to refugees' experience of 'border management policies', particularly when they are impelled to use irregular migration routes in search of protection. Together the compacts represent the latest opportunity to try and achieve international momentum for protection of the rights and interests of refugees and migrants. If history is any measure, Australia's withdrawal from the GCM on the grounds that it is a 'threat to sovereignty' should not have come as a surprise.[120] Certainly, its decision to do so may undermine prospects for the GCM and GCR to strengthen international frameworks for protection of refugees and migrants. As two leading civil society commentators observed when Australia first signalled its intention

---

119 *New York Declaration for Refugees and Migrants,* GA Res 71/1, UNGA, 71st sess, UN Doc A/RES/71/1 (3 October 2016).

120 Chris Merritt, 'UN Migration Pact "a Threat to Sovereignty"', *The Australian,* 3 August 2018, available at: www.theaustralian.com.au/nation/immigration/un-migration-pact-a-threat-to-sovereignty/news-story/f9c795ec8127863e55aacbd9baebb6eb. Withdrawal from the GCM was confirmed in a joint ministerial statement: The Hon Scott Morrison MP, Prime Minister, The Hon Peter Dutton MP, Minister for Home Affairs, Senator the Hon Marise Payne, Minister for Foreign Affairs, 'Global Compact for Migration', joint media release, 21 November 2018, available at: www.foreignminister.gov.au/minister/marise-payne/media-release/global-compact-migration.

to withdraw from the GCM, there were good reasons why Australia should have joined the rest of the world – except most notably Donald Trump's America and Victor Orban's Hungary – in rethinking the way it responds to the global movement of people.[121] First and foremost is that no state can respond to these issues alone.

Conclusion

This chapter has demonstrated that, in the case of Australia, both *who* the refugee is and *how* she got to Australia have historically defined how well she has been received, and that this '*who*' and that '*how*' continue to shape the way we think about, validate and accept as justified the '*why*' of her quest for protection and the '*where*' in which she seeks it. The chapter has endeavoured to show that the way we understand Australia's responses to the refugee journey, and the way those responses fit into a bigger international picture, is highly dependent on historical-political context and perspective. It has sought to show that each part of this framework has a political and ideological dimension that changes, depending on time and place. To that end, it has presented a broader context for understanding and thinking about Australia's protection of refugees, with the intention of enabling the reader to see Australian accounts of and approaches to the refugee journey through a wider lens.

What we have seen in this background is that Australia's approach to refugee protection has long been situation specific and highly differentiated. The narrow scope of the *Refugee Convention* in its initial framing certainly helps to explain Australia's willing accession to it and Australia's responses to refugee movements in the Convention's early years. We have seen that Australia's responses were not just aligned with but also driven by its postwar labour shortages and immigration priorities. It suggests too that the underpinnings of Australia's oft-celebrated decision to become one of the first states parties to the *Refugee Convention* reflected an early form of the 'utilitarian humanitarianism' that has served and suited both Australia's immigration priorities and changing geopolitical interests.

---

121 Carolina Gottardo, 'Migration Compact Will Benefit Australia', *Eureka Street*, 5 August 2018, available at: www.eurekastreet.com.au/article/migration-compact-will-benefit-australia, and Anne Gallagher, '3 Reasons All Countries should Embrace the Global Compact for Migration', *World Economic Forum*, 22 August 2018, available at: www.weforum.org/.

Finally, we have seen how and with what effects and implications states, including Australia, have (re)calibrated and (re)prioritised durable solutions for refugees over time – those durable solutions being resettlement, local integration and voluntary repatriation. We have seen that Australia's attempts to legitimise exclusionist asylum policies by talking up the resettlement program and implying that it is conceptually and statistically adequate as, in the first instance, a response to the global protection crisis and, in the second, a substitute for spontaneous asylum requests, are unconvincing. At the same time, it is also clear that these attempts are entirely consistent with longstanding approaches to refugee protection.

As the chapter demonstrates, the way in which the state of Australia approaches its obligations to protect refugees and asylum seekers is politically tidal, ebbing and flowing with changing perceptions of the national interest. We see that nation-states such as Australia have positioned themselves legally and politically in a state of perpetual resistance to the refugee journey, unable to accept the need to flee and seek safe haven as a reality that is part of the order of things, or even part of the disorder of things. In the New York Declaration and the two global compacts, we see an acceptance of mobility, including the refugee journey, as part of humanity's reality. Despite Australia's withdrawal from the GCM, that acknowledgement must surely be cause for hope.

2

ONCE A REFUGEE, ALWAYS A REFUGEE?

The haunting of the refugee label in resettlement

Melanie Baak[1]

So I have a new name – refugee
Strange that a name should take away from me
My past, my personality and hope
Strange refuge this.
So many seem to share this name – refugee
Yet we share so many differences.

I find no comfort in my new name
I long to share my past, restore my pride,
To show, I too, in time, will offer more
Than I have borrowed.
For now the comfort that I seek
Resides in the old yet new name
I would choose – friend.

Ruvimbo Bungwe, aged 9 or 14 depending on source, from Zimbabwe[2]

1   Acknowledgements: I would like to acknowledge that the thinking and work that informed this chapter was undertaken on the lands of the Nukunu and Kaurna people and pay my respects to ancestors and Elders past, present and emerging. I would also like to acknowledge the work of my colleagues, Emily Miller, Associate Professor Anna Sullivan and Associate Professor Kathleen Heugh, on the research project from which a component of data is used in this chapter. Finally, I'd like to thank all those from across the world who have shared their stories of refugee experiences with me over many years.
2   Iris Teichmann, *Credit to the Nation: Refugee Contributions to the UK* (London: Refugee Council, 2002).

On International Refugee Day 2018, Danijel Malbasa, a Melbourne-based industrial relations lawyer and a refugee of the Yugoslav wars, wrote of his desire growing up to distance himself from his refugee identity. He worked hard to 'scrub out my strong Slavic accent, develop an Aussie drawl, take out the letter "j" from my name, even better anglicise it to "Dan", get out of the ESL class' and in doing this to 'pass' as Australian, to shun all the 'stereotypical baggage that comes with declaring oneself a refugee'.[3] Similarly, my own father was the child of post–World War II refugees from Poland and Russia resettled in Australia. My father began school as Henrik, not speaking a word of English, shortly thereafter he became Henry and fairly quickly forgot most of the Polish and Russian he spoke as a child. Like Danijel and my father, many former refugees have written of the desire to escape the 'refugee' label. Hannah Arendt, for example, in her seminal essay 'We Refugees' suggests that '[i]n the first place, we don't like to be called "refugees". We ourselves call each other "newcomers" or "immigrants"'.[4] Ruvimbo Bungwe (cited above) at a very young age identified the desire to resist the naming 'refugee'.

Both Danijel and my father could take these actions to 'pass' as Australians and shun their refugee backgrounds because they were young, 'white' people of Eastern European refugee background resettled in Australia, and thus had some of the characteristics of 'whiteness' required to pass in Australia.[5] The cultural and ethnic diversity of Australia has shifted significantly since my father was a five-year-old in the 1950s. Jupp identifies that in 1947, Australians were 99 per cent white and 96 per cent Anglo-Celtic.[6] During the peak period of Yugoslav resettlement in Australia in the early 1990s, approximately 82 per cent of Australians spoke English as their first language.[7] The 2016 Australian census identified that 21 per cent of Australians speak a language other than

---

3   Danijel Malbasa, 'I Used to Distance Myself from my Refugee Identity. Now I Own It', *Guardian*, 20 June 2018, available at: www.theguardian.com/commentisfree/2018/jun/19/i-used-to-distance-myself-from-my-refugee-identity-now-i-own-it.

4   Hannah Arendt, 'We Refugees', in *Altogether Elsewhere: Writers on Exile*, ed. M Robinson (Boston: Faber and Faber, 1994), 110.

5   Val Colic-Peisker, '"At Least You're the Right Colour": Identity and Social Inclusion of Bosnian Refugees in Australia', *Journal of Ethnic and Migration Studies* 31, no. 4 (2005), doi.org/10.1080/13691830500109720.

6   James Jupp, *Immigration*, 2nd ed. (Melbourne: Oxford University Press, 1998), 132.

7   James Jupp, 'From "White Australia" to "Part of Asia": Recent Shifts in Australian Immigration Policy Towards the Region', *International Migration Review* 29, no. 1 (1995): 211, doi.org/10.2307/2547002.

English at home and 33 per cent were born outside of Australia.[8] While the ethnic and linguistic diversity of Australia has shifted significantly since the ending of the official 'White Australia' policy in 1973,[9] Australia is still perceived as a 'white nation'. The concept of 'race' has always been and continues to be central to political debates in Australia on issues such as immigration and national identity. These political debates in turn influence the everyday experiences of those who are 'marked' by their race. Having a 'visibly different' appearance, whether on the basis of skin colour or religious markers (such as wearing Islamic dress), results in a very different resettlement experience than those refugees who can pass in the 'invisibility' of 'whiteness' in Australia. While Danijel writes that he has recently learnt to 'own' his refugee identity after 'hiding' it for many years, this raises a number of questions. Why do some people with refugee experience resettled in countries such as Australia feel the need to distance themselves from their refugee background? What are the experiences of refugees resettled in countries such as Australia who can't 'pass' as Australian, whose visible difference can't be erased – whether by virtue of their skin colour or religion or whose audible difference can't be silenced? This chapter explores these questions. First by interrogating the framing of refugees in media, political and broader discourse. Second, by focusing on the experiences of former refugees who have been resettled in Australia.

For those who have lived in uncertain, protracted refugee situations with little hope of repatriation to their countries of birth and limited options for integration into countries of first asylum, resettlement can be seen as a dreamlike aspiration. The numbers of those resettled globally each year are a tiny number of the recognised refugees globally. In the 12 months to June 2018, approximately 102,800 of the recognised 25.4 million refugees, or 0.4 per cent, were resettled.[10] While the number of resettled refugees are a very small percentage of the overall number of displaced people globally, those who are resettled live their lives at the intersection of the multiple framings of refugeeness. They bring the refugee experience into direct contact with the Western frames of understanding what it means

8   'Cultural Diversity in Australia', Australian Bureau of Statistics, 28 June 2017, available at: www.abs.gov.au/ausstats/abs@.nsf/Lookup/by%20Subject/2071.0~2016~Main%20Features~Cultural%20Diversity%20Data%20Summary~30.

9   James Jupp, *From White Australia to Woomera: The Story of Australian Immigration* (Melbourne: Cambridge University Press, 2002), doi.org/10.1017/cbo9781139195034.

10   'Figures at a Glance', UNHCR.org, as at June 2018, available at: www.unhcr.org/en-au/figures-at-a-glance.html.

to be a refugee. In a country such as Australia, for example, where over 220,000 people from refugee backgrounds were resettled in the period from 2000 to 2019,[11] these people, their experiences and the resultant research play a significant role in shaping perceptions and understanding of forced migration and refugees. In the past 20 years, resettlement has mainly been concentrated in a relatively small number of countries, primarily the United States, Canada, Australia, the Nordic countries and, increasingly, Europe. Given the geographical locations in which refugees have predominantly been resettled, interrogating the framing of refugees in these countries is crucial to understanding the ways in which former refugees are likely to be 'seen' and understood in their new home countries.

After resettlement, many former refugees continue to be referred to as 'refugees', even when resettlement entails a formal bureaucratic relabelling as permanent residents and then later as citizens. Labelling of those who have been resettled as 'refugees' continues in much academic[12] and media discourse.[13] This labelling continues for long after former refugees become permanent residents and citizens. For example, a recent research article refers to children born of parents with refugee experience who have lived in the UK for all or most of their lives as 'second generation refugees'.[14] The question becomes: when, if ever, do people who have been refugees stop being refugees (with all of the frames of reference this entails)?

---

11   Janet Phillips, 'Australia's Humanitarian Program: A quick guide to the statistics since 1947', 2017, available at: www.aph.gov.au/About_Parliament/Parliamentary_Departments/Parliamentary_ Library/pubs/rp/rp1617/Quick_Guides/HumanitarianProg; Department of Home Affairs, 'Australia's offshore Humanitarian Program: 2018–19', 2019, available at: www.homeaffairs.gov.au/ research-and-stats/files/australia-offshore-humanitarian-program-2018-19.pdf.

12   See, for example, Mark Brough et al., 'Young Refugees Talk About Well-Being: A Qualitative Analysis of Refugee Mental Health from Three States', *Australian Journal of Social Issues* 38, no. 2 (2003), doi.org/10.1002/j.1839-4655.2003.tb01142.x; Peter Browne, *The Longest Journey: Resettling Refugees from Africa* (Sydney: University of New South Wales Press, 2006); Clemence Due, '"Who are Strangers?": "Absorbing" Sudanese Refugees into a White Australia', *ACRAWSA E-Journal* 4, no. 1 (2008), available at: acrawsa.org.au/wp-content/uploads/2017/12/CRAWS-Vol-4-No-1-2008-1.pdf.

13   See, for example, Piers Ackerman, 'Refugee Fury at Africa Ban; Sudanese: Minister Insulted Us', *Sunday Mail*, 14 October 2007, available at: www.news.com.au/adelaidenow/ story/0,22606,22581759-5006301,00.html (site discontinued); Elissa Hunt, 'Killers who Bashed Sudanese Refugee Liep Gony to Death can be Identified after Herald Sun Campaign', *Herald Sun*, 18 February 2010, available at: www.heraldsun.com.au/news/killers-who-bashed-saudanese-refugee-liep-giny-to-death-can-be-identified-after-herald-sun-campaign/news-story/35af7b625d 754b6d4643a40d072ae026; Ben Schneiders, 'Refugees Fear for Future, Say Leaders', *Age* (Melbourne), 23 October 2007, available at: www.theage.com.au/news/national/refugees-fear-for-future-say-leade rs/2007/10/22/1192940985058.html.

14   Alice Bloch and Shirin Hirsch, '"Second Generation" Refugees and Multilingualism: Identity, Race and Language Transmission', *Ethnic and Racial Studies* 40, no. 14 (2017), doi.org/10.1080/014 19870.2016.1252461.

To interrogate this question, this chapter will highlight the development of frames of understanding the refugee, then dialogue these with everyday experiences of people from refugee backgrounds resettled in countries such as Australia. The chapter presents a small component of a research project conducted with students with refugee experience in secondary schools as well as drawing on literature, writing by people from refugee backgrounds such as Danijel Malbasa[15] and personal experience with people from refugee backgrounds over the past 15 years. This chapter will provide examples of the ways in which 'race' and racialisation of the refugee underpin how refugees are seen and understood as well as the ways in which the refugee label continues to haunt former refugees who are resettled in third countries such as the United States, the United Kingdom, Australia and Canada.

In this chapter I use the term 'haunt' to understand the ways in 'which abusive systems of power make themselves known and their impacts felt in everyday life'.[16] To be haunted, Gordon argues:

> is to be tied to historical and social effects ... these ghostly aspects of social life are not aberrations, but are central to modernity itself ... The ghostly phantom objects and subjects of modernity have a determining agency on the ones they are haunting.[17]

Through tracing the framing of the refugee and the everyday experiences of this framing, I argue that there are 'abusive systems of power' in place that haunt refugees and former refugees and have a 'determining agency' that positions them as always already in deficit and as objects in need of assistance. Through tracing the development of the refugee label and explicating how the label is enacted and experienced in everyday lives, I argue that it is not the refugee label that needs to be escaped/exorcised but the frames of reference through which the refugee experience is understood.

---

15 Malbasa, 'I Used to Distance Myself from my Refugee Identity. Now I Own It'.
16 Avery F Gordon, *Ghostly Matters: Hauntings and the Sociological Imagination* (Minneapolis: University of Minnesota Press, 2008), xvi.
17 Ibid., 190–201.

Framing the refugee

The word 'refugee' can be traced to its origins in the French word *réfugié* that was used to identify the Huguenots, tens of thousands of Reformed Protestant French migrants who escaped the French Catholic monarch to live in other non-Catholic European countries at the time.[18] While the 'legal and moral status'[19] of refugees was crystallised with the development of the *1951 Convention Relating to the Status of Refugees*,[20] the ways in which refugees are understood by the broader population, particularly in countries in which they are given refuge, has shifted and changed, and been influenced by wider cultural and political rhetoric. Canadian historian Michael Ignatieff argues that currently 'new metaphors have entered the democratic body politic, categorizing the refugee not as an individual with rights and a moral claim, but as the invasive other'.[21] Visual, political and discursive fields operate to construct frames that position refugees not only as Other, but as a threatening, undesired Other. Butler argues that certain normative processes operate to 'produce certain subjects as "recognizable" persons and to make others decidedly more difficult to recognize'.[22] Through processes of framing particular populations, such as refugees, these normative processes make refugees inherently more difficult to recognise as subjects and thereby human. In order to understand the ways in which these normative processes have operated to produce refugees as infinitely less 'recognizable' persons, it is important to trace the ways in which refugees have been labelled and understood.

A number of important research articles have interrogated the labelling of refugees. Roger Zetter's original paper 'Refugees and Refugee Studies – A Label and an Agenda'[23] articulated a framing of the refugee that continues in a similar vein 30 years later:

> in the present century it is the word 'refugee' which has increasingly been deployed to describe the millions of uprooted people who have been forced into exile or displaced within their

---

18   Leo Hornak, 'The Word "Refugee" has a Surprising Origin', *Public Radio International*, 20 February 2017, available at: www.pri.org/stories/2017-02-20/word-refugee-has-surprising-origin.
19   Michael Ignatieff, 'The Refugee as Invasive Other', *Social Research: An International Quarterly* 84, no. 1 (2017): 223.
20   *Convention Relating to the Status of Refugees*, opened for signature 28 July 1951, 189 UNTS 150 (entered into force 22 April 1954).
21   Ignatieff, 'The Refugee as Invasive Other', 223.
22   Judith Butler, *Frames of War: When is Life Grievable?*, 2nd ed. (London: Verso, 2010), 6.
23   Roger Zetter, 'Refugees and Refugee Studies – A Label and an Agenda', *Journal of Refugee Studies* 1, no. 1 (1988): 1–6, doi.org/10.1093/jrs/1.1.1.

own countries because of intolerance, war or other human factors. 'Refugee' constitutes one of the most powerful labels currently in the repertoire of humanitarian concern, national and international public policy and social differentiation. The label 'refugee' both stereotypes and institutionalises a status. It is benevolent and apolitical, yet it also establishes, through legal and policy making practices, highly politicised interpretations (Wood 1985). It may designate crisis needs and the associated conditions of poverty and deprivation. Conversely it encompasses longer term issues of resettlement and assimilation.[24]

Zetter's subsequent works, particularly 'Labelling Refugees: Forming and Transforming a Bureaucratic Identity'[25] and 'More Labels, Fewer Refugees: Remaking the Refugee Label in an Era of Globalization',[26] continue to explore the ways in which bureaucratic action forms and transforms the framing and identification, as well as the identities, of refugees. He argues, along with others such as Malkki,[27] that humanitarian agencies and interventions in refugee situations have resulted in a 'focus on refugees as their object of knowledge, assistance, and management'.[28] Chimni develops these arguments, suggesting that through the objectification of refugees, understandings of refugees have been constructed through a 'western strategy to employ *political humanitarianism*'.[29] Through this focus on refugees as an object of knowledge, refugees have become 'an object of concern and knowledge for the "international community," and for a particular variety of humanism'.[30] The objectification of refugees has seen refugees represented as ahistorical, apolitical, victims,

---

24   Zetter, 'Refugees and Refugee Studies – A Label and an Agenda', 1.

25   Roger Zetter, 'Labelling Refugees: Forming and Transforming a Bureaucratic Identity', *Journal of Refugee Studies* 4, no. 1 (1991), doi.org/10.1093/jrs/4.1.39.

26   Roger Zetter, 'More Labels, Fewer Refugees: Remaking the Refugee Label in an Era of Globalization', *Journal of Refugee Studies* 20, no. 2 (2007), doi.org/10.1093/jrs/fem011.

27   Liisa H Malkki, 'National Geographic: The Rooting of Peoples and the Territorialization of National Identity Among Scholars and Refugees', in *Culture, Power, Place: Explorations in Critical Anthropology*, ed. Akhil Gupta and James Ferguson (Durham, NC: Duke University Press, 1997), doi. org/10.1215/9780822382089-002; Liisa H Malkki, *Purity and Exile: Violence, Memory, and National Cosmology among Hutu Refugees in Tanzania* (Chicago: The University of Chicago Press, 1995), doi. org/10.7208/chicago/9780226190969.001.0001; Liisa H Malkki, 'Refugees and Exile: From "Refugee Studies" to the National Order of Things', *Annual Review of Anthropology* 24 (1995), doi.org/10.1146/annurev.an.24.100195.002431; Liisa H Malkki, 'Speechless Emissaries: Refugees, Humanitarianism, and Dehistoricization', *Cultural Anthropology* 11, no. 3 (1996), doi.org/10.1525/can.1996.11.3.02a00050.

28   Malkki, 'Speechless Emissaries', 377.

29   B S Chimni, 'The Birth of a "Discipline": From Refugee to Forced Migration Studies', *Journal of Refugee Studies* 22, no. 1 (2009): 13, doi.org/10.1093/jrs/fen051.

30   Malkki, 'Speechless Emissaries', 378.

'universal humanitarian subjects',[31] in need of 'fixing by state actors and aid providers',[32] as 'undesirable elements disruptive to the national order of things',[33] who are recognised through 'racializing schemes that serve to blacken and stigmatize'.[34]

Photojournalism, film, the media and the state have all shaped the positioning of 'refugees' in particular ways.[35] The images that circulate in the media 'play a central role in framing how refugees are publicly perceived and politically debated'.[36] Media images and political discourses have framed understandings of the refugee such that, on hearing the word refugee, many people imagine images of refugee camps, hunger, war, conflict and trauma. Others think of current political discourses globally around 'asylum seekers', 'queue jumpers', 'terrorists' and fear. International and national discourses around the 'refugee crisis' see current events framed in ways that sensationalise the 'problem' of the refugee.[37] For refugees, certain representational conventions 'have coagulated into a standard discursive mode that one finds routinely in journalistic writing and other news media'.[38] Through representations of refugees as 'needy' victims who have experienced trauma,[39] they are frequently portrayed as

---

31   Ibid.

32   Sara L McKinnon, 'Unsettling Resettlement: Problematizing "Lost Boys of Sudan" Resettlement and Identity', *Western Journal of Communication* 72, no. 4 (2008): 397, doi.org/10.1080/105703108 02446056.

33   Bishupal Limbu, 'Illegible Humanity: The Refugee, Human Rights and the Question of Representation', *Journal of Refugee Studies* 22, no. 3 (2009): 268, doi.org/10.1093/jrs/fep021.

34   Aihwa Ong, *Buddha is Hiding: Refugees, Citizenship, the New America* (Berkeley: University of California Press, 2003), 13.

35   Melanie Baak, 'Murder, Community Talk and Belonging: An Exploration of Sudanese Community Responses to Murder in Australia', *African Identities* 9, no. 4 (2011), doi.org/10.1080/14725843. 2011.614415; Prem Kumar Rajaram, 'Humanitarianism and Representations of the Refugee', *Journal of Refugee Studies* 15, no. 3 (2002).

36   Roland Bleiker et al., 'The Visual Dehumanisation of Refugees', *Australian Journal of Political Science* 48, no. 4 (2013): 402.

37   Marlou Schrover and Willem Schinkel, 'Introduction: The Language of Inclusion and Exclusion in the Context of Immigration and Integration', *Ethnic and Racial Studies* 36, no. 7 (2013), doi.org/ 10.1080/01419870.2013.783711.

38   Limbu, 'Illegible Humanity', 268.

39   Laura Bates et al., 'Sudanese Refugee Youth in Foster Care: The "Lost Boys" in America', *Child Welfare Journal* 84, no. 5 (2005); Brough et al., 'Young Refugees Talk About Well-Being'; Kaaren Frater-Mathieson, 'Refugee Trauma, Loss and Grief: Implications for Intervention', in *Educational Interventions for Refugee Children: Theoretical Perspectives and Implementing Best Practice*, ed. Richard Hamilton and Dennis Moore (London: RoutledgeFalmer, 2004), doi.org/10.4324/9780203687550; Jay M Marlowe, 'Beyond the Discourse of Trauma: Shifting the Focus on Sudanese Refugees', *Journal of Refugee Studies* 23, no. 2 (2010), doi.org/10.1093/jrs/feq013; Robert Schweitzer et al., 'Trauma, Post-Migration Living Difficulties, and Social Support as Predictors of Psychological Adjustment in Resettled Sudanese Refugees', *Australian & New Zealand Journal of Psychiatry* 40, no. 2 (2006), doi.org/10.1080/j.1440-1614.2006.01766.x.

undesirable 'parasites' of the state[40] who are unwilling or unable to find employment,[41] unlikely or unable to succeed at school without significant state-funded support,[42] and unwilling or unable to integrate within the host community.[43] The re-inscription of representations of 'refugees', then, works to preclude refugees from inclusion into the communities to which they are resettled.

These standard discursive modes have resulted in what Adichie refers to as the 'single story'.[44] The 'danger of the single story' is that it serves to rob people of their dignity and make 'our recognition of our equal humanity difficult'.[45] The discourses and images, the 'single story' of refugees, not only haunt the ways in which the broader population understands refugees in the countries in which they first seek asylum, but these framings also follow refugees to the countries in which they are resettled. Through representations of 'the refugee', anonymising and dehumanising narratives are allowed, and even encouraged, to permeate. These singular, deficit views overlook the 'complex and oftentimes contradictory humanity and subjectivity'[46] that underscores how refugees negotiate their lives. It limits

---

40   Mireille Rosello, *Postcolonial Hospitality: The Immigrant as Guest* (California: Stanford University Press, 2001); Alison Saxton, '"I Certainly Don't Want People Like That Here": The Discursive Construction of "Asylum Seekers"', *Media International Australia* 109, no. 1 (2003), doi.org/10.1177/1329878x0310900111.

41   Val Colic-Peisker, 'The "Visibly Different" Refugees in the Australian Labour Market: Settlement Policies and Employment Realities', in *Refugees, Recent Migrants and Employment: Challenging Barriers and Exploring Pathways*, ed. S McKay (New York: Routledge, 2009), doi.org/10.4324/9780203890745.

42   Lutine de Wal Pastoor, 'Rethinking Refugee Education: Principles, Policies and Practice from a European Perspective', *Annual Review of Comparative and International Education 2016*, vol. 30 (2016), doi.org/10.1108/s1479-367920160000030009; Rachel Hek, 'The Role of Education in the Settlement of Young Refugees in the UK: The Experiences of Young Refugees', *Practice* 17, no. 3 (2005), doi.org/10.1080/09503150500285115; Jody Lynn McBrien, 'Educational Needs and Barriers for Refugee Students in the United States: A Review of the Literature', *Review of Educational Research* 75, no. 3 (2005), doi.org/10.3102/00346543075003329; Emily Miller, Tahereh Ziaian and Adrian Esterman, 'Australian School Practices and the Education Experiences of Students with a Refugee Background: A Review of the Literature', *International Journal of Inclusive Education* (2017), doi.org/10.1080/13603116.2017.1365955.

43   Surjeet Dhanji, 'Welcome of Unwelcome? Integration Issues and the Resettlement of Former Refugees from the Horn of Africa and Sudan in Metropolitan Melbourne', *The Australasian Review of African Studies* 30, no. 2 (2009); Kerstin Lueck, Clemence Due and Martha Augoustinos, 'Neoliberalism and Nationalism: Representations of Asylum Seekers in the Australian Mainstream News Media', *Discourse & Society* 26, no. 5 (2015), doi.org/10.1177/0957926515581159; Alison Strang and Alastair Ager, 'Refugee Integration: Emerging Trends and Remaining Agendas', *Journal of Refugee Studies* 23, no. 4 (2010), doi.org/10.1093/jrs/feq046.

44   Chimamanda Ngozi Adichie, 'The Danger of a Single Story' (talk, TEDGlobal 2009), available at: www.ted.com/talks/chimamanda_adichie_the_danger_of_a_single_story/transcript.

45   Adichie, 'The Danger of a Single Story'.

46   Gordon, *Ghostly Matters*, 4.

them to being understood and seen as always and only refugees, with all the ghosts that this entails, and homogenises the multiple lives to a single experience. As Turton has argued, for refugees, the discourse of forced migration:

> helps to make it possible for states, governments and the publics of host countries, especially rich Northern ones, to respond to forced migrants not as individual human beings, people like us, embedded in contingent social and historical circumstances, but as anonymous and dehumanised masses. As people who are members neither of our civil nor our moral community.[47]

With this dehumanisation of the refugee experience, it becomes clear that the lives of refugees have become dissociated from the human in a way that makes their lives less recognisable. To interrogate the ways in which we might shift these frames, Butler argues that it is essential to call these frames into question – 'to show that the frame never quite contained the scene it was meant to limn, that something was already outside, which made the very sense of the inside possible, recognizable'.[48] To do this requires not only the production of new frames, but also a reworking of the existing frames through which it 'becomes possible to apprehend something about what or who is living but has not been generally "recognized" as a life'.[49] While there is effort in the alternative media (i.e. media sources that do not seek to represent government and corporate interests as the mainstream media does)[50] and in various research to produce new frames of understanding the refugee experience,[51] there is still significant work required to rework the existing frames. In the sections that follow, I provide examples from a research project that identify how frames of understanding the refugee are enacted in everyday life. However, the research examples also emphasise the ways people with refugee experience struggle to resist these framings.

---

47   David Turton, 'Conceptualising Forced Migration' (RSC Working Paper No. 12, 2003): 10, available at: www.rsc.ox.ac.uk/files/files-1/wp12-conceptualising-forced-migration-2003.pdf.
48   Butler, *Frames of War: When is Life Grievable?*, 9.
49   Ibid., 12.
50   Edward S Herman and Noam Chomsky, *Manufacturing Consent: The Political Economy of the Mass Media* (Random House, 2010), doi.org/10.2139/ssrn.1977265.
51   See, for example, Melanie Baak, *Negotiating Belongings: Stories of Forced Migration of Dinka Women from South Sudan* (Rotterdam: Sense Publishers, 2016), doi.org/10.1007/978-94-6300-588-3; Behrouz Boochani, *No Friend but the Mountains: Writing from Manus Prison*, trans. Omid Tofighian (Sydney: Picador, 2018); Laurent Van Lancker, *Kalès* (Polymorfilms, 2017); Olivia Woldemikael, 'A Crisis of Definition Rehumanising the Refugee', Real Media, 2017, available at: realmedia.press/a-crisis-of-definition-rehumanising-the-refugee/ (site discontinued).

Research context

This chapter is informed by over 15 years of personal and professional experience living and working with people of various refugee backgrounds in a number of different countries and contexts. As a white Anglo Australian woman who is married to a South Sudanese Australian of refugee background, my understandings are informed by his experiences as well as those of his family, friends and community. I have also spent time living with South Sudanese refugees in Kenya and Uganda. Over the past 11 years I have undertaken a number of different research projects exploring different aspects of the resettlement experience for refugees in Australia and in Scotland, particularly focused on schooling, but also on broader contexts including employment, health and social inclusion. While these experiences inform this chapter, the data presented in what follows largely draw on a project I recently undertook with colleagues entitled 'Improving Educational Outcomes for Students from Refugee Backgrounds in the South Australian Certificate of Education: A Case Study of Two Catholic Secondary Schools'.[52] The aim of the project was to explore how schools support students with refugee experience undertaking the senior secondary certificate of education, and was focused on evaluating an intervention that was introduced in the two participating schools to support students with refugee experience. Case studies were undertaken in two secondary schools. The data included online surveys with school staff (n=34) and students (n=29), one focus group with teachers in each school (n=17), one focus group with students in each school (n=16), and individual interviews with five teachers and five students in each school (n=20). This chapter specifically focuses on themes that arose during the research at one of the schools, which was a girls-only school where approximately 60 per cent of students spoke English as an Additional Language and almost 40 per cent of students came from a refugee background. School staff were requested to identify students from refugee backgrounds for participation; this was usually done by the English as an Additional Language specialist teacher or by an educational support officer who worked closely with the culturally and linguistically diverse students at the school. The school staff reported that students were identified for participation based both on 'visa type' identified in school

---

52   Melanie Baak et al., 'Improving Educational Outcomes for Students from Refugee Backgrounds in the South Australian Certificate of Education Project: A Case Study of Two Catholic Schools' (University of South Australia, 2018), available at: apo.org.au/node/136916.

enrolment records as well as on knowing the students. The study was not specifically about exploring the refugee label or experience. However, what became obvious very early in the project, particularly at the girls-only secondary school, was a reluctance from the students to be identified as refugee background students. Some of the reasons for this possible reluctance to be identified as 'refugee students' will be explored in the sections below.

The haunting of the refugee label: Who is a refugee and for how long?

> The word refugee stalks you through life prefixed to any other subsequent identity you develop in post-refugee life.

> A 'refugee' felt like a prior identity, a political status once ascribed to me that suggested vulnerability, inferiority, alienness, pity – everything I wanted to remove from my idea of myself.[53]

The refugee label, with all the frames of reference it entails, continues to haunt those with refugee experience through resettlement. This label has a 'determining agency' on those whom it haunts.[54] As Malbasa argues, 'the word refugee stalks' suggesting 'vulnerability, inferiority, alienness, pity'.[55] This perhaps goes a long way in explaining why the students in our project were reluctant to be identified as refugee background students. Feedback from the teachers facilitating the recruitment of student participants suggested that the girls did not want to be identified as refugee students. Jacinta, one of the specialist support teachers who worked very closely with students from diverse backgrounds, identified that:

> some of the other girls are like 'I'm not a refugee student what are you talking about' you know 'My parents came here … because they had the skills'. So no acknowledgement whatsoever, a couple of girls in particular … that's why – I guess I can assume that for those girls they didn't want to be part of it because they didn't want to be labelled … And also the fact that they perhaps care about what other people think, their friends – they do care about what people are going to think about them. (Jacinta, school educational support officer)

53 Malbasa, 'I Used to Distance Myself from my Refugee Identity. Now I Own It'.
54 Gordon, *Ghostly Matters*, 190.
55 Malbasa, 'I Used to Distance Myself from my Refugee Identity. Now I Own It'.

The students from refugee backgrounds who undertook the survey, focus group or interviews self-identified as being from a range of national, linguistic, cultural and religious backgrounds including Afghanistan, Burma, South Sudan, Democratic Republic of Congo and 'Muslim'. With the diversity of the school, some students from refugee backgrounds endeavoured to de-identify themselves from the label refugee. Jacinta argued that the young women 'care about what people are going to think about them' and therefore 'didn't want to be labelled'. Instead the girls preferred to identify that their parents came here 'because they had the skills' thereby identifying as skilled migrants, a category of migrant that does not have the negative framing associated with being a refugee. The quote from Jacinta suggests that some of the girls from refugee backgrounds sought to 'hide' their refugee backgrounds in the diversity of the school without having to identify with the 'refugee' label. In a similar way, Ryu and Tuvilla describe Chin youth from Burma, resettled in the United States, as recalibrating 'their refugee identity as a voluntary immigrant' and challenging the 'dominant narrative of refugees'.[56] Danijel Malbasa also identifies with this experience, describing:

> Better to call myself an immigrant, I decided … To regard myself as belonging to a category of migratory humanity that is for the most part uncontroversial, less needy, less 'frightening' than a refugee.[57]

A majority of the students who participated in the focus groups and interviews conducted as part of this project were comfortable with identifying as being from a refugee background. It is assumed that most of those who were uncomfortable with this labelling chose not to participate. However, one female participant, Gloria, a young woman from an African country who was in Year 11 at the time of the research, rejected identification as a refugee, highlighting her father's employment. Gloria was identified by the school for participation in the project based on her refugee background. However, when asked about this, Gloria did not identify as being from a refugee background.

> Interviewer: And so you came when you were two, did your family come as refugees?

---

56 Minjung Ryu and Mavreen Rose S Tuvilla, 'Resettled Refugee Youths' Stories of Migration, Schooling, and Future: Challenging Dominant Narratives about Refugees', *The Urban Review* (2018), doi.org/10.1007/s11256-018-0455-z.
57 Malbasa, 'I Used to Distance Myself from my Refugee Identity. Now I Own It'.

Gloria: Not really. Dad he kind of grew up in the city so he's like
– and so he got offered a job here in Sydney, so he came first and
then we came – he brought us after.

As well as demonstrating Gloria's self-identification as an immigrant, this
excerpt presents two additional questions for labelling refugees. First, if
Gloria did not identify as being from a refugee background, on what
basis was she recruited by the school staff to participate in the research?
Second, even if Gloria was from a refugee background, if she came to
Australia when she was two and she was in Year 11 at the time of the
interview (making her about 17 years old), should this refugee label still
be following her 15 years after arrival in Australia? I hypothesise that the
racialisation of refugees in Australia plays a significant part in the haunting
of the refugee label particularly for those, like Gloria, who are of 'black'
African appearance. In the sections that follow, I first argue for the role of
racialisation in the identification of people as refugees and finally I explore
the question of how long a refugee remains a refugee.

'This black refugee …': Racialisation of the refugee in countries of hegemonic whiteness

Gloria, like other arrivals to Australia of African descent, has become
part of a complex, racialised country. Since colonisation, Australia has
been a nation of settlers.[58] But since this time, the hegemonically 'white'
Australian national identity continues to be unsettled by the presence of
non-'white' Indigenous Australians and the arrival of non-'white' migrants
and refugees. The White Australia policy, which was only officially
disbanded in the early 1970s, aimed to promote and strengthen the 'white'
European national identity. The numbers of 'black' Africans in Australia
has historically been quite low. In 1971, census data estimated that 61,935
African-born people lived in Australia and over 20 per cent of these were
born in South Africa, with a significant number being 'children of colonial
functionaries and Anglo Saxons from Southern Africa'.[59] By 2006, the
African-born population in Australia had increased significantly, with

58   Pal Ahluwalia, 'When Does a Settler Become a Native? Citizenship and Identity in a Settler Society', *Pretexts: Literary and Cultural Studies* 10, no. 1 (2001), doi.org/10.1080/713692599.
59   Graeme Hugo, 'Migration Between Africa and Australia: A Demographic Perspective' (Sydney: Australian Human Rights Commission, 2009): 15.

approximately 248,699, of whom approximately 42 per cent were South African.[60] From the late 1990s, Australia has accepted significant numbers of African-born refugees through the humanitarian entrant program. In the period from 2004 to 2016, the largest sources of resettled refugees to Australia included Burma, Iraq, Bhutan, Somalia, Syria and South Sudan. For a country still rooted in denial of the original owners of the land, a nation founded on ideals of white superiority and with a history of white migration,[61] the significant recent arrivals of refugees, particularly from Horn of Africa countries and Middle Eastern countries, have continued to unsettle these 'white' ideals. Phenotypical characteristics as well as other markers of visible difference, such as Islamic female dress or veils, mark refugees as culturally and/or religiously different from the hegemonically white identity that is still presumed to be 'Australian'.

Gloria was identified by her school as being from a refugee background despite not self-identifying as a refugee and having lived in Australia for 15 of her 17 years. She was of 'black' African appearance. This demonstrates the tendency to conflate blackness with refugeeness in Australia. While Phillips, in her analysis of the labelling of South Sudanese Australians as a refugee group, argues that Sudanese Australians are 'generally *understood* to be refugees',[62] I would take this further to propose that 'black' Africans in Australia are frequently *assumed* to be refugees. The conflation of blackness with refugeeness was also described by participants in my PhD research. My PhD project explored the experiences of belonging for five Dinka women from South Sudan who were resettled in Australia, through in-depth qualitative ethnographic and life history approaches.[63] Achol, for example, described an experience at her daughter's school:

> But when I was moving here this house, I take children to Greenhills Primary School. Other girls to fighting with the Ayak [my daughter] in the school. Other woman coming, she tell me 'This one refugees, refugees … [switches to Dinka] this black refugee. How could she beat my child?' … Then I was called to the meeting, there was a translator, and I had already been informed by Ayak that there was a woman who was angry with me in the school. Then the headmaster asked me through the interpreter,

---

60 Hugo, 'Migration Between Africa and Australia', 16.

61 Jupp, 'From "White Australia" to "Part of Asia"'.

62 Melissa Phillips, 'Convenient Labels, Inaccurate Representations: Turning Southern Sudanese Refugees into "African-Australians"', *Australasian Review of African Studies* 32, no. 2 (2011): 57–79 (emphasis added).

63 Reported extensively in Baak, *Negotiating Belongings*.

and I replied that 'If you people say you don't want my child in the school because she is a black refugee, then I will take her to another school.'[64]

Achol described another mother at her daughter's school identifying her as a 'black refugee' thereby conflating blackness and refugeeness. Ramsay argues that 'experiences of racialisation toward women who are resettled in Australia from Central African countries ... reflect a colonial imaginary and a legacy of postcolonising dominance in Australia' with 'assumptions of difference, dirtiness, and savagery' attached to the women.[65] Similarly, Kumsa, in a study of young Oromo refugees in Toronto argues that the 'refugee' label is used as a label of exclusion to further distance people from belonging to the nation.[66] With the negative framing of the refugee that positions those with refugee background as always in deficit as described above, it is hardly any wonder that those with refugee backgrounds endeavour to find other labels and identities without these framings with which they can be identified.

For African-born Australians, blackness and refugeeness are conflated as a double negative relegating them to a form of perpetual foreignness. In a similar way, the association of Muslim immigrants and refugees with threats of terrorism results in them being 'considered suspicious and consequently less desirable'.[67] This results in visible markers of Islamic faith also being frequently associated with refugeeness. Colic-Peisker further argues that European refugees and immigrants 'do not face their own racial "visibility" as a barrier to inclusion' in Australia.[68] The visible difference of most refugee groups results in the humanitarian resettlement program being 'the most contentious immigration category'.[69] These experiences of visibly different refugees, whose blackness or religious Otherness position them as perpetual refugees, sit in stark contrast to the 'white' Bosnian refugees Colic-Peisker interviewed in her research. The Bosnian refugees, like Malbasa described above, were able to distance themselves from

---

64   Baak, *Negotiating Belongings*, 58–59.
65   Georgina Ramsay, 'Central African Refugee Women Resettled in Australia: Colonial Legacies and the Civilising Process', *Journal of Intercultural Studies* 38, no. 2 (2017): 170, doi.org/10.1080/07 256868.2017.1289904.
66   Martha Kuwee Kumsa, '"No! I'm not a Refugee!" The Poetics of Be-Longing Among Young Oromos in Toronto', *Journal of Refugee Studies* 19, no. 2 (2006), doi.org/10.1093/jrs/fel001.
67   Colic-Peisker, '"At Least You're the Right Colour"', 619.
68   Ibid., 619.
69   Ibid., 619.

their refugee identity, seeing themselves as 'whites in a white country'[70] and recounted being told by other Australians that 'at least you're the right colour'.[71] The racialisation of the refugee in countries of hegemonic whiteness, such as Australia, results in them perpetually being seen as refugees regardless of how long they have lived in Australia.

'I'm still a refugee …'

Gloria, in the excerpt quoted above, came to Australia when she was two. Yet, 15 years later, her school continued to identify her as being from a refugee background. Even if she did arrive on a refugee-related visa, 15 years of a 17-year old's life is a very long time to continue being haunted by the refugee label. It is likely that even if Gloria did arrive in Australia on a refugee-related visa, the most likely visa program she would have come through would have been a family reunification visa through the sponsored Special Humanitarian Visa program, sponsored by her father who was already living in Australia. Resettlement through this pathway facilitates people legally becoming permanent residents in Australia as soon as they arrive. Thus, in the legal sense of the label refugee, Gloria has not been a refugee since her arrival in Australia. However, the informal label of refugee and its concomitant frames of reference have continued to haunt Gloria for 15 years, despite her legal status as permanent resident (and likely citizen). On this basis Ludwig argues that the 'legal refugee status and the informal label refugee are not, and should not be used as, synonymous terms'.[72]

The problem with the continuing haunting of the refugee label for people with refugee experience resettled in Australia was also described to me in my PhD research, outlined above. Abuk, a woman aged in her 50s, described in Dinka:

> But we've been here for years and we are not refugees anymore.
> Now I've been here for about five years and I'm not a citizen,
> I'm still a refugee.[73]

---

70   Ibid., 621.
71   Ibid., 620.
72   Bernadette Ludwig, '"Wiping the Refugee Dust From my Feet": Advantages and Burdens of Refugee Status and the Refugee Label', *International Migration* 54, no. 1 (2016): 6, doi.org/10.1111/imig.12111.
73   Baak, *Negotiating Belongings*, 47.

Despite arriving in Australia through Australia's humanitarian entrant program, and thereby being a permanent resident on arrival in Australia, Abuk's experience was that, even after five years living in Australia, she was still recognised and identified as a refugee. This experience resonates with other people from various refugee backgrounds in contexts of resettlement. Jumsa writes of the experiences of Oromo resettled in Canada, who, despite being citizens for over 10 years, are still seen by others, and therefore themselves, as refugees.[74] Neumann and Gifford argue that 'Australian scholarship largely remains steeped in labelling resettled refugees as refugees well beyond their initial arrival in Australia'.[75] This is an issue not only in scholarship and research, but also in the media as well as political and everyday discourse. While legally the ending of the refugee label is clearly demarcated, there is no finite point at which people stop being seen by others, or in some instances by themselves, as refugees.

Conclusion: Rehumanising the refugee

While labelling resettled former refugees is inherently problematic, as highlighted above, without using labels such as 'refugee' or 'former refugee' or 'refugee background' it is impossible to acknowledge and recognise the previous experiences that people have had prior to resettlement in Australia. The word refugee in and of itself is not the problem: rather, it is the framing and what it represents, the social constructions of what that label means, that results in a negative framing of the former refugee. Reframing the socially constructed understanding of the term 'refugee', while notably difficult, would enable the use of the label 'refugee' without using it to Other through marginalisation and deficit understandings. As Ryu and Tuvilla suggest, in their article exploring the educational experiences of Chin former refugees resettled in the United States, there is a 'dilemma as to how to identify and accommodate their needs while not subscribing to sweeping narratives about the helpless refugees in need of support'.[76]

---

74   Kumsa, '"No! I'm not a Refugee!"'.
75   Klaus Neumann and Sandra M Gifford, 'Producing Knowledge about Refugee Settlement in Australia', in *Critical Reflections on Migration, 'Race' and Multiculturalism*, ed. Martina Boese and Vince Marotta (Routledge, 2017), 116, doi.org/10.4324/9781315645124-7.
76   Ryu and Tuvilla, 'Resettled Refugee Youths' Stories of Migration, Schooling, and Future', 5.

The politics of representation have seen refugees constructed as Others: as victims, lacking agency, in need of humanitarian intervention. This Othering serves to remove the human subjectivity of refugees,[77] dehumanising them through a process that objectifies. As Bakewell has argued, '[b]y staring too hard at "refugees" or "forced migrants", we fail to see their "normality"'.[78] The question then becomes, 'how to reverse this dehumanization and to return the humanity to those from whom categorization has removed all individual attributes'.[79]

To rehumanise requires really listening to and hearing the voices of those who are often not heard. It is important to recognise that really 'hearing' their stories is:

> embodied in the process of mutually recognizing our claims on each other as reflexive human agents, each with an account to give, and account of our lives that needs to be registered and heard.[80]

It is necessary to hear narratives of former refugees and those who are resettled as more complex than those of trauma, disempowerment and victimisation inherent in research, media and public discourse. Rather we need to hear the stories of agency, subjectivity, individuality, resiliency, resentment, fear, hate, love, passion, vulnerability, strength, courage and challenge. This also requires hearing the multiple stories that these voices have to tell. As Adichie has argued:

> Stories matter. Many stories matter. Stories have been used to dispossess and to malign, but stories can also be used to empower and to humanize. Stories can break the dignity of a people, but stories can also repair that broken dignity.[81]

The stories and lives of those from refugee backgrounds can illustrate a complexity that is so quickly lost in research that struggles to be objective and representative. An acknowledgement of this complexity is vital if former refugees are to be understood in their full humanness. As Halpern and Weinstein have observed, '[a] critical step in rehumanization is to view

---

77   Zygmunt Bauman, *Wasted Lives: Modernity and its Outcasts* (John Wiley & Sons, 2013).
78   Oliver Bakewell, 'Research Beyond the Categories: The Importance of Policy Irrelevant Research into Forced Migration', *Journal of Refugee Studies* 21, no. 4 (2008): 449, doi.org/10.1093/jrs/fen042.
79   Jodi Halpern and Harvey M Weinstein, 'Rehumanizing the Other: Empathy and Reconciliation', *Human Rights Quarterly* 26, no. 3 (2004): 567, doi.org/10.1353/hrq.2004.0036.
80   Halpern and Weinstein, 'Rehumanizing the Other', 580.
81   Adichie, 'The Danger of a Single Story'.

another person as a complex, nonidealized individual'.[82] Rehumanising those with refugee experience, beyond the negative, singular stories that are so often represented, requires an acknowledgement that:

> there is no intrinsic paradigmatic refugee figure to be at once recognised and registered regardless of historical contingencies. Instead ... there are a thousand multifarious refugee experiences and a thousand refugee figures whose meanings and identities are negotiated in the process of displacement in time and place.[83]

Listening to the voices and representing them in all their complexity can and will help to rehumanise those with refugee experience. Rehumanising understandings of the refugee would enable a shift such that being a refugee is not seen as a negative experience. It is simply one part of the experience that makes up the lives of complex humans. While it is essential that there is increased recognition that those who are resettled in Australia are no longer officially refugees, people with experience as refugees should feel able to identify with this experience in the knowledge that it will not be seen others as a deficit.

---

82   Halpern and Weinstein, 'Rehumanizing the Other', 574.
83   Nevzat Soguk, *States and Strangers: Refugees and Displacements of Statecraft* (Minneapolis: University of Minnesota Press, 1999), 4.

3

'HIS HAPPY GO LUCKY ATTITUDE IS INFECTIOUS'

Australian imaginings of unaccompanied child refugees, 1970s–80s

Jordana Silverstein[1]

In 1976 one welfare officer working at the Enterprise Hostel – a migrant holding centre in Springvale, Victoria – produced a set of descriptions of the refugee children living there.[2] Of one it was noted that: 'This girl is attractive and very shy, at school she is withdrawn and rarely speaks up'.[3] Of another was written an extensive note documenting her family's life in Timor and noting that: 'All of their property was occupied by various Army forces during the war, and resulted in considerable loss of property'.

1   This chapter was researched and written with funding provided by the ARC Laureate Research Fellowship Project FL140100049, 'Child Refugees and Australian Internationalism from 1920 to the Present'.

2   For recent histories of migrant hostels and holding centres, see, for example, Alexandra Dellios, *Histories of Controversy: The Bonegilla Migrant Centre* (Melbourne: Melbourne University Press, 2017); Catherine Kevin and Karen Agutter, 'The "Unwanteds" and "Non-Compliants": "Unsupported Mothers" as "Failures" and Agents in Australia's Migrant Holding Centres', *The History of the Family* 22, no. 4 (2017): 554–74, doi.org/10.1080/1081602X.2017.1302891; Sara Wills, 'Between the Hostel and the Detention Centre: Possible Trajectories of Migrant Pain and Shame in Australia', in *Places of Pain and Shame: Dealing with 'Difficult Heritage'*, ed. William Logan and Keir Reeves (Florence: Taylor and Francis, 2008), 263–80, doi.org/10.4324/9780203885031; *Hostel Stories: Life in S.A. Migrant Accommodation*, University of Adelaide, available at: arts.adelaide.edu.au/history/hostel-stories/.

3   No author, Report on child, National Archives of Australia (hereafter NAA): B925, V1978/60922 PART 1. To try to ensure anonymity, I have removed the names of the children.

Since her arrival in Melbourne, she had been found to be 'shy to the extent that she was unable to say her name'. This report concluded by noting that:

> At the hostel M socialises well. The only time M and her family were upset, was during the time when her uncle Mr SW was under a deportation order – This however has now been withdrawn and the family hopes that permanent residence will be given.
>
> M has applied for permanency <u>and</u> nominated her parents to come to Australia.
>
> Comment: This family could serve as a model in many ways.[4]

Maintaining refugee settlement services in Australia has, over the years, resulted in a vast bureaucracy and paper trail, with many of these types of reports that describe those who were 'settled' being produced. Oftentimes it has been social workers who played an integral role in facilitating and documenting the lives of refugees living in holding centres – the sites where refugees would first live after arrival in Australia – as they began the process of settling into their new lives. The records from the 1970s and 1980s that these workers left behind in their files, now held in the National Archives of Australia – our national repository of government documents – provide a vital window through which we can catch a glimpse of the ways that governments, and those who help create and implement government policy, thought about the people whose lives they were describing, and controlling.[5]

Looking at some of these writings presents an opportunity to think about the ways in which a category of person – that of the 'refugee child' – has been constructed by and through Australian public policy. This category of person has a long, transnational history, and is importantly understood as historical: like any other legal, social, cultural or political category of person, it is not one that naturally occurs. By confining children in particular places and writing about them in certain ways and with specific vocabularies, government bureaucracies can create a body of knowledge around a population, or a category of person. In this chapter I am interested in thinking about what makes this group of people a visible category, or a defined group, at a particular moment in time, that of the

---

4   F Wositzky, Report on child, NAA: B925, V1978/60922 PART 1.
5   See Kevin and Agutter, 'The "Unwanteds" and "Non-Compliants"'.

late 1970s and early 1980s, and in a particular place, Australia. This is a group that is largely defined around their location in the world – that they are travelling, or have recently travelled fleeing violence and persecution, and seeking a different home – and by their relative age. By exploring the role that bureaucracies, lists and descriptions of people composed by welfare officers, social workers and government department workers play in creating this differentiated group, we can understand the ideas of refugee children that are created. In this chapter, files that predominantly describe and organise Vietnamese and Timorese children will be explored. Through an examination of a set of documents that were created by the bureaucracies surrounding their settlement process, I will explore the ways that these refugee children are understood as a group to be managed. As described by anthropologist, historian and critical theorist Ann Laura Stoler, this is a crucial part of a government's descriptive project: a group is described as a necessary part of the project of managing them.[6] Similarly, historian and political theorist Mahmood Mamdani has asserted that 'the management of difference is the holy cow of the modern study of society, just as it is central to modern statecraft'.[7]

The project of managing people who cross the nation-state's borders is a fundamental part of the Australian national project, and has been integral to Australia's sense of itself since before Federation.[8] By understanding the ways that the bureaucracy describes, controls and produces in order to manage, we get a glimpse of the ways that borders are maintained and populations are controlled. The practices of government that control those who move exist as part of a project of, to use Jennifer Hyndman's phrasing, 'disciplining displacement'.[9] They are a way of governmentally organising people who are on the move. This is part of a broader ideology that determines that the movement of people across borders is something that requires governmental control. Indeed, the notion that the movement of people should be controlled and administered by governments is a

---

6   See Ann Laura Stoler, *Along the Archival Grain: Epistemic Anxieties and Colonial Commonsense* (Princeton, NJ: Princeton University Press, 2009).

7   Mahmood Mamdani, *Define and Rule: Native as Political Identity* (Cambridge, MA: Harvard University Press, 2012), 2.

8   Tracey Banivanua-Mar, *Decolonisation and the Pacific: Indigenous Globalisation and the Ends of Empire* (Cambridge: Cambridge University Press, 2016), doi.org/10.1017/cbo9781139794688; Claire Higgins, *Asylum by Boat: Origins of Australia's Refugee Policy* (Sydney: NewSouth Publishing, 2017). More generally see Hagar Kotef, *Movement and the Ordering of Freedom: On Liberal Governances of Mobility* (Durham: Duke University Press, 2015).

9   Jennifer Hyndman, *Managing Displacement: Refugees and the Politics of Humanitarianism* (Minneapolis: University of Minnesota Press, 2000), xx.

historical one, rather than one that is necessary or natural, even though it may have attained such normalcy in our society as to seem natural and inevitable. On the flip side, could we imagine, for instance, a world in which people move across borders without control: what new languages and forms of government would that produce? What would Australia look like, for instance, without the *1901 Immigration Restriction Act* as a founding document? What would relationships between people look like if they were not being produced through the violence of these modes of description?

In the descriptions that I will explore in this chapter there is some overlap between what we will see and the ways that adult refugees and/or citizen children have been described by social workers. The social workers whose words we are looking at here are part of a long history of social workers in Australia conducting similar work, as Shurlee Swain has documented.[10] Moreover, as I will go into more detail about below, there is overlap in the ways that other racialised populations – in particular Aboriginal children or non-child refugees – have been described by Australian welfare workers. These overlaps arise as a result of a broader history of migration, settler colonialism and racialisation within which the particular documents I am considering here sit. But, as we will come to see, there are important particularities to the words used and the stories told about these refugee children. Understanding that these words and stories serve as a means to control a group living in a particular space and having a certain age is vital to understanding the work that these accounts do. So while language might be borrowed from or shared with other fields of governmental knowledge, and circulate amongst social workers in recurring ways, the words used here do particular work to produce certain meanings and certain outcomes. When coupled with an understanding of the work that the bureaucracy does when it comes to sit in the archive – as I will explore below – we can gain an understanding of how this language works as part of the governmental project of constructing and producing the category of the refugee child. I am looking here at this category as a governmental and bureaucratic one, working to understand how it takes shape as such.

---

10   See, for example, Shurlee Swain, 'Beyond Child Migration: Inquiries, Apologies and the Implications for the Writing of a Transnational Child Welfare History', *History Australia* 13, no. 1 (2016): 139–52, doi.org/10.1080/14490854.2016.1156212. See also Fiona Davis, 'Put Down Your Knitting: Unpicking Social Welfare Professionalisation in 1970s Australia', *Journal of Australian Studies* 41, no. 2 (April 2017): 222–36, doi.org/10.1080/14443058.2017.1308420, and R J Lawrence, *Professional Social Work in Australia* (Canberra: ANU Press, 2016), doi.org/10.22459/PSWA.02.2016.

The stories of themselves that these child refugees would narrate, or that their friends or parents or doctors or, indeed, social workers, would tell, would most likely be vastly different. In this chapter, one story – a small part of a much larger historical story – will be told.

Refugee children, guardianship and documentation

The descriptions of refugee children from the migrant holding centres in Victoria in the 1970s–80s, which sit within the archive of the government bureaucracy, were produced for a number of reasons: as part of reports by government workers arguing for more funding or explaining the workings of the holding centres; as part of the process of keeping track of the children's lives, behaviours, schooling and finances; and as general case file notes. Much of this bureaucracy resulted from the process of documenting the people whose lives were being cared for by the government under the structures of the *Immigration (Guardianship of Children) Act*.[11]

This Act first came into action in 1946 to provide the measures necessary for the minister for immigration to act as guardian for the British boys who had been brought to Australia during World War II.[12] While it has always applied to immigrant children in general, the Act has also applied to child refugees, most particularly since the beginnings of the mass arrival

11   For an overview, see Tamara Blacher, 'Resettlement of Unattached Refugee Children in Victoria, 1975–1979: Placement Alternatives' (Multicultural Australia Paper No. 7, Melbourne: Clearing House on Migration Issues, 1980); Robert Bennoun and Paula Kelly, *Indo-Chinese Youth: An Assessment of the Situation of Unaccompanied and Isolated Indo-Chinese Refugee Minors* (Melbourne: Indo-China Refugee Association of Victoria, 1981).

12   The full name of the Act was 'An Act to make provision for and in connexion with the Guardianship of certain alien children'. It was changed to 'alien' from 'Children outside Australia' in the amendments of 1983, available at: www.comlaw.gov.au/Details/C2004A02801. Its origins in the management of child migrants can also be seen in the report produced by the Senate Standing Committee on Community Affairs, *Lost Innocents: Righting the Record – Report on Child Migration*, 30 August 2001, esp. 11–45, available at: www.aph.gov.au/Parliamentary_Business/Committees/Senate/Community_Affairs/Completed_inquiries/1999-02/child_migrat/report/index. For longer histories of this Act see Jordana Silverstein, '"The Beneficent and Legal Godfather": A History of the Guardianship of Unaccompanied Immigrant and Refugee Children in Australia, 1946–1975', *The History of the Family* 22, no. 4 (2017): 446–65, doi.org/10.1080/1081602X.2016.1265572; Jordana Silverstein, '"I Am Responsible": Histories of the Intersection of the Guardianship of Unaccompanied Child Refugees and the Australian Border', *Cultural Studies Review* 22, no. 2 (September 2016): 65–89, dx.doi.org/10.5130/csr.v22i2.4772.

of unaccompanied refugee and asylum seeker children in the 1970s.[13] While in recent years this Act has proved highly contentious – with some labelling it as providing for the minister to be 'both the jailer and the legal guardian' of children – in the late 1970s it was seen as predominantly a bureaucratic instrument by politicians.[14] Indeed, for some people working in the Immigration ministry and Department of Immigration, it was not of any great significance.[15] The public debate that has occurred about it since the early 2000s, and which occurred in the late 1940s, stands in stark contrast to this era of the late 1970s and early 1980s. In this era, it seems, it was at the level of the social workers, undertaking the face-to-face work with the children in the hostels and group homes, that the workings of the Act were most visible. Ian Macphee, the minister for immigration and ethnic affairs from 1979 to 1982, noted in an interview I conducted with him in 2017, that while he could not remember doing the work of being a guardian under the Act, he was:

> sure that whatever happened if anyone had recommended to me that action be taken in accordance with that I would have, of course, gone along with that. In fact, I would have gone out of my way.

He and other senior officials, he said, took time 'to investigate and weigh up what was in the best interest of the person' because 'they cared. The senior officials cared and I cared'. It was, Macphee remembered, 'just a process based on our humanity'.[16] One of the senior officials of whom Macphee spoke, John Menadue, the secretary of the Department of Immigration from 1980 to 1983, commented in an interview with me in 2017 on the single boys who were 'selected' by Australian immigration officials and brought from displaced persons camps in Vietnam, noting that 'frankly' he did not 'know how well they settled. I don't know', he said.[17]

---

13   Note though that the 1994 amendments changed the legislation so that the minister was no longer responsible for children entering Australia for the purposes of adoption. Senate, Parliament of the Commonwealth of Australia, 'Immigration (Guardianship of Children) Amendment Bill 1993: Explanatory Memorandum', available at: www.austlii.edu.au/au/legis/cth/bill_em/iocab1993427/memo_0.html.

14   Sarah Hanson-Young, 'Motion—Convention on the Rights of the Child', Commonwealth Parliamentary Debates (CPD), Senate, 14 March 2012. See also, for example, Chris Evans, Testimony at Standing Committee on Legal and Constitutional Affairs—Immigration and Citizenship Portfolio—Department of Immigration and Citizenship, Senate Estimates Committee, CPD, 21 October 2008; and Julia Gillard, 'Ministerial Statements—Managing Migration', CPD, House of Representatives, 3 December 2002.

15   Interview conducted by author with Ian Macphee, 3 August 2017, Melbourne. Interview conducted by author with John Menadue, 11 September 2017, Sydney.

16   Interview with Macphee.

17   Interview with Menadue.

The Act has been amended numerous times, but the key provision that the immigration minister is the guardian of all children who are governed by the Act has remained. These children have included those who were under 21 (or, since 1983, 18), were not Australian citizens, and were not accompanied by a parent or a relative over the age of 21 who was to act in the role of a parent or guardian.[18] The minister's guardianship obligations were considered to have ended when the child reached adulthood, when they became a citizen or when they left Australia permanently. The minister has also always been able to delegate some of the responsibilities of guardianship and has regularly done so, particularly to the departments of Social Service or Community Service, or similar bodies.[19] These departments have also been responsible for providing support for refugee and asylum-seeking children who have come to Australia as part of families, and as part of the general settlement services with which they were provided.[20] And it is the workings of the people who conducted these services that will be explored in this chapter.

The guardianship produced by the Act has also provided for the categorisation of refugee children into a number of different groups. From the 1970s, all children governed by this legislation were known as 'isolated'. Under the umbrella term 'isolated' they fell into one of two groups: 'unattached', which meant that they had no relative in Australia to look after them, or 'detached', which meant that they had a relative who was over 21, but who was not a parent. These different categories translated into different funding schemes, housing arrangements, and modes of care from the government and social services, and this was always debated as a problem by those responsible for the day-to-day care of these children.[21] Regardless of the precise term being used, all of these

18   The children governed by the Act were initially referred to as 'immigrant' children, and in an amendment in 1983 this was changed to 'non-citizen'. For all versions of this Bill see Australian Government, ComLaw, 'Immigration (Guardianship of Children) Act 1946', available at: www.com law.gov.au/Series/C1946A00045.

19   This delegation has, at times, required clarification. In response to a minute asking for confirmation of whether the immigration minister's authorisation was required before a child who was governed by the Act was allowed to marry, a memo issued by D J Rose, Senior Assistant Secretary, Constitutional and Financial Branch, Advisings Division, Attorney-General's Department, on 2 June 1977 makes clear that 'this power of delegation only extends to the Minister's powers and functions under that Act', and that the minister (or acting minister) must provide consent 'in person', NAA: A432, A1977/3319.

20   For a discussion of this by someone working in the field, see Confidential Report by the A/Director Regional Services, Ivan Beringer, addressed to the Deputy Director-General, 30 July 1976, NAA: B925, V1978/60922 PART 1.

21   A Working Party on the Problems of Unattached Refugee Children was formed in 1978 to try to deal with some of these problems. It contained representatives from all states, as well as the Commonwealth. See NAA: B925, V1978/60922 PART 1 and PART 2.

descriptors position the child in relation to family and lack of family, and ensure that the guardian is seen as providing a form of family. These refugee children are produced and comprehended as a group through the description of their relation to a caregiver and their relative perceived vulnerability. The descriptions of them contained in the reports I am exploring in this chapter are a further testament to this positioning. Minute detail regarding their behaviour is recorded, indicating that it was thought that they required both care and surveillance, housing and monitoring, schooling and documenting. Guardianship, in this formulation and in these documents, enacts a certain control, at the level of the everyday.

This control came as a result of the vast majority of the refugee children coming to Australia in the late 1970s – children predominantly from Vietnam and Timor, coming normally after having been 'selected' in a refugee camp somewhere in Asia – being housed in migrant hostels on arrival. These were spaces that would provide access to housing, food, English classes and medical care, and would act, as Sara Wills has framed it, as 'frontiers of assimilation', 'hold[ing] together' ideas of Australianness and creating, as Glenda Sluga has made clear, sites of 'material and cultural *discomfort*' for many.[22] While in these hostels, the unaccompanied children would have their lives documented.[23] There were a series of instrumental reasons for this. Firstly, governments were unaware of how many unaccompanied children were in Australia and in each city. Reports on children at each hostel thus functioned as a type of census exercise. Secondly, while the immigration minister was the guardian of these children, responsibilities of guardianship were delegated to the local Department of Social Services, and the departments believed that they required certain information about each child to be known in order for services to be provided. Thirdly, there was the question of funding: as each child was recorded, their funding needs and pensions provided were noted.[24]

---

22   Wills, 'Between the Hostel and the Detention Centre', 268. Quote from Glenda Sluga, and emphasis, in Wills.

23   Indeed, for a number of reasons, the hostels were a key site for the gathering of information. For one child it was noted that the family with which he was living 'left Midway Hostel before case studies were completed and the information on hand is minimal. The Welfare Officer will attempt to home-visit the family as soon as possible, and information gained will be forwarded'. Mary Ralph, Welfare Officer, Migrant Services, 23 August 1976, NAA: B925, V1978/60922 PART 1.

24   A note from M L McCready, Executive Officer, Settlement, to all Settlement Officers, dated 29 August 1979, titled 'Isolated Refugee Children', explains that 'It is extremely important that [reports about the children are] done as Community Welfare Services is relying on these details to have an up-to-date picture of refugee children, isolated or at risk. It also assists Community Welfare Services in submissions for staff to cope with long-term casework demands of this group', NAA: B925, V1978/60922 PART 2.

The government policy framework being used, however, was unclear for many of the workers. In July 1976, the associate director of regional services wrote to the deputy director-general of the Department of Immigration and argued that 'There would appear to be a fairly urgent need to clarify a range of policy issues related to defining responsibility and effective case planning for refugee children'.[25] It was not until 1985 that a cost-sharing agreement between state and federal governments was established – an agreement that remains in place, unaltered, to today.[26] Before this period, arrangements were generally ad hoc.

While some workers at the hostels would provide simple lists, at other times stories about the children were told by welfare and settlement officers. Some of these were full-page reports, containing information such as name, sex, place and date of birth, address, nationality, ethnic origin, 'natural' father and mother, financial support, relatives in Australia, relatives in country of origin, relatives elsewhere, current situation and sections for an expanded background and comment. Others were short paragraphs, headed by a name and birthdate. Of recurring focus throughout the reports were questions of finance, housing and the temperament of the children. Throughout these reports, the voices of the workers dominate, with the chance rarely, if ever, provided for the children to report about themselves. What we learn from these reports, therefore, is not how the children were living their lives, or undertaking their own settlement process, or understanding themselves; instead, we get a glimpse of the discourses and structures of governmental bureaucracy at work. We gain a sense of the ways the social workers and administrators imagined and catalogued the task of managing the migration and settlement of refugee children in Victoria. Through these bureaucratic writings we find just one of the ways in which the category of the 'child refugee' was created. Indeed, this bureaucratic production sits within a long set of histories and practices of governments creating and defining populations, and of international law and instruments such as the Convention on the Rights of the Child – which would come later – providing guidelines that

---

25   Confidential report by the A/Director Regional Services, Ivan Beringer, addressed to the Deputy Director-General, 30 July 1976, NAA: B925, V1978/60922 PART 1.
26   The cost-sharing agreement is available in NAA: A14039, 2520: Cabinet Memorandum 2520 – Immigration and Ethnic Affairs – 1985–1986 Budget – new policy proposal – cost-sharing program for care of refugee minors – Decisions 5059/ER (Amended) and 5667.

national governments variously follow or ignore.[27] In Australia, this forms part of a broad settler-colonial project of control and assimilation, which works to differentiate, often in racial terms, this population.[28]

Descriptions of the children

Within the surveys of the children, there were continued reports on their present and future housing situations. This began before the children arrived in Australia, with cables being sent from officials in Canberra to the Department of Immigration branch in Melbourne noting the settlement officers' decision as to where the children should be placed upon arrival.[29] While children could express a view on where they would live, the ultimate decision rested with settlement officials. As one cable noted, 'confirming' a previous cable regarding three siblings who were 'unattached refugee minors' and were living in 'Singapore having been rescued at sea': there was a 'distant cousin' living in Springvale, who could not 'accommodate' them. The corresponding official wrote that:

> we would wish to send them to Victoria to at least give them some family tie but we would also wish them to be retained as a group in hostel accommodation after initial period in migrant centre.

The 'urgent views' of officials in Melbourne was 'appreciated'.[30]

Once in Australia, the housing arrangements were under constant scrutiny and discussion. Of one child it was reported that:

> He would be happy to live in a large communal house if his friends were also living there, if this cannot be arranged he has a twenty year old friend … [in Oakleigh] with whom he could live.[31]

---

27 For histories of children's rights and international law, as well as Australia's relationship to this law, see, for example, Mary Crock and Lenni B Benson, eds, *Protecting Migrant Children: In Search of Best Practice* (Cheltenham: Edward Elgar Publishing, 2018).

28 See, for example, Patrick Wolfe, *Traces of History: Elementary Structures of Race* (London: Verso, 2016).

29 There are many examples of these cables in NAA: B925, V1978/60922 PART 4.

30 Cable sent from Tarbath to Melbourne, 20 March 1981, NAA: B925, V1978/60922 PART 4.

31 'Timorese Children', no date, NAA: B925, V1978/60922 PART 1.

Another boy was reported as 'prefer[ring] living with his sisters to any other accommodation arrangement'.[32] Of a set of siblings it was written that a settlement officer from Midway Hostel together with a worker from the department 'agreed that the best solution is to try to obtain a flat for them, but we believe that economically they cannot afford to pay for one'.[33] In this way, housing and financial concerns from the department often intersected. Similarly, in an April 1976 report on Timorese unaccompanied children at the Midway Hostel it was noted that the situation with a group of boys was:

> fairly stable. They have caused no problems. They are the boys who are receiving $4.80 per week after the hostel tariff is paid. Financially their situation is inadequate because from $4.80 they need to pay school requisites, clothing, other personal items and medical expenses.[34]

This focus on the financial position of the children recurred throughout the reports, as social workers documented how much money the children had, needed and earned, and what this would mean for their living situation. Some children, it was written, 'reject any form of communal living' and sought employment to support their desire to live together, while others were described as 'not presently receiving any financial support'.[35] In the lists of the children, careful notes were made to explain precisely which government 'benefits' were received.[36]

As social workers tended to do, these workers were also keen to describe the behaviours of the unaccompanied children. In the description of one child it was noted that:

> the Welfare Officer feels that [she] has suddenly been allowed too much freedom and needs welfare follow-up. It would also be beneficial if she found lasting friendships outside of the hostel in the community.[37]

---

32   Ibid.

33   Victoria Undurraga, Settlement Officer, Midway Centre, to Ms Margaret McCready, Executive Officer, Settlement Unit, 21 December 1979, NAA: B925, V1978/60922 PART 3.

34   Assistant Director, Settlement Services Section, 'Report on Timorese Refugees. "Isolated Children"', 14 April 1976, NAA: B925, V1978/60922 PART 1.

35   J Zaia, Welfare Officer, Migrant Services, 'Reports on Timorese Without Parents (Midway)', 7 July 1976, NAA: B925, V1978/60922 PART 1. The report begins by noting that 'These reports are only factual – they will be followed-up with recommendations and suggestions for the children's future'.

36   NAA: B925, V1978/60922 PART 2.

37   'Progress Report on Welfare of Isolated Timorese Children at Enterprise Hostel', 9 April 1976, NAA: B925, V1978/60922 PART 1.

Another child was described as being bound to:

> have many problems settling in Australia. She is functionally
> illiterate. She has little or no concept of time, and combined
> with a very short concentration span, she has great difficulty in
> keeping appointments and performing any kind of organised
> work. [expunged section …] Many efforts have been made to
> help and support her. Catholic Family Welfare had arranged for
> her to live in a hostel with five girls, but she rejected this, she also
> has rejected any other form of alternative accommodation. [She]
> has always lived a 'free life', not bound by any restriction. I do not
> believe institutional care is the answer, but I am unable to offer
> any other alternative.[38]

This girl's description ends there, with the last sentences 'expunged',
presumably by the archivist at the National Archives of Australia, where
these documents are now housed.[39]

These expungements give pause, compelling the historian reading these
archival papers to note the potential ongoing force of the documentation
of these children's lives. Through these lists, as I have indicated,
information is acquired, and certain forms of knowledge produced, about
these children and where they do and can live within society. Where once
these names and descriptions sat within confidential government files,
today they sit in the archives, publicly accessible. This notation, described
above, was created on 7 July 1976, relatively recently, and we can thus
presume that this girl, or people who know her, remain within Australia,
able to access this description. This description is saturated with racialised
ideas of 'appropriate' migrant living and settlement, and also contains
expunged sentences. Some descriptors are, it would seem, judged too
sensitive to be available to the public. Others are deemed suitable to be
made available.

---

38   J Zaia, Welfare Officer, Migrant Services, 'Reports on Timorese Without Parents (Midway)',
7 July 1976, NAA: B925, V1978/60922 PART 1.
39   From looking at the pages in the archives, it appears that certain sentences are covered over
with tape reading 'expunged', and the page has then been photocopied before being re-placed in the
archival file. In the NAA's Recordsearch facility, the file is noted as being 'Open with exception' for
reasons under the *Archives Act 1983* (Cth) para 33(1)(g): would 'unreasonably disclose information
about the personal affairs of a person'. See 'Why we refuse access', NAA, available at: www.naa.gov.
au/help-your-research/using-collection/access-records-under-archives-act/why-we-refuse-access.

Indeed, this expunging is part of the process of racialisation of these children, wherein certain descriptors remain public while others are withheld from view. It is important to note that the archival records of citizen children are withheld from public access for 100 years.[40] The files and papers that I am exploring in this chapter are possible to view, I would guess, because they sit within the record-keeping of immigration, rather than of social services. And while archivists might repeatedly inform me that anything to do with personal, medical or sexual information is withheld from public viewing under the Archives Act of 1983's exemption reason 33(1)(g), the presence and public availability of these types of information suggests that this is not always true.[41]

While we cannot know the mindset of the archivist who ruled this open – and indeed documents like this, which tell the histories of refugee children in Australia, remain viewable throughout the archives – the fact that the file remains publicly accessible requires us to ponder the layers of ethics in using them to write these histories. As I utilise them, then, I am forced to sit with an ambivalence over their usage. Perhaps this ambivalence is essential to the work of the historian – for in colonial archives we can often find materials that describe people without their consent, and that have been made public without their ongoing consent – but in this present political moment, when refugees remain a political battleground within Australian politics, it takes on a particularly potent feeling. These are affective archives, we could say. As I put them to work to craft a narrative, they do emotional work within me, and within the Australian nation.[42] There is a discomfort attached to them. But the historians' discomfort is, of course, beside the point. An ethical usage of these documents and descriptions then, one can only suppose, arises from their use in the service of the seeking of migrant and refugee justice. It lies further in the constant remembering that these are people, with lives, histories, memories and futures, who are being described. Their humanity sits not in these documents but in the lives they have lived.

---

40   I am grateful to Professor Shurlee Swain for alerting me to this point.

41   Medical information is often freely available in these archives, and has appeared in almost every NAA file that I have seen which holds documents dealing with the implementation of this Act.

42   See, for example, Trish Luker, 'Decolonising Archives: Indigenous Challenges to Record Keeping in "Reconciling" Settler Colonial States', *Australian Feminist Studies* 32, no. 91–92 (April 2017): 108–25, doi.org/10.1080/08164649.2017.1357011.

Additionally, I am compelled to wonder, does the public availability of these documents tell us something vital about how the various arms of government imagine, and manage, refugees and their place within Australian society? These documents, it would seem, testify to an idea of these child refugees as being outside the realm of citizenship. If citizen children's archives are kept from public view for longer than non-citizen children's, and difference is not neutral, then these differences can be understood to demonstrate a conception of the personhood of child refugees as being substantively different to that of child citizens. While this might be obvious when considered as a question of legal categories – of course a citizen is different to a non-citizen, some may say – I am interested in what it means when thought through the lens of a history of bureaucratic writing, or governmental practices, or interpersonal relations.[43] What can this tell us about how these children are imagined, and their lives noted down, described and understood? It produces simultaneously both an outsiderness to citizenship and a life lived under government control and surveillance. This is the predicament that many racialised populations face, as they are refused access to the benefits of citizenship, but are saddled with the controlling aspects of government bureaucracy. In this way, these refugee children are experiencing similar types and effects of descriptions and controls that have been used to determine the lives of Aboriginal children and other racialised groups over Australia's history. What distinguishes them is their different position in society: it is the movement across borders, and their position within the Australian community after arrival, that is being placed under surveillance and managed. Those who migrate, and those who are Indigenous, are treated by governments in ways that coincide, but are not the same.

Refugee children are being produced as a group through both the collection of this information by social workers and the like, and then by its retention and public availability through archival practices. Bureaucratic processes of description, collection and retention help to produce a population that can be known, for these instances of refugee children's lives being intimately – and now publicly – documented repeat and repeat. Another child at the Enterprise Hostel was described in the following language: 'His relationship with his aunt … is not good. Amongst the complaints that he lists are that no friends are allowed to visit him in his room,

---

43   See, for example, David Tait, Terry Carney and Kirsten Deane, *A Ticket to Services, or, a Transfer of Rights? Young People and Guardianship* (Hobart: National Clearinghouse for Youth Studies, 1995).

he receives no pocket money', and the next few sentences are expunged.[44] While certain intimate details are determined to be of interest to note, and allowed to be read by the public, a line is drawn somewhere. The precise place is – for those of us who access these documents – inscrutable. But we know that we can read other children described as 'likeable',[45] as 'more mature than her age would indicate, readily displaying responsibility and sensibility',[46] as having a 'well mannered, pleasant personality',[47] and as 'attractive and very shy'.[48] One school was asked to provide a report on two siblings, and of the brother they report that he 'wears very corrective glasses' while the sister 'has no physical problems, in fact she has a most affectionate smile'.[49] Another child's report states that:

> At the beginning he wanted to go back but with the time, he gained friends and his happy go lucky attitude is infectious. He has changed his mind and is definitely FOR AUSTRALIA.[50]

In this notation, as in the one with which I began this chapter, the position of the child refugee in relation to the nation is invoked: there is a move towards incorporating these model child refugees into the nation. Surveillance and description remain part of the process of producing a desired national population.

All of these stories were collected as the result of the existence of the idea of the category of the child refugee, and in the service of the production of that category of person. As noted in the description of the child and her family with which I began this chapter, certain refugees were imagined as 'models' for others by the social workers and settlement service workers who created the reports; certain ideas of what it meant to be a refugee were created through these reports in order to be held up and followed by others. These descriptions of the children existed as both a product of surveillance and a way of creating a category of personage, as well as in order for bureaucrats and public servants to lobby different branches of government to provide funding and support. Thus, a July 1976 report

---

44   F Wositzky, Welfare Officer, Enterprise Hostel, no date, NAA: B925, V1978/60922 PART 1.
45   Ibid.
46   Ibid.
47   Ibid.
48   Ibid.
49   K Richardson, Migrant Coordinator, and K Gough, Principal, Springvale Primary School, 15 July 1976, NAA: B925, V1978/60922 PART 1.
50   Deputy Director General, Victorian Resettlement Co-ordinating Committee, Confidential Note: 'Unattached refugee children still in Victoria', 30 July 1976, NAA: B925, V1978/60922 PART 1.

from the Victorian state government utilised case file reports written about unattached children in order to support their claims for greater assistance and regulation in policy and practice. The cases outlined included descriptions of children's housing and financial arrangements, as well as of their state of mind, and served to be 'illustrative of the difficulties being encountered in effectively planning for these refugee children'.[51]

These documents thus provide us with a glimpse into the genealogy of these categories of person and the ways in which their histories can be written. While these case file notes in some ways propose to outline the stories of the children, to provide seemingly vital information about them, they instead provide a set of discourses about how these refugee children were thought of and written about, how they were surveyed, described and categorised. Certain aspects of their lives were deemed important to document, other aspects discarded. These traces sit within the government archive, providing us with the means to understand the work that government discourse does when relating to, describing and producing certain categories of person.

Conclusion: The work of categorisation

In their use of surveys to gain information about the children, and their management of their housing and thus relationships with others, the Australian welfare departments and their social worker employees sought to tell a set of stories about who these refugee children were, how they would live and what their relational lives in Australia would look like. These stories were collected as the result of the imagining of the category of the child refugee, and in the service of the production of that category of person. This was to be a category of person defined as 'child-like': as requiring care and protection provided by the workers of the state. These descriptions buttressed the existence of this category of person within the population. The dividing up of the population served as a means of exerting control, both of this divided group and of the population at large. In this way, refugee children as a group were circumscribed and defined through their relationship to place, to surveillance and to other peoples. They were kept within a particular political order.

---

51   Confidential Report by the A/Director Regional Services, Ivan Beringer, addressed to the Deputy Director-General, 30 July 1976, NAA: B925, V1978/60922 PART 1.

But alongside this we can read the work of Bashir Bashir and Amos Goldberg, who have written, following Hannah Arendt and Giorgio Agamben, that 'the refugee is precisely the one who stands outside the political order, and is thus by definition a figure that disrupts the established order of things'.[52] This is because, they say, the refugee crosses boundaries, moving around the world and thus inhabiting the world in a manner that disrupts the bounded world of the citizen. If we follow this thinking, which I think can be helpful, we can understand the ways that the bureaucracy tries to contain and annul this disruption: to manage any possible alteration to the political order.

Peter Mares, writing in relation to a recent case of a temporary resident parent being denied permanent residency even though their children and former partner were Australian citizens, explains that there is caution among policymakers that women may fall pregnant in order to remain in Australia: one 'senior government adviser' told him that 'You have to be very careful what visa products you put on the market … People will try to exploit those loopholes'.[53] Could a new way of thinking – one that avoids these racialised capitalist logics – about the place and role of regulation of borders and human movement open up a new way of describing how, and why, people move around the world, and how they should be related to when they do? What other possible languages, or 'grammars' could be used?[54]

We can come to understand that in these documents those who worked within settlement services, or at schools, or in the multitude of other spaces (both bureaucratic and physical) with which the children interacted, produced a set of languages, discourses and grammars about the children. The knowledge that was produced about these children was refracted through the government and social workers' words. As in governmental documents more generally, there was an attempt at silencing. Governments tend to make policy for, rather than with, those who are subjected to that policy. In this case, these refugee and asylum seeker children were doubly infantilised, imagined as unable to speak,

---

52 Bashir Bashir and Amos Goldberg, 'Deliberating the Holocaust and the Nakba: Disruptive Empathy and Binationalism in Israel/Palestine', *Journal of Genocide Research* 16, no. 1 (2014): 90, doi.org/10.1080/14623528.2014.878114.
53 Peter Mares, *Not Quite Australian: How Temporary Migration is Changing the Nation* (Melbourne: Text Publishing, 2016), 93.
54 Liisa H Malkki, 'Refugees and Exile: From "Refugee Studies" to the National Order of Things', *Annual Review of Anthropology* 24 (1995): 516, doi.org/10.1146/annurev.an.24.100195.002431.

both as refugees and as children. This then, perhaps, is part of the work being done in these documents: the production of a group of people who are imagined to rely on being controlled, and having their lives shaped, by the settlement services offered by various layers of government. Even if at times officials might have consulted with children as to where they wanted to live, decision-making power rested with officials, not with the children. These archives that I have examined – and that now share *too much* with the public – are sources of discipline, both discursive and material, and they sit within those practices of the art and vocabulary of government that work to create ideas of what it meant to be a Vietnamese or Timorese unaccompanied child refugee in Australia in the late 1970s and early 1980s.[55]

---

55 Michel Foucault, *Security, Territory, Population: Lectures at the Collège de France 1977–1978*, ed. Michel Senellart, trans. Graham Burchell (Basingstoke: Palgrave Macmillan, 2009), esp. 87–134.

4

'FOREIGN INFILTRATION' VS 'IMMIGRATION COUNTRY'

The asylum debate in Germany

Ann-Kathrin Bartels

The capacity of how many people our country can take in is limited … The burden refugees put on the FRG [Federal Republic of Germany] is too heavy. How should this cramped, overpopulated country be able to take in tens of thousands of people? How should the already strained nature cope with the inevitable consequences of settling more and more asylum seekers? … There is indeed still physical space in this country (maybe it is possible to accumulate the entire world population on the territory of the FRG), but this cannot be the standard. Nature's reserves will not withstand further mass immigration, especially not if from different cultural hearths. And the psychological willingness to accept more refugees of the people, who do not want to lose their homes, is waning too.[1]

---

1   Original: *Aber die Aufnahmefähigkeit unseres Landes ist begrenzt … Die Flüchtlingslast wird zu schwer für die Bundesrepublik. Wie soll dieses enge, übervölkerte Land immer neue Zehntausende aufnehmen können? Wie soll die jetzt schon überstrapazierte Natur fertig werden mit den unvermeidlichen Folgen der Ansiedlung von immer mehr Asylbewerbern? … Platz im rein physische Sinne ist in der Tat noch (vielleicht kann man die ganze Menschheit auf dem Territorium der Bundesrepublik versammeln); aber das kann doch wohl nicht der Maßstab sein. Für weitere Massenzuwanderung, vor allem aus anderen Kulturkreisen, reichen die Reserven der Natur und der Ökonomie nicht, reicht auch nicht die psychische Hinnahmebereitschaft der Bevölkerung, die ihre Heimat nicht verlieren will.* Johann G Reißmüller, 'Diese Last wird zu schwer', *FAZ*, 5 September 1985, 1.

The above quotation was published in the German newspaper *Frankfurter Allgemeine Zeitung* (*FAZ*) in September 1985. Other articles of that time spoke of 'foreign infiltration', 'bogus asylum seekers' or 'legions of displaced persons', and were titled (e.g.) '*Opfer von Schmarotzern*' (*Die Zeit*), '*Die Last wird zu schwer*' (*FAZ*), '*Ohne Grundgesetzänderung geht es nicht. Was tun angesichts der Asylantenflut?*' (*FAZ*).[2] Moderate journalists like Klaus Liedtke, former editor of the weekly magazine *Stern*, held politicians responsible for instilling fear in the population by using terms such as '*Grenzen der Ausländerverträglichkeit*' (limitations to the tolerance of foreigners) and '*Überfremdung des Volkes*' (foreign infiltration). He deemed it careless of them to suggest that Germans had to protect their 'national identity against ever new waves of Asian invaders – disguised as asylum seekers'.[3]

Conditioned by the country's National Socialist past, art 16, §2II GG of the constitution of the Federal Republic of Germany (FRG) guaranteed that '[p]ersons persecuted on political grounds shall have the right of asylum'.[4] Growing numbers of asylum seekers coming to the FRG in the 1980s led conservatives to proclaim that they would abuse the laws of asylum and the constitution. At the time, Theo Sommer, former chief editor of *Die Zeit*, argued that the fierce debate around the right of asylum in Western Germany really would revolve more around the question of the German self-conception as a nation than around the number of asylum seekers coming to Germany.[5] Indeed, the 1980s were a period when the very existence of a German national identity was thoroughly questioned. One existential part of this debate was the '*Historikerstreit*' (Historians' Quarrel) that emerged in 1986 after the *FAZ*-publication of Ernst Nolte's essay *Vergangenheit, die nicht vergehen will*. In his essay, he questioned the singularity of the Holocaust and attempted to newly evaluate its importance for German historiography. The German sociologist and philosopher Jürgen Habermas accused him of writing revisionist history and trying to create an unbroken German national identity based on conservative values. A major controversial discussion of the existence, composition and definition of a German national identity ignited almost

---

2   In English: 'Victims of Social Parasites', *Die Zeit*, 26 April 1985; 'This Burden is too Heavy', *FAZ* 5 September 1985; 'It Cannot be Done Without a Constitutional Change. What is there to be Done Given this Flood of Asylum Seekers?', *FAZ*, 30 October 1986.

3   Klaus Liedtke, 'Die Angst vor den "Kanakern"', *Stern*, 4 September 1986, 3.

4   *Grundgesetz für die Bundesrepublik Deutschland* [Basic Law of the Federal Republic of Germany], available at: www.documentarchiv.de/brd/1949/grundgesetz.html.

5   See Theo Sommer, 'Wegen Überfüllung geschlossen?', *Die Zeit*, 29 August 1986, 1.

at the same time that the asylum debate was gaining momentum, which leads to the question of whether the debates emerged isolated or related to one another.

I argue that it is possible to gain insight into the concept of a German national identity by analysing statements about asylum seekers in newspaper articles, as they can be read as a dialogue about the 'other' amid the German people. The focus of this chapter is on the representation and linking of these debates in newspapers and magazines from February 1985 to January 1987. During these years, the numbers of people seeking asylum in the FRG rose to over 100,000 per annum – to 103,076 in 1988.[6] Against the backdrop of an emerging economic crisis and high rates of unemployment, a heated debate around the intake of asylum seekers and its implications for the German public emerged and peaked shortly before the general election in January 1987. Articles for the analysis stem from the following nationwide West German broadsheet newspapers:

- *Frankfurter Allgemeine Zeitung* (*FAZ*), centre-right, liberal conservative
- *Süddeutsche Zeitung* (*SZ*), centre-left, progressive liberalism
- *Bildzeitung*, centre-right, conservative populist tabloid
- *Frankfurter Rundschau* (*FR*), left-liberal
- *Die Tageszeitung* (*taz*), centre-left/left
- *Die Zeit*, centre-left, liberal.

And additionally, from the weekly news magazines:

- *Der Spiegel*, centre-left
- *Stern*, centre-left.

Initially, around 500 articles on microfilm were sourced for analysis by scanning them for keywords such as 'asylum', 'asylum seekers', 'bogus asylum seekers', 'refugees', 'refugee shelter', 'wave of asylum seekers', 'economic migrants', 'law of asylum', 'national identity', etc. Thematic topics of the newspaper and magazine articles were (e.g.) the FRG's constitution, xenophobia, ethnicity or the right to asylum. These 500 articles were then sifted through by looking more closely at the types of article (descriptive, factual, opinion) and at the headline and content of the

---

6   See 'Table 24: Zahl der Asylbewerber in der Bundesrepublik, 1975 bis 1995', in Ulrich Herbert, *Geschichte der Ausländerpolitik in Deutschland* (Bonn: C.H. Beck, 2003), 263.

articles, the language and tone used in them, and distinguishing between descriptive and opinion pieces. From this, a good understanding of the individual journalist's or writer's political standings could be gathered. It also disclosed how these reflected the specific newspaper's political stance. Around 220 articles were selected for closer analysis.

For the purpose of this paper, the debates around 'asylum' and 'national identity' are regarded as discourse threads. This is based upon the concept of entanglement of discourses according to Siegfried Jäger. He defines discourses as rivers of knowledge through time and acknowledges that they affect individual and collective actions and therewith wield power.[7] Discourses are not an absolute reflection of social realities, but they shape them. Their analysis aims at problematisation, that is, at exposing omissions or contradictions. Furthermore, Jäger assumes that discourses are made up out of different components and layers. Their various threads are formed out of discourse fragments that, in the broadest sense, discuss the same topic. These fragments often refer to several subjects, which results in an entanglement of discourses. Consequently, discourses are not isolated from each other and their intertwining creates a highly branched net of discourse threads.[8]

At the end of this paper, the German debate of the 1980s will be compared to the Australian debate about the arrival of Vietnamese boat people in the 1970s and early 1990s. Conclusions will be drawn about the similarities and dissimilarities of the two debates and the motifs emerging in them. This is of interest, for multiple reasons. First, Germany and Australia have a very different history when it comes to taking in foreigners. Germany has, apart from the guest worker system of the 1950s, '60s and early '70s, never had a proactive immigration system. It does not have a control system or a quota for taking in migrants or asylum seekers. Additionally, Germany has always struggled with the question of what it means to be German. Friedrich Nietzsche proclaimed in 1886 that the question 'What is German?' would never die off.[9] Australia, on the other hand, has been an immigration country from the arrival of the First

---

7   Siegfried Jäger, *Kritische Diskursanalyse: Eine Einführung* (Münster: Unrast, 2004), 132.
8   Jäger, *Kritische Diskursanalyse*, 132; Siegfried Jäger, 'Diskursive Vergegenkunft: Rassismus und Antisemitismus als Effekte von aktuellen und historischen Diskursverschränkungen', in *Historische Diskursanalyse*, ed. Franz X Eder (Wiesbaden: Verlag für Sozialwissenschaften, 2006), 239–52, doi.org/10.1007/978-3-531-90113-8_13.
9   Friedrich Nietzsche, *Jenseits von Gut und Böse: Zur Genealogie der Moral. Eine Streitschrift* (Berlin: Holzinger Verlag, 2013), §244.

Fleet in 1788. It has a well-established immigration system, including a humanitarian system of refugee resettlement that is split into offshore, onshore and special humanitarian programs. The countries had a different comprehension of their 'national identities' – Germany believing in *jus sanguinis*, citizenship through German descent, compared to *jus soli*, birthright citizenship, in Australia (this was abolished in 1986).

Defining 'national identity'

Looking at the political, cultural and technological conditions that gave rise to nationalism in eighteenth-century Europe, the author of *Imagined Communities*, Benedict Anderson, points to the importance the development of newspapers and novels played in forming homogenous groups. Their emergence, combined with the rise of capitalism, he argues, is the point of origin of national consciousness. He refers to nations as '[imagined communities] because, regardless of the actual inequality and exploitation that may prevail in each, the nation is always conceived as a deep, horizontal comradeship'.[10] Even though the single members within a community do not know each other, they share a conception of a superior community to which they belong. 'National identity' is a feeling of belonging that is shared by a group of humans and that produces an idea of a collective as a 'nation' according to Eunike Piwonie, who analysed changes to the concept of 'national identity' in Germany. 'National identity' has an inclusive and an exclusive effect, as it can create or show up differences of the outsiders to a specific community.[11] Part of this 'feeling of togetherness' of a group of people, the creation of a 'we-feeling', is a result of features such as historical territory, language, shared memories, traditions or rights and obligations. The national narrative, built through history and literature, plays a particularly important role as it is internalised and understood as the public's shared history. Considering Germany's National Socialist past, it becomes clear why especially the question about the creation of an identity on the grounds of the nation's past was discussed controversially. According to Claudia Tazreiter, 'ethnic nationalism was a fertile environment for the growth of exclusionary politics in preserving unity against external threats and internal regional,

---

10   Benedict Anderson, *Imagined Communities* (London: Verso, 2006), 7.
11   Eunike Piwoni, *Nationale Identität im Wandel: Deutscher Intellektuellendiskurs zwischen Tradition und Weltkultur* (Wiesbaden: Springer VS, 2012), 46, doi.org/10.1007/978-3-531-18740-2.

religious and social forces'.[12] A clear differentiation from 'Others' plays an important part for the concept of 'national identity', seeing that Germany is generally considered to be an 'ethnic nation'. It builds its concept of identity on the grounds of its cultural and ethnic heritage and the concept of *jus sanguinis* that makes German citizenship an exclusive one.

Heterostereotypes and autostereotypes

One way of creating an 'Other' is by stereotyping. Stereotypes, which help make sense of the world, are passed on through 'socialisation, education, our families, media, propaganda etc.'[13] (social genesis), and are accepted in society as fixed structures. Stereotypes come into existence and change at certain points in time (historical genesis). They play an important role in our everyday lives, as they are resilient and integrative and form our preconceptions, influence the integration of others into society and are the motivation behind social acts, ideologies, politics etc. The historian Hans Henning Hahn defines a stereotype as:

> a (negative or positive) value judgement, which is generally backed by a strong conviction (or the speaker only pretends to be of this conviction if he uses the stereotype specifically with a manipulative intention, thus not himself convinced that the stereotype is true). It is mostly used on humans, specifically on groups of humans which can be defined in different ways: racial, ethnical, national, social, political, religious or confessional, vocational etc.[14]

A stereotype's research value can be separated into three levels: (a) an asserted claim to truth about a person's nature, (b) alleged objectivity about the stereotype's target (the person that is being discussed) and (c) information about the user of the stereotype. Only the last offers actual insight as it reveals the user's perception of the world and much about the society in which the stereotype exists.[15] Stereotypes have two 'sides':

---

12   Claudia Tazreiter, *Asylum Seekers and the State* (Farnham: Ashgate Publishing Ltd, 2004), 88.

13   Hans Henning Hahn, '12 Thesen zur historischen Stereotypenforschung', in *Nationale Wahrnehmungen und ihre Stereotypisierung: Beiträge zur Historischen Stereotypenforschung*, ed. Hans Henning Hahn and Elena Mannová (Frankfurt: Peter Lang, 2007), 18.

14   Hans Henning Hahn and Eva Hahn, 'Nationale Stereotypen: Plädoyer für eine historische Stereotypen-forschung' in *Stereotyp, Identität und Geschichte: Die Funktion von Stereotypen in gesellschaftlichen Diskursen*, ed. Hans Henning Hahn (Frankfurt: Peter Lang, 2002), 20.

15   Hahn, '12 Thesen', 20f.

they show the way others are perceived ('*heterostereotype*') and reveal self-perception ('*autostereotype*'). Conclusions about the worldview of the heterostereotype user can be drawn by analysing both sides.

Heterostereotypical depictions of asylum seekers

It is possible to identify five main heterostereotypes in the newspaper and magazine articles under consideration here:

1. The '*Wirtschaftsflüchtling*' or '*Scheinasylant*' ('economic refugee' or 'bogus asylum seeker') was widely used and assumes that people mainly come to Germany for economic reasons. Attorney Manfred Ritter wrote that, for example, Sri Lankan Tamils would abuse art 16 of the constitution by coming to Germany 'because of the significantly better economic conditions … instead of seeking refuge in neighbouring countries which are linguistically, religious, culturally, climatic and historically more like their own countries'.[16]

2. Criminal offences such as drug trafficking, robbery or prostitution were attributed to asylum seekers. The 'criminal asylum seeker' could not be trusted and certain crimes were attributed to specific nationalities. In an interview with *Der Spiegel* in March 1986, Berlin's Interior Senator Heinrich Lummer said 'but it is the truth'[17] when asked if he really thought Ghanaian women were prostitutes, Sri Lankan Tamils drug traffickers and Lebanese people petty criminals. However, official documents, such as the German Federal Office of Criminal Investigation's paper on crime reduction from 1987,[18] make no reference of a noticeable rise of crimes committed by asylum seekers.

3. People from non-European backgrounds were portrayed as being distinctively 'culturally different'[19] and hence incompatible with German culture. It was implied that asylum seekers from African or

---

16 Manfred Ritter, 'Ohne Grundgesetzänderung geht es nicht: Was tun angesichts der Asylantenflut?', *FAZ*, 30 October 1986, 9.
17 Axel Jeschke and Christian Habbe, '"Gucken Sie sich doch die Leute aus Ghana an": Der Berliner Innensenator Heinrich Lummer (CDU) über seine Pläne zur Verschärfung des Asylrechts', *Der Spiegel*, 17 March 1986, 61–64.
18 Bundeskriminalamt Wiesbaden, *Kriminalitätsbekämpfung als gesamtgesellschaftliche Aufgabe: BKA-Vortragsreihe Band 33* (Wiesbaden: BKA, 1988), 36–38.
19 Ritter, 'Ohne Grundgesetzänderung', 9; or Liedtke, 'Die Angst vor den "Kanakern"', 3.

Asian countries did not want to integrate themselves. Asylum seekers of Muslim belief were defined mainly by their religion and Islam was seen as incomprehensible and threatening. In an *FR* reader's letter, Alfons Winter demanded that 'the entry of Islamists, which come from a completely different culture', should be banned because the FRG would be in danger of 'slowly, but surely turning into an Islamic republic'.[20] Sommer pointed out that Germany had been a country shaped by immigration for centuries and that waves of migrants had shaped its culture over time and eventually always became part of the nation.[21]

4. Asylum seekers were also portrayed as a 'source for social unrest'. According to Reißmüller, the accumulation of more 'economic refugees' could lead to social conflict and result in destabilisation of democracy.[22] Other articles pointed out that the German problems with asylum seekers were home-grown: 'Strict prohibition to work and detention in camps forced foreigners into the role of vexatious outsiders'.[23] Poor hygiene standards and overcrowding in camps resulted in fights and led to growing public resentment.[24]

5. Several articles described the construction of camps and the intake of asylum seekers generally to be the source of 'xenophobia' in Germany. The *Stern* reported that residents of Eggenfelden put up banners that read *'Keine Asylanten nach Eggenfelden! Eltern schützt eure Kinder!'* (No Asylum Seekers in Eggenfelden! Parents, protect your children!)[25] Another article stated how an anonymous caller threatened to send petrol so that the asylum seekers could set themselves on fire[26] and yet another argued that Germans must be stupid allowing asylum seekers in despite high unemployment rates, as this would lead to social conflict.[27]

---

20   Alfons Winter, 'Asylsuchende nach Amerika? Leserbrief', *FR*, 11 August 1986, 2.

21   Sommer, 'Wegen Überfüllung geschlossen?', 1.

22   Johann G Reißmüller, 'So geht es nicht weiter', *FAZ,* 15 July 1986, 1.

23   '"Im Lager ist besser als daheim": Asylgrundrecht – Gütezeichen der Verfassung oder Fehlkonstruktion?', *Der Spiegel,* Nr. 31/1986, 28 July 1986, 32.

24   Josef-Otto Freudenreich, 'Kein Platz für Toleranz', *Die Zeit,* 11 October 1985, 14.

25   Christine Claussen, '"Menschen die keiner will …" Im Bezirk Niederbayern wehren sich Einwohner gegen die Aufnahme von Asylsuchenden', *Stern,* 8 August 1985, 60.

26   See Gerhard Tomkowitz, 'Den Druck im Kessel erhöhen', *Stern,* 4 September 1986, 210.

27   Helmut Böpple, 'Die Deutschen sind … Leserbrief', *Stern,* 28 August 1985, 9–10.

In the following section, the heterostereotypes and autostereotypes of the 'bogus asylum seeker'/'economic refugee' and the 'culturally different asylum seeker' will be examined. The development of the term 'Asylant'[28] and the declassification of asylum seekers as 'Scheinasylanten' is the subject of an article in the *taz* from July 1986. According to author Jürgen Link, the term 'Asylant' was not part of the public discourse until the late 1970s as there were only small numbers of people seeking asylum, mainly coming from communist countries and therefore deemed eligible applicants. In the following years, the term developed into a negatively denoted term to describe asylum seekers. It followed the tradition of other negatively connoted words ending with the affix '-ant', which is also used in words such as '*Ignorant*' (ignoramus) or '*Simulant*' (malingerer). According to Link, 'Asylanten' lost their human face as media and politicians no longer saw them as individual human beings, but rather as a threatening flood or avalanche.[29] Ritter accused asylum seekers of falsifying political persecution in their home countries by 'provoking their government or through joining a radical … organisation'.[30] Equally, Reißmüller thought it indisputable that most of the people coming to Germany were doing so for economic benefits and thus, he noted, natural and economic resources, as well as society's willingness to accept more migrants, were dwindling.[31] Migrants of a different cultural, non-European background were perceived as particularly problematic. While asylum seekers from Eastern Europe were likely to be of Christian belief, followed similar traditions and learned the German language quickly, asylum seekers from African or Asian countries were depicted as unable to adapt and impossible to integrate. Muslim asylum seekers were defined solely through their religion, with Islam perceived as incomprehensible and even threatening. In an article in *Die Zeit*, the journalist Roland Kirbach described the prejudices a Lebanese refugee family faced when they moved into an apartment: Since Muslims would only eat after dark during Ramadan, it was feared that 'the four Omayrat-children would, under the stimulus of hunger, roam the streets and steal lollipops from the German children'.[32]

---

28   'Asylant' is commonly used as a negative term to describe asylum seekers, whereas 'Asylbewerber' is the official term.

29   Jürgen Link, 'Asylantenflut oder "Flüchtlinge raus"', *taz*, 24 July 1986, 5.

30   Ritter, 'Ohne Grundgesetzänderung', 9.

31   Reißmüller, 'Diese Last wird zu schwer', 1.

32   Roland Kirbach, 'Sie beten zuviel: Wertminderung durch eine Moslem-Familie?', *Die Zeit*, 21 February 1986, 14.

Generally, those who are negatively defined are deemed ineligible to be granted asylum, yet the accusation that people would come to Germany only for economic reasons was hard to verify. None of the articles that support restrictions to the laws of asylum questioned the negative terminology. There are, however, articles that criticised the use of such terminology: '*Deichgrafen-Metaphorik*'[33] (dike-reeve imagery or water metaphors) is what Sommer called the extensive use of sea-related terms such as '*Flüchtlings-Springflut, Asylanten-Schwemme, Ausländer-Strom, Einwanderer-Welle*' (refugee spring tide, glut of bogus asylum seekers, stream of foreigners, wave of immigrants) and Rolf Michaelis was surprised that Germans were not ashamed to insult those seeking protection.[34]

It is important to note that the fear of new arrivals from 'different cultures' was strengthened in these articles by adding the attribute 'foreign'. The historical and social origins of this stereotype therefore went hand in hand, as the process of promoting the idea of immigrants as irredeemably foreign was reinforced on different levels of social life. The image of something being 'foreign' became part of the collective symbolism and served as a reference point of orientation within society and helped justify political and social actions. It appears that the stereotypes built on one another and became interdependent, almost forming an argumentative circle. Their social and historical origin can be traced back to the increased use of the terms by the media and in politics in the 1980s. The more often asylum seekers were portrayed negatively, the more these ideas gained legitimacy and were adopted in other public spheres of society.

Autostereotypes

Each stereotype allows for conclusions to be drawn about those voicing it, about their emotions and perceptions of the world, and thus provides insight into the society in which they take effect.[35] Assuming that stereotypes are particularly useful tools for creating 'we'-groups, it can be argued that the depictions of asylum seekers in mid-1980s newspaper articles were primarily used to distance asylum seekers from Germans, intending to ensure that readers did not identify with asylum seekers, but instead rallied against them.

---

33   Sommer, 'Wegen Überfüllung geschlossen?', 1.
34   See Rolf Michaelis, 'Gesang vor der Tür', *Die Zeit*, 1 August 1986, 29.
35   Hahn, '12 Thesen', 21.

The first assertion about the autostereotype is the 'tolerance limit'. This suggests that the FRG had saddled itself with too great a burden by taking in asylum seekers. It includes the allegation of abuse of the right to asylum by '*Scheinasylanten*' by describing applicants negatively. High unemployment rates, criminality, xenophobia and social conflict served as reasons for claiming that the right to asylum should not be granted to 'bogus asylum seekers'. Stressing that large numbers of asylum seekers arrive in the FRG suggests that parts of the German population were concerned about their own living standards. Having experienced the economic miracle of the 1950s and 60s, the German state had moved into an adverse economic situation after 1973 as the oil crisis affected every sector of the German economy. However, despite unemployment rising faster than ever since World War II,[36] the idea of thousands of asylum seekers burdening the economy was unproven. Emotionally loaded terms like '*psychische Hinnahmebereitschaft*'[37] (psychological readiness of acceptance) or '*Interessen der Deutschen*'[38] (German interests) imply that the 'tolerance limit' is not a measurable but rather a subjective limit, suggesting that the exact moment of its excess cannot be determined.

The 'tolerance limit' is supplemented by the idea of 'foreignness' and both blend together to such an extent that their clear distinction is impossible. The fear of foreign infiltration led to a call for a limitation of migration. Bavarian Prime Minister Franz Josef Strauss warned: 'If the situation in New Caledonia gets any worse, we will soon have wogs in our country'.[39] He criticised the unwillingness of asylum seekers and foreigners to assimilate into German culture. Assimilation seemed to be the only acceptable version of integration.

The depiction of asylum seekers as cultural strangers in many articles leads to the question of from where this German fear originates. One cause appears to be the lack of awareness of differences between Germans and non-Germans. The above cited *Die Zeit* article details how the landlord of a Lebanese refugee family was lectured by anonymous callers about the differences between Germans and Lebanese: as they would normally 'live in caves' it would not be necessary to offer them 'a comfortable

---

36   See Table, 'Entwicklung der Arbeitslosigkeit in der Bundesrepublik in den Jahren 1950 bis 1990', *bpb.de*, available at: www.bpb.de/geschichte/deutsche-einheit/lange-wege-der-deutschen-einheit/47242/arbe itslosigkeit?p=all.

37   Reißmüller, 'Diese Last wird zu schwer', 1.

38   Gerhard Kropf, 'Hochtrabend und wirklichkeitsfremd: Leserbrief', *FAZ*, 22 September 1986, 11.

39   Hans Schueler, 'Kein deutsches Ruhmesblatt', *Die Zeit*, 5 April 1985, 7.

apartment with floor heating, tiles, carpets, precious wooden doors and an open fireplace'.[40] Arrivals from Poland, however, were greeted with less suspicion as 'they have the right skin tone, come from a familiar cultural background and learn German quickly'.[41] Different concepts of hygiene, intimacy or time, and also of the roles of family, gender or religion, can lead to misunderstandings between cultures, but it does not preclude their compatibility. If they are nonetheless seen as hindrances, it can be concluded that either a feeling of superiority of one's own culture or a fear of explicit displays of foreign customs are the reason for this.

No concrete evidence is given as to those components of the German culture supposedly in danger, but it is interesting to look at the Prussian virtues that are nominally said to form the basis of the German value system: honesty, modesty, discipline, sincerity, diligence, a sense of justice, a sense of duty and reliability.[42] Asylum seekers in the articles were described as not possessing such virtues. Instead they were depicted as being the exact opposite, as criminal and immoral.

The discourse thread focusing on a tightening of art 16, §2II GG is of significance here. As it guaranteed the right to asylum, the continuous increase in numbers of asylum seekers since the 1970s lead especially conservatives to the perception that the constitution was being abused by asylum seekers. Numerous restrictive measures were taken throughout the 1970s and 1980s to constrain the number of foreigners coming to the FRG: for example, the First and Second Acceleration Laws in 1978 and 1980, which aimed at shortening the procedures for granting the right to asylum or imposing a five-year working ban for asylum seekers in 1982. Interior Senator of Berlin Heinrich Lummer claimed that 'according to the current law of asylum, the entire Red Army and the KGB could march [into Germany] as long as they would only proclaim themselves to be asylum seekers'.[43] Reißmüller and others promoted tightening art 16, §2II GG, a move they deemed long overdue seeing that 'millions, yes dozens of millions' could ask for asylum in the FRG under the current laws, which would lead to a destabilisation of the German democracy.[44]

---

40   Kirbach, 'Sie beten zuviel', 14.

41   '"Die Spreu vom Weizen trennen": SPIEGEL-Serie über Asylanten und Scheinasylanten in der Bundesrepublik (IV): Polen', *Der Spiegel*, 15 September 1986, 109.

42   See Herbert Kremp, 'Preußische Tugenden', *Welt*, 2001, available at: www.welt.de/print-welt/article431886/Preussische-Tugenden.html.

43   Schueler, 'Kein deutsches Ruhmesblatt', 7.

44   Ritter, 'Ohne Grundgesetzänderung', 9.

Asylum seekers were portrayed as threatening to Germany's political system and its values. This becomes particularly apparent when insisting that '*Scheinasylanten*' would abuse the right to asylum: the stereotypical user accuses asylum seekers categorically of exploiting the law and implies that they would flout basic values. This contradicts imagined German – or Prussian – virtues like honesty and sincerity.

Opponents to an amendment of the constitution pointed to the experiences of flight and refuge of the founders of the FRG and to the National Socialist post of the country, and proclaimed that a change to the constitution might sound like a popular idea in an election year, but that it would not be a viable solution. Instead, the reasons for flight should be investigated and stopped around the world.[45] After the general election in 1987, an amendment of the constitution was less contested, but the discussion came to life again in the early 1990s and finally resulted in a constitutional change of art 16, §2II and the so-called safe-third-country regulation in 1992–93.

Focusing on the 'tolerance limit' and 'foreignness', it can be concluded that there is a presumed limit to what German values can withstand and exceeding it could result in their loss. It is interesting to note that a national character is created for asylum seekers even though these migrants have diverse national and cultural origins. Their cultural diversity is reduced to a few negative attributes to give this group a uniform face. Their assimilation is named as the only way to prevent the loss of German values, or even the abandonment of the German nation in the Western part of Germany.[46] This implies insecurity about the building blocks of one's own nation. Talking about 'floods' of asylum seekers suggests that the control and defence of the arrival of asylum seekers is far more important than determining why people flee their home countries. The use of water metaphors reinforces this feeling of overstraining. An objective discussion or respectful interactions with refugees are treated as equally irrelevant.

It can be concluded that a heterogenic group of asylum seekers is moulded into a faceless group with its own national character by means of stereotyping. This group is characterised as being different and parasitic; verifying the claims of these statements seems to be unimportant. The ideas of having a 'tolerance limit' and of not being able to accept the 'foreignness'

---

45   Christian Schütze, 'Politisch Verfolgte genießen Asylrecht', *SZ*, 169/30, 26/27 July 1986, 4.
46   Reißmüller, 'So geht es nicht weiter', 1.

of asylum seekers build upon one another and are interconnected. They merge into the assumption that a subset of the German population lives in fear of the 'other'.

Furthermore, the creation of a negative concept of the asylum seeker as alien appears to be combined with a stylisation of the self-image of the native German. The acceptance of negative stereotypes into the symbol system of the German language implies that the existent image of the 'foreigner' is no longer enough. Negative connotations of foreigners indeed existed in the FRG before the 1980s, most notably through guest worker programs. From 1954 to 1955, a steadily growing number of guest workers and their families came to Germany from countries such as Italy, Spain, Portugal and Greece as well as Turkey, Yugoslavia and Tunisia. After their work contracts expired, many guest workers and their families chose to settle in Germany rather than return to their countries of origin. With the economic recession of the mid-60s and early 70s and rising unemployment, guest worker programs were no longer required and ceased operation in 1973. The permanently settled guest workers started being blamed for problems such as shortages in apartments and jobs, social conflicts and the emergence of a subculture of semi-isolated 'second generation' migrants. The 1980s, however, saw another shift in the discourse and a redefinition of the 'foreigner problem': from guest worker to asylum seeker.

Discourses and stereotyping

Looking at the asylum debate and the national identity debate as discourses, it can be concluded that the two are indeed not occurring separately from one another, but that they are entangled. There is, foremostly, the question of how to handle Germany's nationalist-socialist past and the responsibilities that arise out of it. In his speech commemorating the fortieth anniversary of the end of World War II on 8 May 1985, Federal President von Weizsäcker spoke of learning to accept the nation's past – not in order to overcome it, but to preserve its memory and to learn from it. He ended with the plea:

> Do not let yourselves be forced into enmity and hatred of other people, of Russians or Americans, Jews or Turks, of alternatives or conservatives, blacks or whites. Learn to live together, not in opposition to each other.[47]

These aspects are also mentioned in articles regarding the topic of asylum: for example, when defending and challenging art 16, §2II. While some see Germany's history as a reason to take in asylum seekers, others condemn this as 'mistaken altruism'.

Based on the idea that nations, as a construct, work not only in an inclusive but also an exclusive way, and that 'national identity' is constructed by differentiating it from the 'other', some aspects of the debate on asylum stand out: insisting on the idea that asylum seekers are culturally foreign to Germans indicates the creation of a 'we'-group through the exclusion of 'others'. The resulting feeling of togetherness is based upon ethnic homogeneity and relies on the principle of assimilation of everything deemed to be foreign. The one common denominator for the 'we'-group is fear – fear of foreigners, and fear of related, social problems. Here, stereotyping's impact on public discourses becomes apparent. A negative reputation is the result of linking Asian or African asylum seekers to criminality, cultural differences, social unrests and xenophobia. 'National identity' and the *feeling of togetherness* influence the thoughts and actions of those belonging to the nation and act as strong binding material. This is enhanced specifically by thinking in stereotypes, which has an important and resilient defensive function. Articles promoting immigration do not manage to destroy this negative perception. Instead they label fear of asylum seekers as xenophobia and do not offer an informed elucidation of the pros and cons of immigration. This, however, leads to a growing disparity between supporters and deniers of the right to asylum. Eventually, only two options prevail for a nation: redefining the image of the society by adjusting it to encompass foreigners or attempting to make society fit their idea of it. The actual diversity of the German nation, visible in the presence of former guest workers and their families as well as resettlers, refugees and asylum seekers, clashes with the idea of a national identity based upon ethnic homogeneity. And, ultimately,

---

47 Richard von Weizsäcker, 'Speech by President Richard von Weizsäcker during the Ceremony Commemorating the 40th Anniversary of the End of War in Europe and of National-Socialist Tyranny on 8 May 1985 at the Bundestag, Bonn', *Bundespraesident*, available at: www.bundespraesident.de/SharedDocs/Downloads/DE/Reden/2015/02/150202-RvW-Rede-8-Mai-1985-englisch.pdf?_blob=publicationFile.

the German government took the path of attempting to eliminate the facticity of a multicultural society by imposing more restrictive measures, which culminated in the 'Asylkompromiss' of 1992–93. This new regulation means that those travelling to Germany via a safe third country, or a country of the European Union, cannot ask for asylum in Germany, because they have already passed through a safe country in which they could have asked for asylum. It also introduced the principle of safe countries of origin, which deems certain countries to be safe if they do not, or not generally, produce refugees.

(Dis)similarities in German and Australian debates

Australia's immigration policies had for decades been governed by the *Immigration Restriction Act 1901*, which became known as the 'White Australia policy'. It aimed at encouraging Anglo-Celtic migration and keeping out the Asian races.[48] The post–World War II era saw a shift in Australia's attitude towards non-white, non-European migrants and the White Australia policy was abolished in 1973. Shortly after, from 1975 onwards, Australia witnessed for the first time unauthorised arrivals to the country via boat. While Australia had always taken in refugees from around the world via its humanitarian program and under its obligations to the *1951 Refugee Convention*, this was an unexpected challenge.

After the fall of Saigon to the North Vietnamese Army in 1975, large numbers of Vietnamese fled their country, seeking refuge abroad. The majority of the 80,000 Indochinese migrants arrived in Australia by plane and had previously been formally processed by Australian officials at Malaysian and Thai refugee camps. In April 1976, however, a boat with five Vietnamese men landed in Darwin. They were the first of a total of just 2,059 arrivals by boat that came to Australia between 1976 and 1981.[49] Despite the number of boat arrivals being comparatively low, the reaction from politics and society were largely negative. With a federal election due on 10 December 1977, the arrival of six boats carrying 218 asylum seekers on 21 November 1977 was major news. Both parties 'used

---

48   Andrew Bennetts, *The Mess We're In. Managing the Refugee Crisis* (Camberwell: Trabagem Publishing, 2017), 185.
49   Nancy Viviani, *The Long Journey: Vietnamese Migration and Settlement in Australia* (Melbourne: Melbourne University Press, 1984), 85.

the arrival of Vietnamese asylum seekers to demonstrate their resolve to enforce Australia's immigration laws'.[50] Opposition leader Gough Whitlam claimed that Australia's borders needed to be protected against unauthorised immigration, criminal offences and the spread of diseases, thereby negatively associating asylum seekers with these.[51] He also doubted the legitimacy of the arrivals' asylum claims, proclaiming it 'not credible, 2.5 years after the end of the Vietnam war, that these refugees should suddenly be coming to Australia'.[52] On 25 November 1977, Prime Minister Fraser spoke to a woman on talkback radio, who was concerned that Australia would turn into 'another Rhodesia with a white minority'[53] due to the large number of Vietnamese refugees. This shows just how much the arrival of unauthorised asylum seekers stoked fears of an Asian invasion of Australia. Newspaper articles at the time ranged from being critical of the Fraser Government's and the Opposition's stance, to proclaiming that instead of being eligible asylum seekers, 'Vietnamese Communist agents and rich Thai businessmen are reported to be entering Australia posing as Indo-Chinese refugees'.[54] Other articles equally describe boat arrivals as non-genuine asylum seekers. The arriving Vietnamese would lack the 'lean and hungry look' and showed 'evidence of wealth'.[55] 1977 also witnessed the hour of birth of one of the most resistant images in the Australian asylum debate: the queue. Gough Whitlam motioned that 'genuine refugees' should be accepted, but spoke out against putting refugees 'ahead of the queue'.[56]

The debate around the Vietnamese boat arrivals had no significant effect on the election outcome;[57] it did, however, have influence on the second wave of boat arrivals from 1989 to 1998. Arrivals were mostly from Cambodia and Southern China. While the Vietnamese boat people of the first wave had been granted refugee status and permanent residence, arrivals of the second wave were held in detention for the duration of their claim assessment – some for over two years. This change was partly brought on by a general surge in applications for permanent residency

---

50   Rachel Stevens, 'Political Debates on Asylum Seekers during the Fraser Government, 1977–1982', *Australian Journal of Politics and History* 58, no. 4 (2012): 529, doi.org/10.1111/j.1467-8497.2012. 01651.x.

51   John Mayman, 'Lib Policies Blamed for Viet Influx', *Australian*, 26–27 November 1977.

52   Ibid.

53   'Fraser Warns Refugees', *Sydney Morning Herald*, 26 November 1977, 1–2.

54   *Age*, 25 November 1977, 9. As quoted in Stevens, 'Political Debates', 530–31.

55   *Australian*, 25 November 1977, 6. As quoted in Stevens, 'Political Debates', 531.

56   'Hawke: Return Bogus Refugees', *Australian*, 29 November 1977, 1.

57   Stevens, 'Political Debates', 529.

from applicants who had arrived in Australia legally. Australian historian Geoffrey Blainey referred to this as having 'turned the White Australia Policy inside out'.[58] According to polls quoted by sociologist Katharine Betts, the Australian public's attitude towards boat arrivals toughened from 1977 to 1979 and again in 1993, with larger numbers of people wanting to send boat arrivals back.[59]

At first glance, similarities between the German debate of the 1980s and the Australian debates of the 1970s and 1990s become apparent. The sudden influx in the numbers of asylum seekers led to an intensifying public debate in both countries and eventually to toughened regulations. The 'Asylkompromiss' in Germany in 1992–93 and the introduction of mandatory detention in Australia in 1992 are good examples of this.

It is interesting to note that the arguments brought forward in the public debates are very similar. In both debates the genuineness of asylum seekers is questioned, with the idea of them seeking a better life, rather than fleeing from prosecution, dominating. This can be seen, for example, in the address to the House of Representatives of the Rt Hon. Ian Macphee, member of the Liberal Party, in March 1982,[60] as well as in the remarks from Manfred Ritter in the *FAZ* in 1986.[61] Rachel Stevens distinguishes between three functions of the 'seeking a better way of life' argument:

1. trivialising the conditions from which asylum seekers were fleeing
2. exaggerating the threat posed to the Australian nation by, potentially large numbers of, asylum seekers
3. creating a separation between those fleeing impoverishment and those fleeing political persecution.[62]

Comparing these three lines of arguments with the German debate, it can be stated that especially Stevens' second point ties in with the idea of the 'tolerance limit' – the extent to which a nation can accept asylum seekers

---

58 Geoffrey Blainey in Warrnambool in March 1984, quoted in Michael Kirby, 'Australian Population, Multiculturalism and the Road from Warrnambool: The Hon Justice Michael Kirby CMG: The Opening Address delivered at the Second General Conference of the Australian Population Association, Sydney, 8 December 1984', *Journal of the Australian Population Association* 1, no. 2 (1985), 61.
59 Katharine Betts, 'Boat People and Public Opinion in Australia', *People and Place* 9, no. 4 (2001): 40–41.
60 Stevens, 'Political Debates', 538.
61 Ritter, 'Ohne Grundgesetzänderung', 9.
62 Stevens, 'Political Debates', 538.

before it may collapse economically or culturally. This is comparable to the exaggerations used by Reißmüller, who speaks of potentially 'millions, yes dozens of millions' of people that could try to seek asylum in the FRG[63] or Berlin's Senator of the Interior Heinrich Lummer, who claimed that 'according to the current asylum law, the entire Red Army and the KGB could march [into Germany] as long as they would only proclaim themselves to be asylum seekers'.[64]

Insisting that arrivals by boat would 'jump the queue' reveals a level of 'foreignness' of asylum seekers. The creation of an imaginary queue in which those seeking asylum are lining up leads to the suggestion that boat arrivals are disrupting this orderly line by jumping straight to the top. They would therewith cheat those asylum seekers who arrived in Australia by plane, for example, out of their spot in the queue. This is not only used to contrast boat people negatively from other asylum seekers, to show them as undeserving of being granted refugee status, but also as an emotive descriptor in that it is used to make boat arrivals look like criminals. This creates a divide between the 'them' and the 'us' – asylum seekers and Australians.

What is interesting to note in the Australian debate, however, is that insisting on a differentiation between 'genuine asylum seekers' and boat people who 'jump the queue' creates a justification for adopting tougher regulations and the move to mandatory detention for boat arrivals. It serves to legitimise these tougher stances, as it claims that those asylum seekers following the proper channels are more deserving of being granted a place in Australia than others. The idea of a jumpable queue is not something that features in the German debate.

1980s Germany was a country that many felt had an obligation to assist asylum seekers due to the experiences during World War II; it was also struggling to come to terms with its 'national identity' and the significance of an increasingly foreign population. Australia, on the other hand, was and is a country whose 'national identity' is deeply connected with the concept of migration. The arrival of Vietnamese asylum seekers to Australia in the 1970s was only the first test for a country that had only recently abolished its White Australia policy and was presumably still coming to terms with a more multicultural, non-White identity.

---

63   Ritter, 'Ohne Grundgesetzänderung', 9.
64   Schueler, 'Kein deutsches Ruhmesblatt', 7.

PART II
Flashpoints in Australian refugee history

5

THE OTHER ASIAN REFUGEES IN THE 1970s

Australian responses to the Bangladeshi[1] refugee crisis in 1971

Rachel Stevens[2]

If I was to ask you to imagine Asian refugees in the 1970s, what images would spring to mind? I suspect you would think of Vietnamese refugees, either on a boat drifting in the South China Sea or perhaps in an overcrowded camp in Malaysia. These are iconic images of Asian refugees in the 1970s and with little wonder. The Vietnamese exodus was dramatic, sudden and was the result of Western, primarily American, military intervention in the region. Furthermore, with the resettlement of over 1.4 million Indochinese (Vietnamese, Laotian and Cambodian) refugees throughout Western countries from April 1975 to 1991, these South-East Asian migrants have had a visible impact on cities across North America, Western Europe and Australia.[3] If not the Vietnamese

---

1   At the time of the conflict, Bangladesh was known as East Pakistan. I will use the contemporary term 'Bangladesh', unless quoting directly from archival material or discussing the history of the region.
2   This research was generously supported by a National Library of Australia Fellowship, funded by the Past and Present members of the National Library Council in 2018.
3   Rachel Stevens, *Immigration Policy from 1970 to the Present* (New York: Routledge, 2016): 108; Seamus O'Hanlon and Rachel Stevens, 'A Nation of Immigrants or a Nation of Immigrant Cities? The Urban Context of Australian Multiculturalism', *Australian Journal of Politics and History* (hereafter *AJPH*) 63, no. 4 (2017): 556–71, doi.org/10.1111/ajph.12403.

refugees, then perhaps you thought of Ugandan Asians, the 27,200 ethnic Gujaratis who were forcibly expelled by Ugandan President Idi Amin as part of his government's 'Africanisation' strategy in 1972–73.[4]

The resettlement of Indochinese refugees, mostly in North America, Australia and France, and the arrival of Ugandan Asians in Britain and other countries were significant events in recent refugee history. Not surprisingly, these two refugee movements have attracted considerable scholarly attention.[5] But in terms of numbers, these refugee populations were dwarfed by the 10 million Bangladeshi refugees who fled to India to escape violence in their home country. Largely forgotten in public memory outside of South Asian communities, the Bangladesh refugee crisis of 1971 received saturation worldwide media coverage at the time and attracted extensive humanitarian relief from governments, aid agencies, the United Nations and religious organisations.

This chapter aims to extend the conventional narrative of Asian refugees during the 1970s to include Bangladeshi refugees. Specifically, it explores the ways that Australians of diverse backgrounds engaged with the unfolding refugee crisis in 1971 and examines how they sought to provide humanitarian relief to the millions of Bengali refugees languishing in camps in India. It asks: Who were the Australians that empathised with the plight of Bangladeshi refugees? And why did they care for distant Asian refugees, many of whom were non-Christians and with socialist leanings? The efforts of Australians to aid Bangladeshi refugees is perplexing: during the second half of the twentieth century, the Australian Government traditionally gave preference to the resettlement of European anti-communist refugees and, later, South-East Asian refugees over

---

4   Samia Nasar, 'We Refugees? Re-defining Britain's East African Asians', in *Migrant Britain. Histories and Historiographies: Essays in Honour of Colin Holmes*, eds Jennifer Craig-Norton, Christhard Hoffmann and Tony Kushner (London: Routledge, 2018): 138–48, doi.org/10.4324/9781315159959-16, and Panikos Panayi, ed., *The Impact of Immigration: A Documentary History of the Effects and Experiences of Immigrants in Britain Since 1945* (Manchester: Manchester University Press, 1999).

5   For recent scholarship of Vietnamese refugees, see the voluminous work of Nathalie Huynh Chau Nguyen; for recent publications on the resettlement of Ugandan Asians in Britain, see Becky Taylor, 'Good Citizens? Ugandan Asians, Volunteers and "Race" Relation in 1970s Britain', *History Workshop Journal* 85, no. 1 (2018): 120–41, doi.org/10.1093/hwj/dbx055; Yumiko Hamai, '"Imperial Burden" or "Jews of Africa?" An Analysis of Political and Media Discourse in the Ugandan Asian Crisis (1972)', *Twentieth Century British History* 22, no. 3 (2011): 415–36, doi.org/10.1093/tcbh/hwq059.

other persecuted groups.[6] These were the exiles with whom Australians sympathised. We shared their struggle against communism and the tyranny of authoritarian dictatorships. But the Bangladeshi refugees did not fit this typical mould and the cross-sectional support they received from the Australian public is, prima facie, counterintuitive.

Two Pakistans, many problems: A brief history to the 1971 conflict

The Islamic State of Pakistan emerged from the Partition of British India in 1947. Its two wings, West Pakistan (current-day Pakistan) and East Pakistan (Bangladesh), were over 1,200 miles apart. These territories were hastily devised by Sir Cyril Radcliffe, a London judge, in under six weeks. This Partition line, which is now known as the Radcliffe line, cut through 450,000 km² and affected the lives of 88 million people. The idea behind the Partition was to separate Muslim-majority areas from Hindu-majority areas, but given the religious diversity in the northern parts of India, this task was not as simple as it sounded. West Pakistan had sizeable Sikh and Hindu populations around the Punjab while in East Pakistan, around 16 per cent of the population was Hindu.

Although the created state of Pakistan was conceived on the assumption of Muslim solidarity, ethnic and linguistic differences between the two wings created frequent instability within the fledgling nation. In Pakistan, the government bestowed official status on English and Urdu, the latter considered the language of Islam in South Asia. Neither official language, however, was widely spoken. According to the 1961 Pakistani census (the most relevant census for the 1971 war), 99 per cent of East Pakistanis spoke Bengali. Meanwhile, two-thirds of West Pakistanis spoke Punjabi, the remainder speaking Urdu, Sindhi or Pashto. Given the dominance of Bengali in East Pakistan, East Pakistanis had long agitated unsuccessfully for official language recognition. The failure of the Pakistani Government to recognise Bengali as an official language was an affront to the rich literary tradition among Bengalis.

---

6   For histories of Australian resettlement of central and eastern European refugees, see Jayne Persian's *Beautiful Balts: From Displaced Persons to New Australians* (Sydney: NewSouth Publishing, 2017) and Vasilios Vasilas, *When Freedom Beckons: The Hungarian Revolution of 1956 and the Jewish Hungarian Journey to Australia* (Sydney: Vasilios Vasilas, 2017).

Even the idea of Muslim solidarity overcoming all other differences proved to be a myth in Pakistan. West Pakistani elites believed that, even though East Pakistanis had Muslim names and identified as Muslim, they were in fact 'Hindu at heart'. West Pakistani elites also saw Bengalis as uncivilised and effeminate. As one West Pakistani commander commented, East Bengal was 'a low-lying land of low-lying people'.[7] The idea that Bengalis were weaker than West Pakistanis had long colonial roots, fostered by the British when they recruited most of the military from the Punjab, the north-western province of British India. Punjabis believed that, as the selected military caste, they were racially superior to other ethnic groups in British India. This belief held through the postcolonial years, with most of the armed forces recruited from West Pakistan. These racial stereotypes, a fear of foreign Hindu influence and linguistic differences rendered East Pakistanis outsiders and 'strangers in their own land', which in turn provided fertile ground for the mass killings that would follow in 1971.[8]

West Pakistani chauvinism arguably enabled the central government to treat its eastern province as a colony and a market, ripe for exploitation.[9] Despite being the more populous province with 76 million people, and the main supplier of income to the national economy through exports of jute and rice, East Pakistanis were deprived of enjoying the fruits of their labour. Government revenue, development projects and foreign aid expenditure were all directed to West Pakistan. West Pakistanis also had access to well-paid government jobs: Islamabad became the national capital in 1967 and home to the civil service; the Pakistan Armed Forces were headquartered in neighbouring Rawalpindi. With this relative prosperity, 75 per cent of all imports to Pakistan were shipped to the western province while East Pakistanis endured endemic poverty punctuated with regular natural disasters. Two such disasters hit East Pakistan in 1970 and exacerbated ill will between the two provinces. The monsoonal floods in July were followed by a cyclone and tidal bore in December. Collectively, hundreds of thousands perished. While international aid poured in, the central government in Islamabad was slow to act and indifferent to the suffering of East Pakistanis.

---

7   Donald Beachler, 'The Politics of Genocide Scholarship: The Case of Bangladesh', *Patterns of Prejudice* 41, no. 5 (2007): 467–92, 477–78, doi.org/10.1080/00313220701657286.
8   Yasmin Saikia, 'Insāniyat for Peace: Survivors' narrative of the 1971 war of Bangladesh', *Journal of Genocide Research* 13, no. 4 (2011): 475–501, 486, doi.org/10.1080/14623528.2011.625739.
9   Srinath Raghavan, *1971: A Global History of the Creation of Bangladesh* (Cambridge, MA: Harvard University Press 2013).

Pakistan held its first democratic elections in 1970. As a watershed moment for a country plagued by corruption and dictatorships in its short history, a sense of optimism filled the air. However, the elections did not go to plan, at least from the perspective of the ruling elite in West Pakistan. Pro-autonomy East Pakistani party, the Awami League, won an absolute majority of the seats out of the newly formed 313-seat national assembly, including 167 out of 169 seats allocated to East Pakistan. With its absolute majority, the Awami League could enact its autonomy program and install its leader, Sheikh Mujibur Rahman, as the prime minister of Pakistan. Of course, the prospect of relinquishing power to a Bengali was unacceptable to the ruling class in West Pakistan. Unwilling to forego power, Pakistan's military dictator Yahya Khan delayed convening the new assembly, which in turn, triggered mass outrage in East Pakistan as Bengalis believed they had been robbed of their electoral victory. Mass protests and strikes soon followed, paralysing the East Pakistani economy.

At midnight on 25 March 1971, the West Pakistani armed forces invaded East Pakistan under the cover of darkness. Their aim was to quash the uprising through brute force and, while they were there, to '[teach] them [Bengalis] a lesson'.[10] In practice, this meant burning villages, destroying crops, capturing and raping of hundreds of thousands of women, and killing agitators, namely, students, intellectuals, Awami League activists and, most of all, Hindus. Approximately 80,000 West Pakistani troops entered East Pakistan, followed by an additional 100,000 paramilitary and civilian armed forces. The West Pakistani forces, however, were met by 175,000 East Pakistani guerrillas who were supported, materially and morally, by India. When India intervened directly in the war in December 1971 – for strategic, political and humanitarian reasons – they deployed 250,000 troops on two fronts. Simply out-powered and overrun, West Pakistan surrendered and East Pakistanis declared their independence, adopting the name Bangla Desh (Land of Bengal).

This brief, peripheral conflict left destruction on an unimaginable scale: the deaths of 1.5 million by conservative estimates; 3 million by Bangladeshi estimates. To escape widespread and indiscriminate violence,

---

10   Quotation is from British High Commissioner to Pakistan, Cyril Pickard, in 1971. See Angela Debnath, 'British Perceptions of the East Pakistan Crisis 1971: "Hideous Atrocities on Both Sides"', *Journal of Genocide Research* 13, no. 4 (2011): 421–50, 428, doi.org/10.1080/14623528.2011.62574 4, and Simon C Smith, 'Coming Down on the Winning Side: Britain on the South Asia Crisis, 1971', *Contemporary British History* 24, no. 4 (2010): 451–70, 456, doi.org/10.1080/13619462.2010.518410.

millions of East Pakistanis fled for their lives. By the end of the conflict, 10 million refugees were living in camps in India, specifically in West Bengal. There were a further 20 million Bengalis internally displaced within East Pakistan. These statistics are all the more staggering when one considers that the East Pakistani population was 76 million at the time. With 30 million internally displaced or refugees in India, nearly two in five East Pakistanis were uprooted during their war of liberation from Pakistan. The mass killings during the 1971 war have been deemed by some researchers as constituting genocide, and the Bangladeshi Government explicitly promotes this view. However, other scholars argue that the violence was multidirectional and opportunistic, and that there was no systematic attempt to exterminate a race of people. Putting this debate to one side, there is a consensus that the armed forces and militia inflicted widespread suffering on civilians: in the words of one Bihari woman, 1971 was 'the year of anarchy and end of humanity in Bangladesh'.[11]

International involvement and scholarly silence

Given the scale and regional significance of the Bangladesh War of Liberation and ensuing refugee exodus, one may assume that historians, anthropologists, political scientists and/or sociologists have extensively documented and analysed this event. However, this is not the case. To be sure, archival materials are difficult to access: government documents in Bangladesh were destroyed by the Pakistani armed forces in the final days of the conflict; Pakistani government archives on this topic remain closed.[12] Feminist South Asian scholars based in the West have highlighted the

---

11   Quotation comes from Christian Gerlach, *Extremely Violent Societies: Mass Violence in the Twentieth Century* (Cambridge: Cambridge University Press 2010), chapter 4, doi.org/10.1017/cbo9780511781254. For scholarly debate on the extent and nature of violence during the 1971 war, see Beachler, 'The Politics of Genocide Scholarship'; A Dirk Moses, 'The United Nations, Humanitarianism and Human Rights: War Crimes/Genocide Trials for Pakistani Soldiers in 1971', in *Human Rights in the Twentieth Century*, ed. Stefan-Ludwig Hoffman (New York: Cambridge University Press 2011): 258–80, doi.org/10.1017/cbo9780511921667.017; Wardatul Akmam, 'Atrocities against Humanity During the Liberation War in Bangladesh: A Case of Genocide', *Journal of Genocide Research* 4, no. 4 (2002): 543–59, doi.org/10.1080/146235022000000463; Sarmila Bose, 'The Question of Genocide and the Quest for Justice in the 1971 War', *Journal of Genocide Research* 13, no. 4 (2011): 393–419, doi.org/10.1080/14623528.2011.625750, and her generalist book, *Dead Reckoning: Memories of the 1971 Bangladesh War* (London: Hurst Publishers 2011).
12   Raghavan, *1971*, 11.

gendered nature of violence during the conflict. Through interviews with survivors and perpetrators of sexual violence in Bangladesh, researchers including Bina D'Costa and Yasmin Saikia have provided a voice to civilians normally rendered silent.[13]

There is scant research on the actions of international actors during this conflict. What limited scholarship there is, is typically top-down and government-oriented, examining foreign policy cables, speeches and government action or inaction, or media portrayals. Drawing on recently declassified government archives, scholars have considered the responses of the governments of the United States, Canada, the United Kingdom and India to the crisis.[14] However, this focus on state actors does not match my own reading of events in which Australians of a variety of backgrounds mobilised, lobbied and fundraised to provide aid for Bangladeshi refugees despite government indifference to the calamity.

In this chapter, I make three main arguments. First, grassroots activism was a significant force in shaping government policy. Throughout 1971, there was a schism between community attitudes in favour of humanitarian intervention and Australian Government policy to remain neutral, avoid interfering in an internal Pakistani matter and donate as little money as possible to generate positive publicity for the government. During the refugee crisis, the Australian Government provided cash and in-kind aid to Bangladeshi refugees gradually, only increasing the donated amount in response to public pressure. In terms of refugee relief, resettlement in Australia was never an option; the Indian Government that temporarily settled the 10 million refugees needed cash to buy materials for shelter, food and medical care. In the end, the Australian Government became a leading donor nation, a fact even more remarkable given the small population base of 12 million people in 1971. By the end of February 1972, the Australian Government had provided US$5,055,072,

---

13 Bina D'Costa, *Nationbuilding, Gender and War Crimes in South Asia* (London: Routledge, 2010); Yasmin Saikia, 'Beyond the Archive of Silence: Narratives of Violence of the 1971 Liberation War of Bangladesh', *History Workshop Journal* 58, no. 1 (2004): 275–87, doi.org/10.1093/hwj/58.1.275.

14 Gary J Bass, *The Blood Telegram: Nixon, Kissinger and a Forgotten Genocide* (New York: Alfred A. Knopf, 2013); Raghavan, *1971*; Richard Pilkington, 'In the National Interest? Canada and the East Pakistan Crisis of 1971', *Journal of Genocide Research* 13, no. 4 (2011): 451–74, doi.org/10.1080/14623528.2011.625741; Debnath, 'British Perceptions of the East Pakistan Crisis'; Janice Musson, 'Britain and the Recognition of Bangladesh in 1972', *Diplomacy & Statecraft* 19, no. 1 (2008): 125–44, doi.org/10.1080/09592290801913767; Sonia Cordera, 'India's Response to the 1971 East Pakistan Crisis: Hidden and Open Reasons for Intervention', *Journal of Genocide Research* 17, no. 1 (2015): 45–62, doi.org/10.1080/14623528.2015.991207.

a figure only exceeded by Scandinavian/northern European nations, the Netherlands (US$5,754,247), Sweden (US$6,000,584), West Germany (US$19,771,298), and major powers, the USSR (US$20,000,000), the UK (US$38,182,132) and the US (US$89,157,000).[15] But substantial Australian Government aid may well have never happened had it not been for public activism.

Second, the Bangladeshi refugee crisis in 1971 created a coalition of disparate groups from a cross-section of Australian society who otherwise had little in common. Unlike many other social causes, aid to Bangladeshi refugees had broad appeal to the right and the left. It appealed to left-wingers who abhorred West Pakistan's seemingly colonial policies towards its eastern wing, pacifists shocked by the wanton violence and mass killings, Christians who sought to remedy Third World poverty and inequality, and internationalists who wanted Australia to play a leading role in world affairs, especially in Asia. Importantly, due to saturation media coverage in 1971, this conflict and refugee exodus galvanised ostensibly apolitical citizens into action. This conflict was easy to understand, its villains and victims easy to identify. The imagery of starving refugees on TV and in the newspaper was evocative; the statistics of up to 3 million deaths, 10 million refugees and a further 20 million internally displaced, for a region of 76 million people, were difficult to comprehend but impossible to ignore. This refugee crisis appealed to Australians' morality and humanity, regardless of political affiliation, religion, profession, age or class.

Third, Australian involvement in the Bangladesh Liberation War was significant because it demonstrated a deep and multifocal engagement with Bengal, a region not usually associated with Australian foreign policies, whether in relation to defence or development. When we think of Australia's engagement with Asia, particularly since 1945, we may reasonably think of military action in Japan, Korea or Indochina, humanitarian efforts in South-East Asia, the complicated relationships

---

15   Offers of Assistance Made By/Received from Foreign Governments up to 24-2-1972, Contributions from governments to the Focal Point – General File, Series 1, Classified Subject Files, Fonds 11, Records of the Central Registry, Archives of the United Nations High Commissioner for Refugees, Geneva.

with Indonesia and mainland China or colonial endeavours in the Pacific.[16] In short, Australians look north. Maybe it is time Australians look north-west.

There are a number of distinct groups of Australians who were active in providing aid and relief to Bangladeshi refugees, such as political activists (including students), humanitarian organisations, Christian groups and Australian diplomats stationed in the region. In this chapter, I will focus on the actions of two groups: diplomats (or public servants) and Christians. Due to word restrictions, it would be too ambitious to include a discussion on humanitarian groups and political activists, and therefore these two populations will be the subject of future publications. I have classified individuals and organisations according to their overarching affiliation and the values that inform their activities. However, the distinctions between the four groups are not perfect and there are occasions of overlap, for example, in the case of Christian student activists. Furthermore, the demarcation between each of these groups does not intend to obscure the links between them. On the contrary, the evidence indicates that individual actors during this event did not operate in a vacuum; rather, they were part of, and impacted by, larger networks.

The diplomats

The National Library of Australia holds a number of transcribed oral histories of career diplomats, the public servants who spent most of their professional lives stationed at various embassies abroad who offer fascinating firsthand accounts as they witnessed major events in world history. These oral histories are supplemented with the memoirs and

---

16 For recent Australian scholarship on histories of humanitarianism in Asia, Agnieszka Sobocinska, 'A New Kind of Mission: The Volunteer Graduate Scheme and the History of International Development', *AJPH* 62, no. 3 (2016): 369–87, doi.org/10.1111/ajph.12268; Joy Damousi, 'The Campaign for Japanese-Australian Children to Enter Australia, 1957–1968: A History of Post-War Humanitarianism', *AJPH* 64, no. 2 (2018): 211–26, doi.org/10.1111/ajph.12461; on relations with Indonesia and China, see Peter van der Eng, '*Konfrontasi* and Australia's Aid to Indonesia during the 1960s', *AJPH* 55, no. 1 (2009): 46-63; Billy Griffiths, *The China Breakthrough: Whitlam in the Middle Kingdom, 1971* (Melbourne: Monash University Publishing 2012); on histories of development, see Nicholas Ferns, '"A New Hope for Asia?" Australia, the United States and the Promotion of Economic Development in Southeast Asia', *AJPH* 64, no. 1 (2018): 33–47, doi.org/10.1111/ajph.12422; on histories of colonial involvement in the Pacific, see Stephen Henningham, 'Australia's Economic Ambitions in French New Caledonia, 1945–1955', *Journal of Pacific History* 49, no. 4 (2014): 421–39, doi.org/10.1080/00223344.2014.976915; Bruce Hunt, *Australia's Northern Shield: Papua New Guinea and the Defence of Australia since 1880* (Melbourne: Monash University Publishing, 2017).

research papers of the diplomats, some of which were self-published and are unlikely to be held at other libraries. In this section, I will focus on three key diplomats: Francis Stuart, the Australian high commissioner to Pakistan, based in Islamabad, West Pakistan; Jim Allen, deputy high commissioner to Pakistan, based in Dhaka, Bangladesh; and Sir Keith Waller, who was secretary of the Department of Foreign Affairs from 1970 to 1974.[17] All three public servants played a significant part in liaising between the William McMahon Government, UN agencies and the Indian and Pakistani governments. But that is where the similarities end between the three individuals.

Jim Allen

James Lawrence Allen, known as Jim Allen, was definitely not a typical Australian diplomat.[18] Born in north-east India to Australian, missionary Methodist parents, the first language he spoke was Urdu. As a child, Jim's parents would ask him questions in English and he would reply in Urdu. During his adolescence, Jim attended boarding school in Adelaide, then studied at the University of Adelaide, graduating with honours in classics. As a new graduate, Jim dreamed of joining the Indian Civil Service. He travelled to London to sit the civil service exam but just fell short of acceptance into the highly esteemed Indian Civil Service. Bitterly disappointed that he could not realise his lifelong dream, Jim returned to West Bengal and worked as an English lecturer before enlisting in the British Imperial Forces to fight in World War II.

After the war, Jim worked briefly with Lord Richard Casey, the Australian who served the British Empire as governor of Bengal from 1944 to 1946. Jim joined the Australian High Commission in New Delhi as third secretary, becoming a permanent member of the Australian Foreign Service in 1946. During this time, he witnessed firsthand the tumultuous Partition of India and the creation of Pakistan, an event that unleashed communal and sectarian violence on an unprecedented scale.

---

17   Unless it is a direct quotation, I will use the indigenous spelling of 'Dhaka' rather than the Anglicised spelling 'Dacca' throughout this chapter.
18   The following discussion is based on: 'James Allen interviewed by Mel Pratt for the Mel Pratt Collection [sound recording]', 1976, typed transcript, National Library of Australia (NLA), ORAL TRC 121/76, available at: nla.gov.au/nla.obj-214917676.

Allen was posted to Dhaka as deputy high commissioner in 1969, a post he held for five years. Importantly, Allen had a native's proficiency in Bengali. While other diplomats in Dhaka took crash courses in Bengali, they could not shake their foreign accent. Because Allen's mother tongue was Urdu, this helped him gain fluency in another Indo-Aryan language, Bengali. While stationed in Bangladesh, Allen mingled with peasants and workers throughout the countryside with ease. He could also make jokes in Bengali – a true indicator of fluency – which made him very popular with the locals. Because of this, Allen was widely admired and respected throughout Bangladesh, a fact that gave the Australian Government enormous kudos as Bangladesh emerged as an independent state.

In his oral history interview, Allen recalled the beginning of hostilities in Bangladesh:

> On the night of Thursday the 25th March Pakistani forces surged out of their Cantonments in all the major industrial/urban centres and started machine gunning anybody in sight – students in particular, polices, people on duty, shopkeepers … that went on for a few days in the urban centres, and of course all Bengalis fled into the countryside. Then the army fanned out into the countryside and continued this massacre in the villages … 1971 was a very sad and unhappy year.

> There was a tremendous amount of cruelty and inhumanity going on all over the country … Quite frankly I had difficulty in getting the message across to Canberra. At the working level, I had the feeling there was a strong continuing pro-Pakistan bias, matched by an equally strong continuing anti-Indian bias. I had the feeling that some of my criticisms of what the Pakistan Army and the Pakistan Government was doing in East Pakistan were not all that welcome back in Canberra, at any rate on the working level.

What we have here are contesting interpretations over the conflict, its causes and how to respond. Jim Allen persevered with relaying his message to his superiors in Canberra, and with the backing of UN observers and other third parties, his perspective eventually gained traction. As Allen recalled 'my story, told from the point of view of the Bengali people, finally prevailed'.[19]

---

19   Ibid., 10–11.

Despite wanton violence, Allen and his wife Marion 'bravely stuck it out' in Bangladesh, choosing not to relocate to safer surrounds.[20] The Allens were very active in relief efforts for refugees and internally displaced persons, providing food, shelter and clothing for refugees in the countryside, and later providing rehabilitation work for widows destitute after the war. Interestingly, these relief efforts were funded privately from friends and acquaintances back in Australia, independent of his work for the Australian Government. Jim Allen also liaised closely with aid agencies in Australia as well as Australian Baptist missionaries in Bengal, which will be discussed later in the chapter.[21]

Francis Stuart

Francis Stuart was the Australian high commissioner to Pakistan, as well as Afghanistan, from 1970 to 1973. He was based in Islamabad, West Pakistan, some distance from his deputy, Jim Allen, in Dhaka. The two diplomats provide a clear contrast: while Allen had spent much of his life in South Asia immersed in the local cultures, Stuart had been a career diplomat and globetrotter, and had been posted in diverse countries such as Cambodia, the Philippines, the United Arab Republic (the brief union of Syria and Egypt) and Poland. Allen and Stuart also understood the conflict in Bangladesh differently. Allen was sympathetic to the view of Bengalis and admired Indian humanitarian efforts during the refugee crisis. Stuart, on the other hand, was unabashedly pro–West Pakistan and anti-Indian. During the conflict, Stuart communicated to the Australian Government that the ongoing conflict was a 'civil war and not a war of independence against alien rule'.[22] The conflict-as-civil-war perspective of Stuart influenced Australian Government policy at first. However, the Australian Government would revise its policy and rhetoric by October 1971 in response to the public outcry at West Pakistani atrocities, and arguably, the persuasiveness of Jim Allen.

While Jim and Marion Allen were working tirelessly to help the internally displaced in the countryside of Bangladesh, Stuart was frustrated by communication difficulties. He wrote in his memoir that:

---

20   Francis Stuart, *Towards Coming of Ages. A Foreign Service Odyssey*, Australians in Asia Series, March 1989 (Brisbane: Griffith University, 1989), 230.
21   J L Allen to Moira Lenore Dynon, Letter 1972 [manuscript], 1972. NLA MS 3118.
22   Stuart, *Towards Coming of Ages*, 230.

> Most of the time the telex network was overloaded or closed down,
> or the Pakistani authorities refused to transmit messages in code.
> At times, we were isolated except for messages carried through the
> Khyber Pass to or from Kabul.[23]

Isolated from communication and distant from the theatre of war,
Stuart became focused on how the Indian Government, he believed,
was using the crisis to shift the balance of power in the region in the
pursuit of Indian hegemony. This focus arguably became an obsession at
the expense of other issues, particularly humanitarian. What is striking
about Stuart's writings is that he seemed removed from what was going
on in Bengal and also Australia, completely misreading public sentiment.
In a condescending tone, Stuart wrote that the Australian public:

> Could not be expected to interest itself in the 1971 affair. To the
> extent it followed things at all it [the Australian public] saw the
> Bangladesh conflict in black and white terms, as the suppression
> of a nationalist struggle for freedom against an imperialist
> military dictatorship.[24]

Stuart also commented that 'the Australian view of the situation as
a liberation struggle against colonialism was simplistic, even puerile'.
Out of touch with public activism and humanitarian endeavours in
Australia, Stuart appears oblivious to the multitude of Australian responses
to the Bangladeshi refugee crisis. Stuart also extended his dismissiveness
to Prime Minister William McMahon, who he deemed a political
opportunist who deliberately harnessed a foreign crisis to further his
domestic political goals. This cynical depiction of McMahon may well
have been true but the prime minister was certainly not the first nor the
last politician to leverage external events for political gain.

In short, the high commissioner for Pakistan, Francis Stuart, and his
deputy, Jim Allen, held diametrically opposing views, an issue perhaps
exacerbated by their distance of over 2,000 km. It was up to the secretary
of the Department of Foreign Affairs, Sir Keith Waller, to make sense of
the conflicting information and pass on recommendations to Australia's
then novice foreign minister, Nigel Bowen.

---

23   Ibid., 234.
24   Ibid., 240.

Sir Keith Waller

Secretary from 1970 to 1974, Waller shared Stuart's pro-Pakistan bias, commenting in his memoirs that the Australian Government had been traditionally wary of the Indian Government since the time of Menzies. Despite general apprehension about Hindus, Waller noted that, traditionally, the Australian Government had good relations with Bengal, both the eastern part in Pakistan and the western part in India, dating back to when Australian Lord Casey was governor of Bengal as well as the longstanding involvement of Australian Baptist missionaries in the region.[25]

Sir Keith was very close to Lord Casey, who remained active in foreign policy circles until his death in 1976. They would often converse over the phone during this period. Given Casey's experience in Bengal, Waller leant on him for advice on the ensuing crisis in South Asia. Importantly, Lord Casey respected Jim Allen, describing Allen as 'remarkably well fitted for his difficult task' of deputy high commissioner in Dhaka.[26] It is hard to say with any certainty, but the close relationships between Allen and Casey, and between Casey and Waller, meant that Jim Allen's position trumped the arguments of his superior, Francis Stuart, who remained isolated and irate in Islamabad.

In addition to providing aid for the refugees, the Australian Government was the first Western nation to recognise the newly declared state of Bangladesh in early 1972. And more than that, the Australian Government forged a coalition of Western and non-aligned countries to recognise Bangladeshi independence, forcing the Pakistani Government into a corner and stopping them from retaliating. Waller was at the centre of the quite complex diplomatic task, organising with Australian ambassadors and high commissioners across the globe and in real time, persuading allied countries to get on board and support Bangladeshi recognition. In Waller's words, the Australian Foreign Service 'mounted a vigorous diplomatic effort to get a number of countries' to recognise Bangladesh.[27] At this time, major Western powers were reluctant to

25   Sir Keith Waller, *A Diplomatic Life: Some Memories*, Australians in Asia Series, July 1990 (Brisbane: Griffith University, 1990), 45–46.
26   Diary entry, 12 April 1969 in 'Lord Casey's diaries, 1965 – June 1976', vol. 29, Box 31a, subseries 4.4 Lord Casey's diaries (photocopies), series 4 Diaries and Letterbooks, Casey family. Papers of the Casey family, 1820–1978 [manuscript], NLA MS 6150.
27   Waller, *A Diplomatic Life*, 46.

recognise the independence of a secessionist province: the US Government refused to recognise Bangladesh as it was closely allied with Pakistan; the Canadian Government feared recognition would fan the flames of its own rogue province, Quebec; the UK Government were hedging their bets; and the Japanese Government had adopted a 'wait and see' approach. Thus, the Australian Government's formal recognition of the People's Republic of Bangladesh was a case of it showing regional leadership and sticking its neck out to support the independence of a vaguely socialist, predominantly Muslim nation.

Christians

Christians were major aid donors who helped provide relief for Bangladeshi refugees and were pivotal in making the Bangladeshi refugee crisis a non-partisan issue. Both Protestants (mostly Anglicans, Methodists and Baptists) and Catholics were equally active in mobilising, lobbying and fundraising for Bangladeshi refugees and overcame sectarian divisions to work collaboratively on the issue. Leaders within the various Christian churches were also very effective lobbyists, with ready access to the Prime Minister's Office, and their seniority within the church bestowed a certain gravitas on their views. Unlike ordinary constituents who wrote to the prime minister and received a reply from the prime minister's private secretary, church leaders received replies direct from the prime minister himself, suggesting that their letters were read by McMahon while other constituent letters did not pass the secretary's desk.[28]

Len Reid

Len Reid was an outspoken advocate for cash donations to the Indian Government to run the refugee camps. He was a Christian first and a politician second. After a couple of terms in the Victorian Parliament, he was elected the federal member for Holt, an electorate in the outer south-eastern suburbs and urban fringe of Melbourne. He was a Liberal politician, though he acted like more of an opposition MP and was a constant thorn in the McMahon Government's side. Reid established

---

28 Example letters from constituents and the clergy can be found in 'Constituent correspondence, June 1971': Files 47 and 49, Box 442, Series 17 Prime Minister 1967–72, William McMahon and Liberal Party of Australia, Papers of William McMahon, 1949–1987 [manuscript], NLA MS 3926.

the Christian charity, *For those who have less* in 1962, an organisation dedicated to addressing poverty and famine in India, Pakistan and Nepal. Driven by Christian values of service to God and helping the poor with humility and service, he believed it was 'God's will and our privilege to help'.[29] He strongly advocated what he termed 'sacrificial giving'. What constituted sacrificial would vary from person to person, but the point was that the degree of giving should be so significant that one should suffer as a result. Giving is not about feeling good about yourself, he reasoned: it's about sufferance. Quoting Mohandas Gandhi, Reid explained that whenever one person suffers voluntarily, it relieves someone else of suffering: 'everyone who fasts gives bread to another who needs it more – everyone who makes some sacrifice helps someone else somewhere'.[30]

Reid's Christian beliefs were at the forefront of his appeal to Australians, invoking references to the Crusades. He argued that, as a Christian community, 'we must take more responsibility for the great human problems that confront so many people around the world' and it is up to the non-government sector 'to campaign more vigorously. If necessary, they should crusade'.[31] Reid's rhetoric was at times confrontational, challenging Australians to put into action their Christian values. In his words, 'If Australia is to continue to call herself a Christian community, we can no longer procrastinate while millions face famine conditions'.[32]

As a member of parliament, Reid travelled to West Bengal on behalf of the government, visiting some 30 refugee camps. With each camp home to approximately 5,000 refugees, Reid estimated that he had seen the lived conditions affecting 150,000 refugees. During this visit, he consulted with government, inter-government and non-government organisations on the ground. With this knowledge, he lobbied the McMahon Government to do more during the refugee crisis in 1971 and for reconstruction and rehabilitation during 1972. In one letter to the prime minister, Reid wrote:

29 Len Reid, *The Tragedy of Those Who Have Less* (Melbourne: Fraser & Morphet, 1973), 23.
30 Ibid., 7, 13, 63.
31 Ibid., 25.
32 Ibid., 62.

> I know the Australian people to be generous and fair minded and where there are injustices they react strongly, for these reasons it will be necessary for us to raise our Aid priorities … The people in Australia will soon demand that we accept a greater responsibility in these countries and I feel we could well seize the initiative.[33]

Reid dedicated much of his only term in the Federal Parliament to lobbying the Australian Government to increase its aid commitment to Asia. It appears that he did so purely for compassionate reasons and was not interested in grandstanding or accounting tricks to impress the public. Specifically, Reid advocated for cash over material (or in-kind) donations.

He was a straight shooter and didn't hold back in his correspondence with the prime minister. Reflecting on events the previous year, in March 1972 Reid wrote:

> During this [refugee] crisis I repeatedly stated that India and the United Nations needed cash – not goods – to provide immediate relief for the refugee. However, my pleas might just as well have come from a junior office boy in the Foreign Office for all the notice that was taken.
>
> I might add I had good reasons for suggesting a cash donation of $10M for the refugees, as I had spent some time visiting a number of refugee camps during the Monsoon, and also had on the spot discussions with Mrs Gandhi and the Government of Pakistan, and they stressed their most urgent need was cash to purchase goods locally … Whoever made the decision not to send cash made the wrong decision, and it appears to me the less said on this issue the better.[34]

To clarify, cash donations are generally preferred by aid groups over in-kind donations. Cash can be sent quickly and used to purchase goods on the ground almost immediately. In-kind donations incur significant freighting charges and take time to transport to the refugee camps. There is also the view that in-kind donations are self-serving, for example, giving business to Australian companies when cheaper alternatives were available

---

33 'Letter. L. S. Reid, Member for Holt to the Rt Hon. William McMahon', 2 November 1972, File 114m Members' Correspondence. R., Box 449, Series 17 Prime Minister 1967–72, William McMahon and Liberal Party of Australia, Papers of William McMahon, 1949-1987 [manuscript], NLA MS 3926.
34 'Letter. L. S. Reid, Member for Holt to the Rt Hon. William McMahon', 30 March 1972, File 114, NLA MS 3926.

closer to India. In-kind donations are thus a self-beneficial method to inflate artificially the aid budget and thus maximise positive publicity in the media and with the voting public, as well as earning political capital with other nations. Reid was perhaps ill-suited to the *realpolitik* in Canberra, not lasting more than one term in the Federal Parliament. His insistent calls for Australians to abandon their addiction to material possessions in pursuit of higher ideals no doubt closely aligned with other active Christians, namely, Baptist missionaries.

Baptist missionaries

Australian Baptist missionaries first worked in Bengal in 1882 and continue to work in Bangladesh to this day. Since 1882, over 250 individuals or couples have worked in the region, including 28 individuals who served during the early 1970s. Although these Christians provided aid to local communities in crisis, it should be clear that humanitarianism was not their raison d'être. Even amid the mass destruction and loss of life during the Bangladesh Liberation War, Baptist missionaries remained optimistic about prospects for Christian conversion of Bengali Muslims. In their end of year report in 1971, the South Australian Baptist Union commented:

> The outcome of the events [in Bangladesh] are what now concern us, and these are not only *thrilling*, but challenging. *Opportunities for effective evangelism among Moslems in Bangla Desh are more promising today than for many years.* The Mission is, therefore, looking to God to raise up the men and money to embark on concentrated evangelism in the new nation. How will we respond to the challenge of a nation that is looking for a satisfying faith? [Italics added][35]

Along with their evangelism, the South Australian branch of the Baptist Church provided material aid from afar, including food parcel delivery, medical care and other relief supplies for refugees.[36]

The Australian Baptist Church also sent missionaries to Bangladesh to promote Christianity in the region. When hostilities broke out in March 1971, there were 17 individuals working in the region, including three

---

35   South Australian Baptist Union Incorporated, *Handbook for 1971–1972: Programme and Reports for Autumn Assembly 1972* (Adelaide: Publisher Unspecified, 1972), 58.
36   Ibid., xvii.

married couples.[37] Most of the Australian missionaries chose to return home or continued their work in India. However, three individuals – Rev. Ian Hawley, Miss Betty Salisbury and Miss Grace Dodge – stayed in Bangladesh throughout the war. They were based in the north at Mymensingh in a compound with 80 refugees, a town that Hawley later described as 'an awful place of death'. In a 2005 piece, Ian Hawley remembered that:

> Every night in Mymensingh during the months of November and December [1971] people were arrested on any pretence, with the Army's consent. Fanatical Muslims, it would seem, were given a free hand to kill whoever they wanted to kill. They unashamedly left victims' bodies on the edge of a river … Vultures and dogs feasted on them. The bodies of others were cut into pieces and thrown down wells. I have seen these wells full of dismembered bodies and also corpses being eaten by dogs on the river bank. How a person can act with such unrelenting savagery and utter contempt for the sacredness and value of human life is beyond all comprehension.[38]

Australian missionaries were unharmed during the conflict, though their properties were damaged and ransacked. Grace Dodge, one of the Australian missionaries, believed that the retreating West Pakistani Army torched the countryside in a final attempt at destruction, leaving the natural environment appearing more like the Australian bush after a fire than the verdant plains associated with Bengal. The local Christian community in Bangladesh had a low death rate as the Pakistani armed forces and militias targeted Hindus, as well as dissenters and professionals.[39] Australian Baptists sought divine wisdom to understand the unfolding conflict and to remain brave among escalating dangers. The missionaries maintained their faith and, in fact, saw the conflict as an opportunity to improve their standing with the locals and acceptance in the community. Beyond their missionary goals, Australian Baptists provided practical compassion for refugees, sheltering vulnerable populations – such as women and children – from the army.[40]

---

37   Tony Cupit, Ros Gooden and Ken Manley, *From Five Barley Loaves: Australian Baptists in Global Mission 1864–2010* (Melbourne: Mosaic Press, 2013), 124.
38   Ian Hawley, 'Reflections on the 1971 Civil War in Bangladesh', *Our Yesterdays: A Publication of the Victorian Baptist Historical Society* 13 (2005): 7–23, 19.
39   Grace Dodge, 'Birisiri Mission or Bunker Mission?' *Vision (Australian Baptist Missionary Society Magazine)* March 1972, 3, 5.
40   Dodge, 'Birisiri Mission or Bunker Mission?'.

Australian Council of Churches

The Australian Council of Churches (ACC) is the peak body representing Anglican, Protestant and Orthodox churches, with its global headquarters in Geneva. Missionary zeal was also evident in this organisation, though there was an awareness that such proselytising could backfire. In a report sent to the World Council of Churches, ACC staff writer Bruce Best observed that Christians would be able to play a more prominent role in postwar Pakistan and Bangladesh but warned that students in particular were becoming dissatisfied with 'what they see as the pietism of the churches and the "missionary" mentality'. Best believed that young students were more likely to support Christianity in its practical dimension, especially projects that promoted social and economic equality rather than adhering to Christian theology alone. While postwar Bangladesh presented fertile ground for conversion, Best worried that it may be more than the local missionaries could control, commenting that 'this growing group [of students] may well become a radical force in the very near future'.[41]

Operationally, the ACC focused on advocacy, both at the top echelons of society and among local citizens. Crossing sectarian divisions, the ACC collaborated with Australian Catholic Relief to lobby the government for more refugee aid and encourage officials to find a diplomatic solution to the conflict. In a joint letter to the prime minister on 4 June 1971, the directors of Australian Catholic Relief and the ACC urged the government to keep the burgeoning crisis 'under constant review and to make further substantial grants as the opportunities occur'.[42] At the local level, the ACC dispatched circulars to all parish ministers throughout Australia, encouraging them to pray and seek donations from their congregants. In one such letter on 9 June 1971, the president of the ACC, Reverend David Garnsey, bishop of Gippsland in Victoria, reminded ministers

---

41 Bruce Best, Report: 'East and West of a Disaster, 7 February 1972' in File: East Pakistan Refugees – Relief Action 1972, Box 425.05.110: Projects East Pakistan Relief and Rehabilitation Service 1972, Series 425: Commission of Interchurch Aid, Relief and World Service (CICARWS), 1948–1992, Sub-fond: Programmes (1911–), Paper Archives of the World Council of Churches, Geneva.

42 'Letter. Wm. C. Byrne Executive Director, Australian Catholic Relief and E. H. Arblaster, Secretary-Director, Division of World Christian Action, Australian Council of Churches, to the Rt. Hon William McMahon, MP, 4 June 1971' in Folder: Pakistan, East and West, 1964–71, Box 117, Records of the Australian Council of Churches, 1911–1990, NLA MS 7645, MS Acc96.075.

of the imperative of Christian compassion. He wrote, 'The Christian Churches have long felt a special responsibility to care for refugees who are forced to place themselves at the mercy of their fellowmen'.[43]

The ACC was the go-to destination for Christians wishing to volunteer their services in the refugee camps in India. The director of ACC, Reverend Ted Arblaster, received a number of letters from doctors and nurses, as well as Christian leaders, wishing to work on the ground. The rationale behind the offers of voluntary service ranged from evangelical to practical. Beginning with the evangelical, Mrs Maureen Bomford from Sydney wrote to Arblaster on 15 June 1971:

> Would the Australian Council of Churches be willing to send me to the Prime Minister of Pakistan?
>
> I know that God would be with me, in this undertaking and I am confident I could gain guarantee and security for the safe return of 6 ½ million refugees.
>
> For ten years I have been corresponding to all Prime Ministers, including Pakistan, and I have sent at least four letters this year to the present Prime Minister. I know that if the Australian Council of Churches have faith in me, God would do the rest.
>
> The biggest problems need the shortest way for solution. This would have God's approval.[44]

Other Christians based their expressions of interest on more practical grounds than religious. In a telephone conversation with Ted Arblaster, nurse Caroline Clough explained that her background and vocational training made her an ideal volunteer. In a scribbled hand-written note documenting their telephone conversation, Arblaster noted that Ms Clough was born in Calcutta and emigrated in 1947, aged 20. She spoke Hindustani (Hindi/Urdu) and was a trained nurse and practised at Wollongong's Port Kembla Hospital. Importantly, Clough had experience in nursing cholera, a skill particularly relevant as the refugee camps had endured a cholera outbreak that very month. Not wishing to limit her

---

43 'Letter. The Rt. Rev. David A. Garnsey, Bishop of Gippsland, President, Australian Council of Churches to Parish Ministers. 9 June 1971' in MP' in Folder: Pakistan, East and West, 1964–71, Box 117, Records of the Australian Council of Churches.

44 'Letter. Mrs Maureen Bomford to The Rev. E. H. Arblaster, 15 June 1971' and 'Letter. The Rev. E.H. Arblaster to Mrs Maureen Bomford, 22 June 1971' in Folder: Pakistan, East and West, 1964–71, Box 117, Records of the Australian Council of Churches.

usefulness though, Clough affirmed that she would 'do anything' to help the refugees in the camps.[45] Arblaster also received offers of service from doctors Beryl Barber and Peter Bass, as well as (presumably nurses) Misses Betty Andersen and Dorothy Platt. Arblaster forwarded the contact details of these individuals to the executive secretary of the Australian refugee aid organisation Austcare, which was operating a medical clinic in a refugee camp.[46] However, all requests for volunteering on the ground were universally rejected as the refugee camps were well serviced by local health professionals in India. The ACC reiterated that Australian Christians could help most by offering cash donations and prayers.

Conclusion

This chapter draws our attention to a major event in recent refugee history that has largely been forgotten outside of South Asian communities. It is hard to believe that a refugee crisis on this scale has been overlooked for so long. The declassification of government archives in Western countries should facilitate research into this topic. However, government archives only provide a limited perspective, outlining bureaucratic machinations and policy debates. Though these areas are valuable to historians, government sources cannot shed light on the actions of individuals and organisations outside of government.

The lack of historical scholarship on the Bangladeshi refugee crisis is problematic, as it implicitly leads to the conclusion that this event does not matter or warrant remembrance. It also implies that individual Australians did not care or do anything to address the suffering of others. Too often, the Bangladesh Liberation War and international involvement – if it is ever mentioned – is reduced to the charity concert in New York City in August 1971 that was initiated by Beatle George Harrison. This focus on the actions of one celebrity in New York City obscures the actions of an array of individual Australians who mobilised, prayed, lobbied government, fundraised and travelled to the region to contribute something, *anything*, to aid the Bangladeshi refugees in India. Furthermore, Australian diplomats and Christians were active from the early months of the conflict and at

45   Scribbled note of conversation between the Rev. E H Arblaster and Mrs Caroline Clough, in Folder: Pakistan, East and West, 1964–71, Box 117, Records of the Australian Council of Churches.
46   'Letter. The Rev. E.H. Arblaster to Mr Parish, Executive Secretary of Austcare, 22 June 1971' in Folder: Pakistan, East and West, 1964–71, Box 117, Records of the Australian Council of Churches.

the forefront of the broad-based movement to provide aid to Bangladeshi refugees. Their commitment to this cause was strong, and in the case of the missionaries and the Allens, they stayed in Bangladesh at considerable risk to their own safety. Despite government inertia and equivocation, Christians and diplomats challenged their political leaders to do more for these Asian refugees, and failing that, took matters into their own hands.

6

RACE TO THE BOTTOM

Constructions of asylum seekers in Australian federal election campaigns, 1977–2013

Kathleen Blair

Issues pertaining to asylum seekers have long been the focus of negative political and public interest, with such interest intensifying in the lead-up to and throughout federal election campaigns. The 1977 federal election was the first in Australian history in which both major parties appealed to the public's unease about the arrival of asylum seeker boats. In fact, much of the anti–asylum seeker rhetoric to which Australians are now accustomed made its first appearance in the 1977 debates. However, the arrival of Vietnamese 'boat people' at that time became what analysts term a political 'non-issue'.[1] It was not until the arrival of the MV *Tampa*, in August 2001, that the long-running debate on asylum seekers and refugees was brought to the fore in an election campaign and, arguably, impacted the election outcome. A tough approach to asylum seekers has been a feature of many federal election campaigns since, culminating in 2013 with the Liberal Party's now-infamous slogan, 'Stop the boats!', aptly summarising both government policy and public attitudes. This chapter

---

1   D Butler, 'Introduction', in *The Australian National Election of 1977*, ed. H R Penniman (Canberra: Australian National University Press, 1979), 15.

explores the use of anti–asylum seeker sentiment in these three federal election campaigns, 1977, 2001 and 2013, and, in doing so, charts the origins of contemporary anti–asylum seeker discourse.

The arguments made by political leaders across the span of these four decades are remarkably similar, with political leaders borrowing from both their predecessors and their opponents. Contemporary concerns about 'economic refugees', 'queue jumpers' and 'illegals' are not unique to the twenty-first century. However, as the number of asylum seekers arriving by boat increased exponentially – approximately 2,000 asylum seekers arrived in the first wave from 1976 to 1979, compared to almost 45,000 between 2009 and 2013 – so too did the degree of cruelty in the government's efforts to dispel and exclude asylum seekers. The last two decades of Australian politics has seen both major political parties engaged in a 'race to the bottom', attempting to outdo one another with cruel and unusual punishments for those seeking Australia's protection.

The first 'boat people' and the 1977 federal election

On 27 April 1976, the *Kien Giang* arrived with the first Vietnamese asylum seekers on board.[2] The five 'boat people' were issued with one-month temporary visas the day after their arrival and were eventually granted permanent residence, without fuss. Neither the government nor the media paid much attention to their arrival. However, as more boats began to arrive, disquiet about asylum seekers grew among Australians. Community attitudes began to shift from indifference to widespread concern.[3] Fears about the introduction of exotic diseases and the effectiveness of the authorities' surveillance of Australia's coastline grew louder, particularly when a boat was found to have reached Darwin unnoticed by the Australian military.[4] Amid these increasing concerns, Prime Minister Malcolm Fraser announced that the 1977 federal election

---

2   Department of Immigration and Ethnic Affairs, *Australia and Indo-Chinese Refugees, 1976–1980: A Chronology* (Canberra: The Department of Immigration and Ethnic Affairs, 1981), 3.

3   L Riddett, 'The Gateway and the Gatekeepers: An Examination of Darwin's Relationship with Asia and Asians, 1942–1993', *Journal of Australian Studies* 19, (1995): 65–67, doi.org/10.1080/14443059509387237.

4   Klaus Neumann, *Across the Seas: Australia's Response to Refugees: A History* (Melbourne: Black Inc., 2015), 268–69.

would be held on 10 December. While issues pertaining to refugees and asylum seekers were not hotly debated in the first few weeks of the campaign, political debate erupted on 21 November when six boats carrying 218 people arrived in Darwin in a single day.[5]

The Labor Party was quick to fuel the fears the public held about asylum seekers, attempting to use the issue of boat arrivals for electoral gain. Senator Tony Mulvihill, Labor's acting Immigration spokesperson, criticised the Fraser Government for its lack of 'selectivity on Indo-Chinese refugees', implying that at least some of the Vietnamese asylum seekers were not 'genuine'.[6] Then Labor Party leader, Gough Whitlam, made a complementary argument when he questioned the legitimacy of Vietnamese 'boat people', arguing that 'genuine refugees' should be accepted (clearly insinuating that those arriving by boat were not genuine), but that the government should not put refugees 'ahead in the queue over people who have been sponsored and who are already coming here'.[7] This imaginary queue, soon to become one of the most powerful images in the anti–asylum seeker discourse, served to distinguish between 'good' immigrants or refugees and 'bad' asylum seekers.[8]

Arguments about the 'genuineness' of refugees arriving by boat centred on their supposed wealth and the lack of an appearance of destitution. It was argued that some of the refugees were 'pseudo-refugees': 'they just don't look like refugees or people who have suffered or have had the trauma of that long trip'.[9] The idea that people who were not visibly destitute and suffering could not possibly be refugees featured prominently in statements made by trade union officials and political leaders.[10] Asylum seekers were consistently described as 'illegal immigrants', aspersions were cast on their 'moral fibre', and it was argued that they were not refugees because of their supposed wealth.[11]

---

5   Nancy Viviani, *The Long Journey: Vietnamese Migration and Settlement in Australia* (Melbourne: Melbourne University Press, 1984), 73–74.

6   Tony Mulvihill, 1977, quoted in Rachel Stevens, *Immigration Policy from 1970 to the Present* (New York: Routledge, 2016), 108–9.

7   'Hawke: Return Bogus Refugees', cited in Gerard Henderson, 'Girt by Sea: Correspondence', *Quarterly Essay* 6 (2002): 86.

8   Jane McAdam, 'Australia and Asylum Seekers', *International Journal of Refugee Law* 25 (2013): 435–48, doi.org/10.1093/ijrl/eet044.

9   Stack 1977, cited in Neumann, *Across the Seas*, 271.

10   Viviani, *The Long Journey*, 78–79; Neumann, *Across the Seas*, 270–76; Rachel Stevens, 'Political Debates on Asylum Seekers during the Fraser Government, 1977–1982', *Australian Journal of Politics and History* 58, no. 4 (2012): 530–532, doi.org/10.1111/j.1467-8497.2012.01651.x.

11   Neumann, *Across the Seas*, 270–76.

The Labor Party were also intent on playing to a latent fear of invasion. Labor leaders urged the Fraser Government to 'make it clear that Australia is not going to open the floodgates ... We will have to try and find a way of showing our sympathy while stopping the flood of what basically are illegal immigrants'.[12] Labor used the arrival of Vietnamese asylum seekers to demonstrate their resolve to enforce Australia's immigration laws. Whitlam argued that Australia needed to increase its border enforcement policies to prevent unauthorised immigration, drug trafficking and the import of diseases, thereby associating asylum seekers with illegal activity and dangerous illnesses.[13] To achieve this, he suggested buying new patrol boats to guard the Australian coastline.[14] Mulvihill also called on the Fraser Government to 'make an example' of some of the unauthorised arrivals: 'We have to turn a few of them around and send them back to South-East Asia under naval escort'.[15]

In the 1977 election campaign, the Labor Party used several different arguments to cast doubt on the asylum claims of boat arrivals. Asylum seekers arriving by boat were portrayed as wealthy economic migrants attempting to 'jump the queue' by entering Australia without authorisation and they were unfavourably contrasted with 'legal' immigrants and 'genuine refugees'.[16] Militarised and punitive responses, such as the turning back of boats and increasing border security, were proposed. Labor was intent on harnessing xenophobic sentiments and the public's fear of invasion for electoral gain.

The Liberal Fraser Government also used the arrival of asylum seeker boats to demonstrate to voters that they too could act tough on asylum seekers. On 16 November, the immigration department for the first time did not immediately grant entry permits to a group of asylum seekers and initially did not allow them to disembark their vessel. While the department issued them with visas 24 hours later, the initial refusal and an accompanying statement by Minister for Immigration Michael MacKellar, in which he announced that his department would urgently assess the implications of unauthorised entry, suggested the government was adopting a tougher approach.[17] This 'tougher' approach was further

---

12   Quoted in 'Eighth Vessel on Way', 1977, cited in Neumann, *Across the Seas*, 270–71.
13   Stevens, 'Political Debates on Asylum Seekers', 530–32.
14   Stevens, *Immigration Policy*, 108–9.
15   Neumann, *Across the Seas*, 270–76.
16   Ibid., 270–76; Stevens, 'Political Debates on Asylum Seekers', 530–32.
17   Neumann, *Across the Seas*, 269.

illustrated by statements made shortly after the arrival of the six asylum seekers boats on 21 November. Minister for Foreign Affairs Andrew Peacock said that Australia could not 'continue to indefinitely accept Asian refugees arriving unannounced by sea', and that 'Australia could not be regarded as a dumping ground'.[18] Fraser himself issued a warning that 'some Vietnamese who landed in Australia might have to be deported'.[19] MacKellar reiterated this view by insisting that those who arrive by boat unannounced would not necessarily be allowed to resettle in Australia.[20]

While these statements from Fraser and MacKellar suggest a proposed escalation in border enforcement policies and resistance to the admission of authorised immigration, numerous examples also exist of a more 'compassionate' discourse in the 1977 campaign on behalf of the Liberal Party. For example, in the initial stages of the campaign, while Labor was quick to manipulate public concern over economic issues, drawing attention to the supposed economic consequences of accepting boat arrivals, MacKellar swiftly challenged these assertions. In response to Whitlam attempting to distort migrant employment figures, MacKellar stated:

> It is surprising and unfortunate that Mr Whitlam should seek to make political capital out of the employment problems of the 20,000 refugees, evacuees and Lebanese who have sought sanctuary in Australia in the past 18 months … These people have come to Australia mainly to survive and to build a new life out of the tatters of civil war and internal conflict in their former countries. The Fraser Government has seen this offer of sanctuary as the first priority.[21]

MacKellar consistently challenged the Labor Party's attempts to exploit the public's concerns over the economy and boat arrivals throughout the campaign. He dismissed allegations that rich migrants were posing as refugees to come to Australia, addressed concerns over the high levels of unemployment amongst new migrants by contextualising

---

18   'Peacock Warns', cited in Neumann, *Across the Seas*, 273.
19   'Fraser Warns Refugees', *Sydney Morning Herald*, 26 November 1977.
20   Stevens, *Immigration Policy*, 109.
21   Michael MacKellar, 1977, cited in Michelle Peterie, '"These Few Small Boats": Representations of Asylum Seekers During Australia's 1977 and 2001 Elections', *Journal of Australian Studies* 40, no. 4 (2016): 446, doi.org/10.1080/14443058.2016.1223150.

migrant unemployment as a normal stage in the settlement process, and highlighted Australia's responsibility to prioritise the safety of refugees and asylum seekers over one's ability to contribute to the nation's economy.[22]

MacKellar appeared intent on placating those anxious about boat arrivals and not allowing Labor to exploit the issue. However, he also seemed anxious not to appear too critical of those who expressed concern. He sought to balance the fears and anxieties of the electorate about border security with humanitarian concern: 'We have to combine humanity and compassion with prudent control of unauthorised entry or be prepared to tear up the Migration Act and its basic policies'.[23] Like many ministers both before and after him, MacKellar emphasised the need for border control. However, he did not use this discourse to cultivate fear. Instead, he sought to justify the Fraser Government's policy of increasing Australia's refugee intake. For example, when MacKellar announced the decision to send immigration officials to Southeast Asia to process asylum seekers, he argued it was 'essential that entry to Australia was controlled' and that assisting 'the orderly international processing of refugees … [would] avoid the need for genuine refugees to make the hazardous voyage to Australia'.[24] MacKellar was keen to ensure that any action taken by his department was 'leavened with humanity and compassion for the plight of genuine refugees'.[25]

For much of the campaign, the Liberal Party's statements were merely reactive. They spoke out against the unfounded claims made by the Labor Party, challenging negative stereotypes as they began to gain momentum. However, less than two weeks before election day, the Fraser Government went on the offensive. In reference to Mulvihill's earlier statement, the two ministers committed their Liberal Government not to '"make examples" of boat refugees by indiscriminately turning some of them back', and not to 'risk taking action against genuine refugees just to get a message across', as doing so 'would be an utterly inhuman course of action'.[26] Viewed through the lens of Australia's contemporary asylum seeker debate, these sentiments from the Liberal Party are remarkable. MacKellar's statements

22   Peterie, '"These Few Small Boats"', 444–46.
23   Neumann, *Across the Seas,* 273.
24   Michael MacKellar, 1977, cited in Peterie, '"These Few Small Boats"', 443.
25   Ibid., 443.
26   Joint statement by Andrew Peacock and Michael MacKellar, cited in Neumann, *Across the Seas*, 279.

humanised those arriving by boat, portraying them as needy people who were deserving of help, and underlined Australia's legal and moral duty to respond to this 'human tragedy'.

The 1977 campaign exemplifies a contestation of power in which asylum seeker discourses were key. While the Labor Party attempted to convince voters that asylum seekers were 'bad' and that they should, therefore, vote for the party that would expel/reject them, the Liberal Party sought to do the opposite. The 1977 campaign was the first in Australian history in which the major parties appealed to the public's unease about unauthorised boat arrivals. The 1977 campaign was, however, also the first in which a senior government minister advocated a policy response to refugees that was not populist, and forcefully asserted the government's right and responsibility to pursue such a response. Despite their efforts, the Labor Party's attempts to make the arrival of boats a key election issue were unsuccessful; political scientists agree that the issue of boat arrivals did not influence the election outcome.[27] When voters were asked to name the issues most important to them in the campaign, they nominated unemployment, inflation and economic management rather than immigration and border control.[28] However, the language and arguments employed by political leaders to justify the exclusion of Vietnamese boat people introduced key phrases and ways of speaking about the arrival of 'boat people', many of which continue to influence contemporary debates on asylum seekers.

The race to the bottom

Since the first sustained arrival of asylum seeker boats, various policies have been enacted, slowly legalising and normalising the criminalisation and dehumanisation of people seeking asylum. Between 1989 and 1995, the second cohort of asylum seekers, mainly from South China and Cambodia, arrived. Concern over their uncontrolled and sporadic arrival saw the Hawke/Keating Labor Government establish laws for the (often prolonged) detention of asylum seekers arriving in Australia; in 1992 this detention become mandatory. Gerry Hand, then immigration minister, rationalised detention practices on the basis that it would deter prospective

27 Clem Lloyd, 'A Lean Campaign for the Media', in *The Australian National Elections of 1977*, ed. H Penniman (Washington: American Enterprise Institute for Policy Research, 1979), 246.
28 R K F, 'Australian Political Chronicle, July–December 1977: The Commonwealth', *Australian Journal of Politics and History* 24, no. 1 (1978): 75–80.

asylum seekers. He was determined to send a clear signal 'that migration to Australia may not be achieved by simply arriving in this country and expecting to be allowed into the community'.[29]

Between 1996 and 2001, the third cohort of people seeking asylum, mainly from Iraq and Afghanistan, arrived. The then Liberal Howard Government introduced the practice of linking the nominal quota for the onshore and offshore programs. They also introduced the *Border Protection Legislation Amendment Act 1999*, which enabled immigration and customs officers to board, search and detain vessels in international waters. In October 1999, Temporary Protection Visas were introduced for asylum seekers arriving in Australia without a valid visa who were found to be refugees.[30] These legislative measures were designed to protect humanitarian resettlement places for refugees who arrived in Australia via the humanitarian program or with a valid visa, thereby reinforcing the dichotomy between 'queue jumping' boat arrivals and 'genuine' refugees. Further, the government argued that temporary protection removed the incentive for asylum seekers to risk their lives at sea while still providing effective protection for those who continued to do so. However, the policy failed in these deterrence aims. The Australian Government had ignored the forces (e.g. persecution and war) that were driving Middle Eastern refugees to flee and seek asylum in Australia in the first place. As such, rather than declining, the number of asylum seekers arriving by boat increased dramatically. These increasing numbers culminated in late August 2001, bringing the issue of asylum seekers, for the first time, to the forefront of a federal election campaign.

Border protection and the 2001 federal election

Border protection was a major issue in the 2001 federal election and arguably determined its outcome.[31] In 2001, Australia experienced enormous rises in asylum seeker boat arrivals – 5,516 arrived in 2001

---

29   Gerry Hand, 1992, cited in Stevens, *Immigration Policy*, 126.

30   Hossein Esmaeili and Belinda Wells, 'The "Temporary" Refugees: Australia's Legal Response to the Arrival of Iraqi and Afghan Boat People', *UNSW Law Journal* 23, no. 3 (2000): 224–45.

31   Ian McAllister, 'Border Protection, the 2001 Australian Election and the Coalition Victory', *Australian Journal of Political Science* 38, no. 3 (2003): 448, doi.org/10.1080/103611403200013398 5; David Marr and Marian Wilkinson, *Dark Victory* (Crows Nest: Allen & Unwin, 2003).

alone, almost double the year before.[32] Securing Australia's border provoked more political and public attention as a result. Further, from late August onwards a series of events resulted in the issue of 'border protection' dominating much of the campaign. The two most significant events were the *Tampa* crisis and the related debate about how to deal with asylum seekers, and the September 11 terrorist attacks (9/11) in the United States and its implications for defence and foreign policy. Doubts put forward by politicians about the character of people seeking asylum in Australia were even more effective following these events. For the first six months of 2001, Labor had enjoyed a comfortable poll lead over the Liberals.[33] However, support for the Labor Party began to dissipate after the *Tampa* crisis and 9/11. In the end, the party that won the 2001 election had promised to 'stop the boats'.

On 26 August, a Norwegian freighter, the MV *Tampa*, rescued 438 people seeking asylum whose boat began to sink while en route to Australia. On the grounds that the incident took place in Indonesian waters, the Australian Government refused the *Tampa* permission to enter Australian territory. After an extended debate and a stand-off lasting several days – in which the *Tampa*, with the 438 asylum seekers, merely floated off Australia's coast – a compromise was reached with New Zealand agreeing to take 150 of the asylum seekers. The remainder were sent to a hastily established processing centre on the Republic of Nauru, where their claims for protection were to be determined.

Throughout the 2001 election campaign, the Australian Government constructed the *Tampa* asylum seekers as a threat to national sovereignty and as antithetical to the Australian way of life. In doing so, Howard manufactured a shared Australian national identity built on the values of generosity and egalitarianism or 'a fair go'. These values were positioned as distinctly Australian and were defined through allusions to the asylum seeker. A key feature of Howard's portrayal of these Australian values was the assertion that they were under threat.

---

32 Janet Phillips and Harriet Spinks, 'Boat Arrivals in Australia since 1976' (background note, Department of Parliamentary Services, 2013), 22.

33 McAllister, 'Border Protection', 446; Ian McAllister, 'The Federal Election in Australia, November 2001', *Electoral Studies* 22 (2003): 382.

A discourse of 'Australian generosity' towards migrants and refugees was crucial to Howard's construction of national identity. To demonstrate this generosity, Howard explicitly and repeatedly referred to the generosity of Australia's refugee program and highlighted Australia's reputation as a good international citizen:

> Australia has a record in relation to caring for refugees of which every member of this House should be proud. No nation in the last 50 years has been more generous or more decent in relation to refugees than has Australia ... But that does not mean that we are abandoning in any way our right to decide who comes here; nor shall we ever abandon our right to refuse to allow people to be landed in this country ...[34]

Howard used the discourse of generosity to work up a positive image of Australians as 'open' to new arrivals, and conversely, a negative one of asylum seekers as threatening Australia's rights and national interest. This contrast acts as a disclaimer for Howard's subsequent assertion of sovereign rights, framing this as 'we are exercising our rights, but we are still generous'. In this conception, Australians are willing to welcome those who come through the right channels, with the right intentions, into the national space.

Political leaders also used the value of egalitarianism to present practices of exclusion and oppression as legitimate and to discredit asylum seekers as 'queue jumpers'. Political leaders used the 'queue' metaphor to represent the offshore immigration application system as a 'fair go' and asylum seekers arriving in Australia by boat as acting unfairly.[35] Claims that people seeking asylum by boat should not be allowed into Australia were justified on the basis that they had 'jumped the queue' and were receiving unfair advantages over other migrants and refugees. 'Jumping the queue' is a violation of impartiality and fairness and effectively positions 'queue jumpers' as violating these central Australian values.

---

34   Danielle Every and Martha Augoustinos, 'Constructions of Australia in Pro- and Anti-Asylum Seeker Political Discourse', *Nations and Nationalism* 14 (2008): 571, doi.org/10.1111/j.1469-8129 .2008.00356.x.
35   See also Danielle Every and Martha Augoustinos, 'Constructions of Racism in the Australian Parliamentary Debates on Asylum Seekers', *Discourse and Society* 18 (2007): 411–36, doi.org/10.1177/ 0957926507077427; Carol Johnson, 'The 2002 Election Campaign: The Ideological Context', in *The Centenary Election*, ed. J Warhurst and M Simms (Brisbane: University of Queensland Press, 2002), 32–49; Peterie, '"These Few Small Boats"', 433–47.

Political leaders drew on the idea of Australia as a generous and fair nation to construct and contrast two groups – 'fair Australians' and 'unfair asylum seekers'.[36] On the one hand, Australia was presented as kind and charitable and as having a deep-seated value to give a fair go to all. By implicit comparison, people seeking asylum by boat were positioned as unfair and anti-egalitarian, as morally antithetical to key Australian values and even as taking advantage of Australia's generosity. This positive/negative contrast is a common strategy in anti-immigration discourses[37] and, in this context, saw Australian values necessitate the rejection of asylum seekers. That is, to ensure the 'fair go' is maintained, Australia could not accept 'queue jumpers'.

The juxtaposition of these values functions to link inclusive and exclusive discourses. Howard consistently encouraged Australians to connect with a positive image of themselves as 'open' to new arrivals and effectively promised to safeguard 'Australianness' through the management and exclusion of potential threats to Australian values.[38] He gave voters permission to see their desire to manage immigration flows as a legitimate reaction to the threat presented by asylum seekers. Further, given that these discourses emerged in an election campaign, he emboldened voters to exercise their desire to manage immigration flows by voting for the political party that promised to do so.

The Australian public was largely supportive of Howard's response to the *Tampa*, reflecting both a history of opposition to new arrivals and increasing negative public sentiment. An *Age* poll found that 77 per cent of Australians agreed with Howard's decision to refuse the asylum seekers entry to Australia.[39] NewsPoll also reported that 50 per cent of respondents believed that *all* boats should be turned back.[40] Immediately following the incident, the Coalition received a 5 per cent increase in

---

36 Every and Augoustinos, 'Constructions of Australia', 574.

37 Teun van Dijk, 'Political Discourse and Racism: Describing Others in Discourse', in *The Language and Politics of Exclusion: Others in Discourse*, ed. S Riggings (London: Sage, 1997), 31–64.

38 Stephanie Younane Brookes, 'Exclusion and National Identity: The Language of Immigration and Border Control in Australian Federal Election Campaigns, 1903–2001' (paper presented at the *Australian Political Science Association Conference*, 2010).

39 Katharine Betts, 'Boat People and Public Opinion in Australia', *People and Place* 9, no. 4 (2001): 41–42.

40 NewsPoll, 'Asylum Seeker Poll: 4/9/2001', *Australian*, available at: polling.newspoll.com.au/image_uploads/cgi-lib.6364.1.010901asylum.pdf (site discontinued).

the polls.[41] Public support for the Howard Government increased even further after the September 11 terrorist attacks, with the Liberals achieving a 15 percentage point lead over Labor.[42]

The sense that the *Tampa* represented an attack on Australia, rather than a compounded tragedy for those aboard, continued to escalate through to the final days of the campaign. The *Tampa* affair and the government's subsequent response set the stage for the 2001 election campaign, in which the government both generated and capitalised on the public's unease toward asylum seekers, and foregrounded Howard's now-infamous declaration: 'We will decide who comes to this country and the circumstances in which they come'.[43]

On 11 September 2001, two months before election day, a terrorist attack on the World Trade Centre Twin Towers and the Pentagon in the United States occurred, killing almost 3,000 people and injuring over 6,000 others, and triggering an international 'war on terror'. Within 48 hours of the terrorist attacks, and in an environment of suddenly and dramatically heightened concern over international terrorism, political leaders drew an explicit link between asylum seekers and terrorism. Defence Minister Peter Reith warned that the unauthorised arrival of boats 'can be a pipeline for terrorists to come in and use your country as a staging post for terrorist activities'.[44] Howard cautioned: 'Australia had no way to be certain terrorists or people with terrorist links, were not among the asylum seekers trying to enter the country by boat from Indonesia'.[45] Along with Reith, Howard was 'deliberately inflaming fear' by conflating the issue of asylum seekers with the newly emergent terrorist threat.[46] These attacks and the Howard Government's subsequent response catalysed border protection and, by extension, asylum seekers as a crucial issue of the 2001 federal election campaign.

Even when direct relationships were not drawn, Howard and Ruddock's phrasing encouraged the association of asylum seekers with terrorism. In his policy launch speech, Howard constructed the arrival of asylum seekers

41   McAllister, 'Border Protection', 44.
42   McAllister, 'The Federal Election in Australia', 382.
43   John Howard, 'Liberal/National Coalition 2001 Federal Election Campaign Launch' (speech delivered at Sydney, NSW, 28 October 2001), Election Speeches, available at: electionspeeches. moadoph.gov.au/speeches/2001-john-howard.
44   'Australia Links Asylum Policy to US Attack', *BBC News*, 13 September 2001.
45   David Marr, *Panic* (Collingwood: Black Inc., 2011), 280–81.
46   Marr, *Panic*, 233.

as an issue of 'national security' and spoke about the need for Australia to 'protect its borders' as 'a proper response to terrorism'.[47] As Australia was then preparing for involvement in the US military campaign, the Howard Government's discussion of asylum seekers as a defence issue conflated them with the enemy of 9/11. Howard highlighted the role of the Australian Defence Force (ADF) in intercepting boats, describing it as one of their most significant responsibilities,[48] and effectively solidified the transformation of Australia's borders to a battlefront. Throughout the campaign, a border protection discourse was employed by Howard and his party to make the arrival of asylum seekers appear as a challenge to the physical safety of Australians, to Australian national identity and to national sovereignty.[49] These constructions sought to reassure a concerned electorate that the government were doing whatever it took to prevent the arrival of the so-called threat.

The 'border protection' issue further fuelled the government's electoral advantage when, on 7 October, the *Olong*, a boat travelling to Australia from Indonesia with people seeking asylum, became the first to confront Operation Relex.[50] Official reports detail a series of events in which, after attempts to escort the vessel back to Indonesia, the *Olong* began to sink. Men, women and children, supported by life jackets, began jumping for their lives into the sea. The navy officers present assisted the 223 passengers to life rafts, diving into the water themselves to help the frightened passengers. This, however, was not the story the government told to the Australian public. Howard and Ruddock accused the asylum seekers of 'throwing their children overboard' in a 'premeditated' attempt to pressure the Australian authorities to rescue them.[51] Images were released, proffered as 'absolute fact' that asylum seekers threw their children overboard when

---

47   Howard, 'Liberal/National Coalition 2001 Federal Election Campaign Launch'.

48   Peterie, '"These Few Smalls Boats"', 441.

49   Every and Augoustinos, 'Constructions of Australia', 574; Every and Augoustinos, 'Constructions of Racism', 530; Alison Saxton, '"I Certainly Don't Want People Like That Here": The Discursive Construction of "Asylum Seekers"', *Media International Australia* 109, no. 1 (2003): 109–20, doi.org/ 10.1177/1329878x0310900111; Kieran O'Doherty and Martha Augoustinos, 'Protecting the Nation: Nationalistic Rhetoric on Asylum Seekers and the *Tampa*', *Journal of Community and Applied Social Psychology* 18 (2008): 576–92, doi.org/10.1002/casp.973.

50   Operation Relex is the name given to the ADF border protection operation conducted between 2001 and 2006. It formed part of the Howard Government's response to the *Tampa* incident and enabled the ADF to intercept, detain and turn back boats carrying asylum seekers.

51   Kate Slattery, 'Drowning Not Waving: The "Children Overboard" Event and Australia's Fear of the Other', *Media International Australia* 109 (2003): 93–108, doi.org/10.1177/1329878x0310900110; Ruddock quoted in Natalie O'Brien, 'Overboard Incident "Never Happened"', *Australian*, 12 July 2001.

they were really images of adults and children fleeing their sinking vessel to save their lives.[52] The government's claim that people seeking asylum had thrown their children overboard generated a media frenzy and further enabled the Howard Government to demonise asylum seekers.

Throughout the 2001 campaign, people seeking asylum were constituted as culturally different and incompatible with Australians. This negative discourse was emboldened after the 'Children Overboard Affair'. Campaigning in the aftermath of *Tampa* and 9/11, Howard described Australia's military support of the United States as a decision to 'defend the values we … hold dear'.[53] Howard framed 'values' as a battleground and constructed those with different beliefs as the enemy. He created a benchmark of 'Australianness' and portrayed asylum seekers as the antithesis of the Australian 'us'. The Howard Government's portrayal of Australia as a decent country involved an emphasis upon family. Howard and Ruddock stressed Australia's morality by describing both the attention the navy paid to women and children during boat interceptions and the government's decision to house a number of women and children in 'alternative' detention facilities.[54] Juxtaposing this representation of Australians as family people, in the aftermath of the 'Children Overboard Affair', asylum seekers were portrayed as abusers of children:

> I can't comprehend how genuine refugees would throw their children overboard. I find that it is against the natural instinct, people leave a regime, leave a country, flee persecution to give a better life and to give a future to their children. Not to put it at risk.[55]

While these threats to children were baseless, the stories told by government ministers portrayed asylum seekers as inhumane, barbaric 'others' who did not possess basic human qualities of parental devotion. Further, he reserved the qualities of humanity and morality for Australians, condemning asylum seekers not only for their violation of Australian ideals but for their violation of 'natural instinct'. In stark contrast to MacKellar's representation of asylum seekers in 1977, in which he suggested that

---

52   Reith quoted in O'Brien, 'Overboard Incident'.
53   Howard, quoted in Peterie, '"These Few Small Boats"', 438.
54   Peterie, '"These Few Small Boats"', 440.
55   John Howard, 'Press Conference Melbourne' [interview transcript], PM Transcripts, Department of Premier and Cabinet, 8 October 2001, available at: pmtranscripts.pmc.gov.au/release/transcript-12104.

Australia's humanity would be jeopardised if asylum seekers were not treated well, Howard and Ruddock cast doubt upon the humanity of asylum seekers, effectively dehumanising them.

Howard's campaign against asylum seekers, together with the events of 9/11, was instrumental to his re-election. As Ian McAllister's analysis of the 2001 Australian Election Study (AES) shows, almost one in four voters mentioned refugees and asylum seekers, defence or terrorism as their major election concern, with the Coalition being, by far, the most preferred party to handle these issues.[56] In contrast to the 1977 election, which saw MacKellar attempt to humanise and contextualise Australia's boat arrivals, in 2001 the Howard Government condemned people seeking asylum for not having progressed through the appropriate resettlement channels and constructed them as undeserving outsiders that posed a threat to Australia's sovereignty, safety and identity. The Howard Government's fervent campaigning on 'border protection' 'clearly manipulated the circumstances of people seeking asylum for electoral gain'[57] and, in doing so, paved the way for the campaigns conducted by the Liberal Party under the leadership of Tony Abbott in 2010 and, again, in 2013.

The 2013 federal election: Stopping the boats

The fourth cohort of boats, between 2009 and 2013, saw by far the largest number of asylum seekers reach Australian shores – almost 45,000 over five years; 30,000 of which arrived in 2012–13.[58] For the three years prior to the 2013 election, as the number of arrivals continued to increase, then-leader of the Liberal Party Tony Abbott engaged his party in a longstanding campaign that was largely responsible for focusing the public and media's attention on the arrival of people seeking asylum – keeping this issue at the top of the political agenda. While Australians have long

---

56   McAllister, 'Border Protection', 451.
57   Senate Select Committee on a Certain Maritime Incident, *Report of the Senate Select Committee on a Certain Maritime Incident* (Canberra: Parliament of Australia, 2002), 478.
58   Phillips and Spinks, 'Boat Arrivals in Australia since 1976', 22.

expressed disdain for the arrival of people seeking asylum,[59] the Liberal Party's emphasis on this issue saw it increase in importance to voters. The 2010 AES reports that, when asked how important the issue of asylum seekers and refugees was, 37 per cent of voters stated it was 'extremely important' to them.[60] This increased to 46 per cent in 2013[61] (close to the 50 per cent of voters who felt the same way in 2001).[62] The majority of respondents (41 per cent) also believed the Liberal Party's policies were closest to their own views on this issue – only 19 per cent of respondents felt the same way about the Labor Party. Both major parties capitalised on this issue in the 2013 federal election campaign, attempting to outdo each other in terms of introducing tough asylum seeker policies and, in turn, win the support of the voting public.

On 19 July 2013, two weeks before the official federal election campaign was announced, and three weeks after regaining leadership of the Labor Party by disposing Julia Gillard as prime minister, Kevin Rudd announced a Regional Resettlement Arrangement between Australia and Papua New Guinea, stating: 'As of today, asylum seekers who come here by boat without a visa will never be settled in Australia'.[63] These remarks were unprecedented. Neither side of politics had ever stated that asylum seekers identified as refugees would be permanently denied resettlement in Australia. Rudd acknowledged it was a 'hard-line' decision, but argued that 'our responsibility as a Government is to ensure that we have a robust system of border security and orderly migration'.[64] Despite this policy announcement and a subsequent announcement of a similar deal with the nation of Nauru, the Labor Party did not actively seek to promote their new-found policy stance. During the 2013 campaign, the Labor

59   See for example, Murray Goot and Ian Watson, *Population, Immigration and Asylum Seekers: Patterns in Australian Public Opinion* (Canberra: Department of Parliamentary Services, 2011); Ian McAllister and Sarah Cameron, *Trends in Australian Political Opinion: Results from the Australian Election Study, 1987–2013* (Canberra: Australian National University, 2014); Betts, 'Boat People and Public Opinion', 41–42.

60   Ian McAllister, Clive Bean, Rachel Kay Gibson and Juliet Pietsch, *Australian Election Study, 2010* (Canberra: Australian National University, Australian Data Archive, 2011).

61   Clive Bean, Ian McAllister, Juliet Pietsch and Rachel Kay Gibson, *Australian Election Study, 2013* (Canberra: Australian National University, Australian Data Archive, 2014).

62   Clive Bean, David Gow and Ian McAllister, *The 2001 Australian Election Study* (Canberra: Australian National University, Australian Data Archive, 2007).

63   Bianca Hall and Jonathan Swan, 'Kevin Rudd to Send Asylum Seekers Who Arrive by Boat to Papua New Guinea', *Sydney Morning Herald*, 19 July 2013.

64   Ibid. This policy position was a reversal of the position Rudd took when first coming into office in 2007. Within two months of his first prime ministership Rudd had abolished Howard's Pacific Solution and those asylum seekers who had been sent to Nauru were brought to Australia.

Party focused on 14 broad election policy pledges that did not refer to 'asylum seekers', 'boats' or 'borders'.[65] Labor's policy to support offshore processing and the settlement of asylum seekers in Papua New Guinea was aimed at shutting down debate on an issue that was a Coalition strength.[66] It could be assumed that the policy position they took and the limited campaigning they did on this issue was out of a desire to neutralise the issue while trying to attract or retain voters sympathetic to the Coalition's position.

In stark contrast to the Labor Party, the Coalition wittingly pursued the asylum seeker issue and, with the news media, effectively raised its prominence as an election issue.[67] Abbott's Liberal Party, like their predecessors, recognised political advantage in campaigning on asylum seeker boat arrivals. Within one week of Labor's policy announcement, the Liberal Party responded by releasing their official 'Operation Sovereign Borders' policy proposal, promising to 'stop the boats' by taking even tougher action on people seeking asylum.[68] Liberal policy was primarily framed in terms of border protection and national security. They promised a military-led operation against 'illegal arrivals', consistent with the punitive position of former prime minister John Howard. The Coalition identified 'border protection' as an election priority in their 12-point 'Real Action' plan and again in their shortened six-point plan, which included a pledge to 'deliver stronger borders' and 'stop the boats'. In less than a month they released three policy documents: *The Coalition's Operation Sovereign Borders Policy, The Coalition's Policy to Clear Labor's 30,000 Border Failure Backlog* and *The Coalition's Policy for a Regional Deterrence Framework to Combat People Smuggling,* cementing not only their commitment to 'protecting Australia's borders' but also asylum seekers as a key election issue.

---

65   'Australian Labor Campaign Media: Media Releases and Transcripts' [data resource], Pandora, National Library of Australia, viewed 3 October 2017, available at: pandora.nla.gov.au/pan/22093/20130906-0237/www.alp.org.au/campaign_media.html.

66   See Sara Dehm and Max Walden, 'Refugee Policy: A Cruel Bipartisanship', in *Double Disillusion: The 2016 Australian Federal Election*, ed. A Gauja, P Chen, J Curtin and J Pietsch (Canberra: ANU Press, 2018), doi.org/10.22459/dd.04.2018.26, for a discussion of the impact of this political bipartisanship in the 2016 election.

67   Andrea Carson, Yannick Dufresne and Aaron Martin, 'Wedge Politics: Mapping Voter Attitudes to Asylum Seekers Using Large-Scale Data During the Australian 2013 Federal Election Campaign', *Policy and Internet* 8, no. 4 (2016): 478–98, doi.org/10.1002/poi3.128.

68   Liberal Party of Australia and the Nationals, *The Coalition's Operation Sovereign Borders Policy* (Barton: Liberal Party of Australia and the Nationals, 2013).

In the 2013 campaign, Abbott's Liberal Party emulated the arguments made by Howard and his government in 2001, actively demonising and dehumanising people seeking asylum by boat. Political candidates, ranging from shadow ministers to future backbenchers, adopted a threat discourse, emphasising that Australia needed to strengthen and secure its borders. The arrival of asylum seeker boats was framed yet again as an affront to Australian sovereignty and safety and security, with political leaders linking these issues, where possible, to broader social issues.

Controlling the arrival of asylum seekers and refugees emerged as an important theme, with both the Coalition and Labor emphasising the importance of determining and controlling what type of people came to Australia and how they arrived. The Coalition's endorsement of this notion of control was cemented in Howard's infamous campaign speech in the 2001 campaign. In the 2013 campaign, there were several instances in which Coalition politicians and policy documents directly quoted this speech when discussing their promise to 'stop the boats'. All three policy documents variously stated:

> It was Prime Minister John Howard who declared that 'we will decide who comes to this country and the circumstances in which they come'. This was a statement of national sovereignty which underlined the need for Australia to control our borders. A Coalition government will restore real policies that live up to this declaration. This is our country and we will decide who comes here.[69]

The Coalition's consistent references to Howard's words served to not only cement their current commitment to protecting the Australian people but also functioned as a reminder that they had never wavered in this commitment and had successfully protected it in the past.

Throughout the campaign, Liberal Party candidates were consistent in referencing the perceived shortcomings of the Labor Government regarding border protection, drawing comparisons between the increased number of boat arrivals that occurred under the Rudd/Gillard government and the relatively few arrivals under the preceding Howard Government.

---

69   Liberal Party of Australia and the Nationals, *The Coalition's Policy for a Regional Deterrence Framework to Combat People Smuggling* (Barton: Liberal Party of Australia and the Nationals, 2013), 7.

> Labor's border failure is the consequence of Labor's failed policies and failed resolve. Labor weakened Australia's borders by abolishing the proven border protection policy regime established by the Howard Government and has provided an open invitation to the people smugglers through their six years in office.[70]

Again, this reference to the 'Howard era' served a strategic purpose. Candidates typically want their electorate to make voting choices using criteria that are based on dimensions favourable to themselves; thus, candidates will often raise issues that they or their affiliated party are seen to be the 'owners' of. Issue ownership posits that the longstanding parties hold reputations for their ability to handle certain issues.[71] These reputations, in turn, provide candidates with credibility over issues associated with their party. By increasing the salience of party-owned issues, the Liberal Party was able to stack the campaign agenda with issues that emphasised their strengths while simultaneously highlighting their opponent's weaknesses.

Unlike in 2001 when the government was forced to deal with events that kept the asylum seeker issue in the public eye, in 2013, aside from the continued arrival of boats, no such events occurred. As such, the Coalition attempted to manufacture concern and interest by focusing on the increased number of arrivals and exaggerating the issues associated with this influx:

> This is a national emergency. When you've had almost 50,000 illegal arrivals by boat, you have a crisis on your borders; and in the end, the first responsibility of government is national security. If you don't control your borders, to that extent, you are losing sovereignty over your own nation.[72]

The Coalition used the increased number of arrivals to construct asylum seekers as a threat to the national interest and the so-called integrity of Australian borders. The issue of protecting and securing/resecuring Australia and its border was a core component of the Coalition's campaign. One of the Coalition's key campaign promises was to deliver a 'safe, secure

---

70   Liberal Party of Australia and the Nationals, *Operation Sovereign Borders Policy*, 3.
71   David Damore, 'The Dynamics of Issue Ownership in Presidential Campaigns', *Political Research Quarterly* 57, no. 3 (2004): 391–97, doi.org/10.2307/3219849.
72   'Tony Abbott Transcript – Joint Press Conference' [press conference transcript], Liberal Party of Australia, 2013, available at: members.nsw.liberal.org.au/tony-abbott-transcript-joint-press-conference-brisbane (site discontinued).

Australia'. This promise of safety and security was then aligned with the ubiquitous promise of 'stopping the boats'. The Coalition effectively framed the arrival of asylum seekers as a threat, communicating that Australia could not be safe or secure while asylum seeker boats continued to arrive on Australian shores. In contrast to the 2001 campaign, in which explicit links were drawn between the arrival of people seeking asylum by boat and the threat of international terrorism, the 2013 campaign saw both major parties engage in this rhetoric in a more discreet manner. It could be argued that explicit statements that constructed asylum seekers as a threat to national safety were no longer necessary as this narrative was already so embedded in public opinion.

The Coalition's representation of asylum seekers was also determinedly militaristic. Terminology such as 'military-led response', 'tactical responses', 'targeted military operation' and even 'Operation Sovereign Borders' explicitly connected people seeking asylum by boat to the Australian defence forces. The use of this terminology in conjunction with the exaggerated language of 'border protection *crisis*' and 'national *emergency*' sought to prime the electorate into a state of concern over boat arrivals, with the militaristic language reinforcing the severity of this issue and, ultimately, justifying the government's proposed response.

Another function of the asylum seeker discussion that is more subtle, but in its own way more profound, is how the number of boat arrivals is amplified, not because of its intrinsic qualities as a threat to sovereignty and border security, but because of its usefulness as a broader political proxy. The primary issue the 2013 campaign revolved around was the management of Australia's economy. While Rudd focused on Australia's AAA rating and how his government overcame the global financial crisis, Abbott emphasised the size of Labor's debt and deficit in comparison to the preceding Howard Government. While these issues were largely spoken about as separate to asylum seekers and border control, the Coalition conflated the two by discussing the costs associated with the increased boat arrivals:

> Between 2007–08 and 2013–14, the budget for managing illegal boat arrivals has blown-out by $10.3 billion. This is real money that could have been spent on Australian schools, hospitals or improving our infrastructure.[73]

---

73   Liberal Party of Australia and the Nationals, *Operation Sovereign Borders Policy*, 3.

The Liberal Party sought to use the asylum seeker issue as a proxy for the broader concerns of the electorate. Issues of diminished access to education and healthcare, underfunded infrastructure and unaffordable housing etc. all created fertile ground for a national debate by shadow play and proxy, whereby asylum seekers were framed as placing additional strain on already depleted resources and government services.

The construction of asylum seekers as a threat to resources was also prominent in local-level campaigning. Various candidates attempted to localise their party's national campaign by drawing on real concerns of their electorate and framing the arrival of asylum seeker boats as a challenge to said issues. A prominent example of this was when Liberal candidate Fiona Scott related asylum seekers to issues of traffic congestion and hospital waiting times:

> It's [asylum seekers] a hot topic here because our traffic is overcrowded.

> My recommendation is go and sit in the emergency department of Nepean hospital or go and sit on the M4, and people see 50,000 people come in by boat, that's more than twice the population of Glenmore Park.[74]

Political candidates skirted over important electoral issues and used asylum seekers as either a scapegoat or deflection to avoid addressing these problems. In doing so, they created a sense of unfair imposition by framing the influx of boat arrivals as responsible for one's economic struggles; political leaders both generated and capitalised on these feelings of deprivation at the hand of the asylum seeker, effectively communicating to their constituents that the easiest way to solve these problems was to 'stop the boats'.

One of the most notable features of the rhetoric on asylum seeker boat arrivals throughout the 2013 campaign was the reticence of political leaders to use categories such as *asylum seekers* or *refugees* to describe this group. Rather, political leaders consistently used variations of the more ideologically loaded 'illegal boat arrivals'. This language depicts *asylum seekers* who arrive in Australia by boat as illegitimate and, more seriously, as criminal. It is important to note also that, by referring to this group as

---

74   Fiona Scott, 'Liberal Candidate Fiona Scott Links Asylum Seekers to Traffic Jams', *ABC News*, 2 September 2013, available at: www.youtube.com/watch?v=y9i9OQHkpOM.

illegal boat arrivals, as opposed to *asylum seekers* or *refugees*, political leaders sought to sever the linguistic reminder that these people are in fact seeking safety and protection. Instead, this choice of terminology disconnects them from the reasons for seeking asylum and delegitimises their legal entitlements and rights, while simultaneously criminalising their actions and positioning them as a threat. This construction again served to justify and necessitate the government's and opposition's 'hard-line' policies.

In contrast, the term 'genuine' was used to describe those *refugees* processed overseas and later resettled in Australia. The construction of these two distinct groups, 'genuine refugees' and 'illegal boat arrivals', served to reinforce the illegitimacy of the latter:

> More than 14,500 desperate people have been denied a place under our offshore humanitarian programme because those places have been taken by people who have arrived illegally by boat. These people are genuine refugees, already processed by United Nations agencies, but they are denied a chance of resettlement by people who have money in their pocket to buy a place via people smugglers.[75]

The dichotomous categories of 'illegal boat arrivals' and 'genuine refugees' were determined through discussions on the mode of arrival of asylum seekers, the notion of a 'queue' and the wealth of irregular arrivals, thus creating implicit criteria used to delineate between illegitimate and undeserving asylum seekers and legitimate and deserving refugees.

The frameworks developed by the Coalition in response to the various events that occurred throughout 2001 proved crucial to the Coalition's 2013 campaign. However, unlike the 2001 election, in which people seeking asylum by boat were explicitly connected to terrorism, had their morality questioned and were positioned as being at odds with Australian values, the 2013 campaign saw these themes emerge much more obscurely. These concerns/fears were already so salient among the population that political leaders no longer needed to draw these explicit connections, they just needed to gently remind the public that these anxieties were still valid.

---

75   Liberal Party of Australia and the Nationals, *Operation Sovereign Borders Policy*, 3.

Conclusion

Despite Australia's history of refugee resettlement, opposition to people seeking asylum has always existed and has often been the dominant discourse. While the events of 2001 mark a significant change in Australia's refugee history, much of the way we talk about asylum seekers began in 1977. Constructions of asylum seekers as 'illegal', 'queue jumpers' and as a threat to Australia's sovereignty and security have been in circulation since the very first cohort of 'boat people'. Political leaders have since borrowed and built on the language and policies of both their predecessors and their opponents, strategically tailoring their arguments to the 'threat of the day'. Constructions of asylum seekers as criminals in the late 1970s emerged once again in 2001 and were reappropriated after the events of 9/11 in which asylum seekers were then portrayed as terrorists. This discourse proved so pervasive that by 2013 political leaders merely needed to remind their constituents of the supposed security imperatives of increased boat arrivals.[76]

Political leaders have consistently used (or at least attempted to use) the respective increase in boat arrivals to their electoral advantage. While this was not as effective in the 1977 campaign as it was in 2001 and 2013, the debates that emerged set a precedent for future discussions about asylum seekers. The misrepresentation of asylum seekers as illegitimate and the use of this issue as a proxy for other electoral issues proved useful for political parties seeking electoral gain. As such, in pursuit of public support, both major political parties have been engaged in a 'race to the bottom', ensuring that the rhetoric they use and the policies they introduce are tougher than their opponents.

---

76 Sara Dehm and Max Walden's analysis of the 2016 election reveals yet again the pervasiveness of the construction of people seeking asylum as threats to Australia's security and identity in political discourse: see Dehm and Walden, 'Refugee Policy: A Cruel Bipartisanship'.

7

BEHIND THE WIRE

An oral history project about immigration detention

André Dao and Jamila Jafari in conversation

André Dao is a writer of fiction and non-fiction. He is the co-founder of Behind the Wire, an oral history project documenting people's experience of immigration detention, a producer of *The Messenger* podcast and coeditor of *They Cannot Take the Sky*. He is also the deputy editor of *New Philosopher* magazine.

Jamila Jafari is a Hazara from central Afghanistan. Her people's story is a centuries-long struggle for justice. The Hazaras are an indigenous people of modern-day Afghanistan who can be traced back as early as the fourth century. For hundreds of years, the Hazaras lived in their independent homeland known as the Hazarajat. In the 1890s, the British crown funded the Pashtun King's first campaign of genocide against the Hazara. Sixty per cent of the Hazara population was killed, millions more were tortured and sold into slavery and many others fled into exile. Jamila came to know about Behind the Wire and wanted to share her story to highlight the realities of immigration detention in Australia. She is a university student and has a keen interest in writing, politics and the community sector.

Discussion

We rarely hear from the asylum seekers and refugees who are the target of Australia's much-debated immigration detention regime. Behind the Wire is a multi-platform oral history project that seeks to address this imbalance by amplifying the voices of people who have experienced immigration detention. The coordinators of the project, who have not experienced detention, sought to do so by having lengthy, in-depth conversations with 'narrators' about their experiences, both inside and outside detention. Those conversations were then edited into short stories that were collected in a book, *They Cannot Take the Sky* (Allen & Unwin, 2017). Some of those stories were also filmed or audio recorded to form a museum exhibition of the same name. Throughout the interviewing and editing process, the aim was for narrators to feel as much ownership over their own stories as possible. In the following conversation, Behind the Wire coordinator André Dao speaks with one of the project's narrators, Jamila Jafari, about what it was like for her to share her story.

André Dao (BTW coordinator): The idea for Behind the Wire came about in 2014, when Sienna Merope and I started talking about the lack of depth and complexity in media representations of asylum seekers and refugees in Australia, especially of their experiences in detention. Even in the positive stories, there's so often a predictable narrative, and little more than a few soundbites from the person themselves. And there was hardly ever any detail about detention itself. We wanted to find a way to address that gap, because in our day jobs we were meeting people who had been in detention with the most incredible stories, and no platform for telling them. So our initial motivation was to find a way to make sure these voices – which should be the most important in this conversation – were part of the public discussion about immigration detention. We also wanted to surprise people who perhaps only had a cursory familiarity with Australia's refugee policies, or subvert their expectations, because there's been so much ink spilt on the 'issue' that people have very fixed, abstracted ideas about what it means to seek asylum. We hoped that in the course of doing this, helping people tell their stories of detention, that our narrators would get something out of the process too. But I've always been hesitant to make assumptions on that front, so I'm hoping that that's something we can explore in this conversation. In particular, Jamila, you were one of the narrators who contacted us about being involved, and I'm very interested to know why? And how the experience of telling your story matched up with what you were expecting?

Jamila Jafari (BTW narrator): Growing up, I was often disheartened that the public had a very narrow perception of who the people in detention were and why they had come to Australia. As you've discussed, while there were personal accounts being broadcast in the media, I also felt that these snippets and soundbites were too inadequate to paint an accurate picture of people's refugee experiences. I often thought about what telling the full story in its rawest form would entail.

For most of my schooling years, I would dread being asked to write creatively by my teachers. What was I supposed to write about? I lacked imagination and had nothing to inspire me. Or so I thought.

In the last two years of school, without giving it any forethought, I found myself writing about Hazara people and people seeking asylum. I began writing short stories about characters, themes and issues that resonated with me and were inspired by my lived experience as a Hazara-in-exile. In my Year 11 English exam I wrote about my people's struggle to enlighten themselves in a land where target killings created a barrier to accessing education. My main character risked death every day to attend school because she knew the power of her pen was mightier than her enemy's bombs and bullets. In my Year 12 drama exam I performed a monologue about a little girl coming to Australia on a boat.

The feedback I received from those assessments motivated me to keep going with my new-found approach. I had once been the girl trying to avoid being seen as different but now I wanted my peers to know I was one of those 'boat people', all in the spirit of inviting dialogue and understanding. One day, I asked a close friend of mine, 'What would you have thought about Muslims and boat people if you and I had never met?' She said, 'I guess I would've believed everything my Dad tells me'. We both fell silent upon realising the impact our friendship had made.

This became a profound moment for me and it is the reason why I reached out to Behind the Wire. I had something to say and I saw that Behind the Wire was willing to help me be heard. I was pleased with the team's ethical approach to giving me, as a narrator, the platform to stand up and speak out – on my own terms – and to be consulted at every step of the way.

By sharing my experiences, I don't expect parliament to unanimously vote overnight in closing down the camps, although that would be wonderful. I don't expect xenophobes to hand me flowers and cake because they now want to make amends. I simply want to show people my undiluted human emotions and experiences and I genuinely believe the change of heart will come naturally.

My story writing, my lunchtime conversations with school friends and my involvement with Behind the Wire have all been my small way of magnifying the human element about how we are treating those who've come from across the seas in the national conversation. My parents raised me to appreciate the power of words and the effect they can have on societies. This is my way of trying to effect change.

André: One of the things that struck me throughout the project was how working with Behind the Wire was often only one of many ways that people talked about these issues. So it's interesting for me to see that that's the case for you as well, that you've spoken with friends and family, as well as using more creative forms like short stories and drama.

Actually, the question of form was something we thought about a lot as editors. Because the conversations we had with narrators would usually go for a few hours – across different days – it was necessary, just from a readability point of view, to cut the transcripts down. But then we were faced with a dilemma: what could we cut? And of course, length wasn't the only factor – we wanted readers to get some of the raw impact that we felt as interviewers sitting down and speaking to people about their personal experiences; at the same time we wanted the stories as a whole to reflect the diversity of detention experiences, without our preconceived ideas of what the 'important' details would be.

Our main approach to this challenge was to try and work as closely as possible with narrators on the editing of their transcripts. But in practice this varied – some narrators said they were happy for us to shape those lengthy conversations into more structured narratives, while others were closely involved in changes, almost going line by line through their stories. Jamila, my memory is that you worked pretty closely with us on your story, so I'm interested in hearing how you approached that side of the project. Did it feel very different from the 'telling' part? And how did you go about thinking about what were the important details?

Jamila: The conversations I had with Zoe Barron, the Behind the Wire volunteer who interviewed me, and the transcript that followed, was the first time I had a good amount of my refugee experience written down on paper. Since Zoe and I had met a few times in relaxed and casual settings I felt comfortable sharing more information with her. During the editing process, I took out information that I felt was quite personal for me. I consciously decided that that sort of information would be best relayed in a real-time face-to-face conversation rather than in written texts or other media formats.

Having conversations with people about topics that are important to me has always been very sacred to me. Ask any of my close friends and they will tell you I sometimes cannot stop chatting away! For some parts that I had removed, I felt that they were unnecessary as I knew I had gone off on a tangent again, which is also why I was happy for the editors to polish down some paragraphs into more succinct texts.

André: It's interesting that you mention face-to-face conversations being a better medium for relaying certain kinds of information. That was something we tried to keep in mind for another iteration of our project, an exhibition at the Immigration Museum in Melbourne. For the exhibition, we had the opportunity to use video, so we decided to film some of the narrators from the book delivering direct-to-camera monologues taken from their longer published stories. The videos were displayed in small booths where the audience could sit and essentially be face-to-face with someone telling their story.

The feedback we got from audience members was very positive. The Immigration Museum said that the exhibition had particularly high engagement rates, and lots of people – including school groups – left notes about how the videos had impacted on them. Jamila, your videos are a great example of how powerful the videos could be – every time I watch one of them I'm struck by how much emotion comes through in your voice, your mannerisms – even your silences. But I'm also conscious that the videos were a big ask for our narrators, and really very different to speaking to an interviewer, off-camera, in a lengthy conversation. How did you find speaking on camera? Did you have to prepare differently than for your conversations with Zoe? And did you feel like the video format allowed you to express more? Or was it more of an inhibition?

Jamila: As I reflect upon that experience now, I realise I didn't do anything drastically different to prepare. Because speaking on camera is slightly different to a real-time conversation, I had to bear in mind that the audience was not in front of me to listen and ask me further questions. Hence why I made sure to include any details I thought someone may potentially ask.

Each media format has its own strengths and weaknesses. The power of a video is in its ability to capture the things a book cannot: the pitch in a voice, the facial expressions, the silences. In my case, these things happened voluntarily and I think it really helped me to say what I wanted to.

I had intended to speak in a calm, neutral tone on camera. But when I watched the videos for the first time, I was really surprised to find that my emotions were so obvious in my voice. Where my voice trembles or my pitch rises a viewer can tell when I am anxious or excited. I was slightly confronted to realise I was a bit like an open book in those videos. But I had to tell myself it was okay to sometimes let myself be honest about how my experiences made me feel. It's not always in the best interests of a newsreader to tell the masses how government policies affected my life, so if I didn't allow myself to show emotion, to be human, then who would?

Through these videos, I hope the public is able to get a glimpse, however small it may be, of certain elements of my experience and the experiences of other people that the mainstream media has been reluctant to broadcast for nearly two decades.

The following is an extract from Jamila's story. She was five years old when she fled Afghanistan with her mother and younger brother in 1999. After travelling by boat from Indonesia, they were intercepted in Australian waters, and were eventually taken to the detention centre in Woomera, South Australia.

The word 'freedom'

We had the initial interview, and it was in a lovely, clean, air-conditioned building – really different from the dongas. There was a desk, an interviewer, an interpreter, and a chair. Mum sat on the chair as she was being interviewed, and my brother and I had to sit on the floor. I think they gave us a piece of paper and a few coloured pencils to occupy us with. And, I mean, it should have been something enjoyable to do but what was I supposed to draw? Razor wire all around me? That's all I'd seen ever since I'd arrived here.

So, once you've been initially interviewed, they transfer you over, make room for the other new arrivals. The other donga we were moved to was much bigger and it had a small living area, a corridor and three bedrooms on each side. Each bedroom had two bunk beds. So we took one of the rooms there, there were other Hazara families in the other rooms. And these other Hazara families, they were, I think, the epitome of what detention does to children. The psychological effects detention has. The lady, she had quite a few children. She had two older boys: one was 14 and the other was 12. She had lots of girls as well. When I think of detention, what I saw with them are a big part of the memories I have.

Woomera was the most notorious detention centre in Australia. There were lots of protests and riots and that sort of thing while we were in Woomera. I saw adults and children with their lips sewn, bruised and all this stuff. The 14-year-old and the 12-year-old, they both had their lips sewn. The mother too.

During one of the riots on 26 January 2000, I was standing there and there was arguing going on. There was screaming, people screaming out, 'Freedom! Freedom!' It was the middle of the desert during the really hot season and the conditions were just unbearable. I remember the 14-year-old, he had some kind of blade. He'd written out the word 'freedom', he cut that into his skin, his left forearm – I'm sorry this is so graphic – his skin's ripped open, his blood's dripping, and he's screaming out, 'We want freedom!'

I could never remove that image from my head. It's so vivid. And his voice is … it's shaking, there's so much pain in his voice. Like, a 14-year-old! Doing that to himself! And all the other adults, older children, protesting and screaming out, 'Freedom, freedom, freedom.' When I think of my childhood, that is one of the main words that I remember, like it's been engraved in me, and I have never … I wish I could, I wish I could remove those images from my head. But, I can't. It's impossible.

After the boy cuts himself, next thing I hear are people screaming and crying out because a man has climbed right to the top of the fence and then he just jumps off the fence. He lands on a coil of razor wire and people are shrieking, they're crying out. Everyone is so surprised. As he lands, his weight causes the coil to bounce, so he bounces a few times like a heartbeat. His arms are all cut up because of the razor and he's bleeding. There's a documentary about him, called 'The Man Who Jumped'. He didn't die, but the conditions in the detention centre drove him off the edge, literally. You wouldn't do that if you were completely sane, you know?

And those boys, they were so damaged, honestly. They did a lot of hectic things but I just admired them so much for their fearlessness, their boldness and their bravery. It's not an easy task to sew your lips together, to go on a hunger strike, to then resort to cutting into your own flesh. You couldn't help but admire them for having those personality traits in the face of such hopeless times. I think there were other people who felt the same way about them, even people older than them.

PART III
Understanding refugee histories and futures

8

FROM DAHMARDA TO DANDENONG VIA DENPASSAR

Hazara stories of settlement, success and separation

Laurel Mackenzie

The chapter draws on interviews conducted with three post-settlement refugee Hazaras living in Victoria who described their journeys from Afghanistan to Australia. These interview participants saw themselves as having overcome obstacles and hardships to arrive at a place of active participation in Australian life. All three interviewees described themselves as successful, having achieved their goals of escape, resettlement and – in most cases – family reunification. This last is significant as all three narratives highlight the importance of family, rather than simply being stories of individual effort. The driving motivation of each story's protagonist was clearly to bring their families to safety: individual success or happiness in each case is bound up with that of family and community. The narratives in this chapter reveal a shared humanity as the people in them describe resettlement experiences both as triumphs and difficulties.

Underlying each of these stories is the invisible hand of Australian immigration policy, which provides the legal context in which people seek asylum in Australia. The experience of coming to Australia is not just an experience of emergent immigrant identity, but also includes the shattering encounter with immigration policy that indefinitely detains people and causes families to be heartbreakingly separated. Excerpts from Salmi's, Hassan's and Jahan's narratives give a sense of how policy frameworks manifest in the lived experiences of real people. To further emphasise the real-life impact of policy on human lives, their stories are framed here in the context of their embodied interviews, drawing attention not just to the events contained within the stories, but to the act of telling and sharing the stories as part of lived experience.

In 2011, I started making regular weekly visits to the Melbourne Immigration Transit Accommodation (MITA) facility, then used to indefinitely hold unaccompanied minors, young men under 18 years of age who had come alone by boat to Australia to seek asylum, while their refugee claims were processed. Along with other visitors, I met members of oppressed minority groups including Tamils from Sri Lanka, Banglas from Bangladesh, Rohingyas fleeing Burma, stateless Kurds, Syrian Palestinians, Afghan Hazaras, and others, including two teenage boys from Indonesia who had been picked up on suspicion of being people smugglers. These last two were not seeking asylum but were held there because there was nowhere else to send them – they were too young to be sent to Melbourne Immigration Detention Centre (MIDC), the higher-security facility reserved for immigration activities specifically defined under the Australian criminal code (including visa over-stayers). They are not the focus of this chapter – I mention them to illustrate the perceived lack of clarity around immigration policy within the detention system. Other manifestations of this included the inconsistent yet indefinite lengths of sentences, and the unclear processes that determined who was awarded visas and why. The two young fishermen were simply sent back to Indonesia after a few months.

The young men who remained had strong reasons not to want to be sent back to their countries of origin. A common thread ran through many of the stories we heard: frequently the head of the family had been killed or had vanished in suspicious circumstances, and the rest of the family had put their money together to send their eldest son to freedom. The hopes of their families rested on the shoulders of many of the young men we met – something that I came to appreciate more with repeated visits. Their concerns for the future were not just for their own survival, but their families and communities as well.

We took in gifts of food and coloured pencils, brought in musical instruments and board games, and conducted impromptu English classes. The kinds of support we were able to offer seemed futile at times. However, the young men detained at MITA told us that these small things helped to make them feel less isolated and more socially connected, as the processing of their claims dragged on interminably. This finding is reflected in research by British criminology researchers into prison and detention centre conditions Mary Bosworth and Blerina Kellezi, who recommend 'greater communication and interaction with the local community' as a strategy in mitigating the high levels of depression caused by isolation within immigration detention centres.[1]

Over the next couple of years MITA changed. MIDC was nearing capacity, so MITA expanded to contain a larger population of inmates than just unaccompanied minors. Security was tightened, and higher fences were built. A friend and I took clarinet reeds to an Iranian grandfather and, with other activists and advocates, raised enough money to buy a computer for a Palestinian Syrian artist who drew political cartoons. One day I registered for a visit and went in by myself to meet a young Afghan Hazara man who had just arrived. He beat me at table tennis, and we watched the grey Melbourne sky transformed by a rainbow. I found myself buoyed by his optimism and sense of hope, the rainbow a perfect visual metaphor. Later that year, a friend and I held a celebration dinner when two other Hazara men were released from detention. They told us their stories, eloquently and passionately. Their stories comprised a complex mix of individual adventure, culturally specific references, narratives of persecution and flight, and elements of self-reflection that implied a conscious shift towards what it might mean to become Australian (rather than Afghan) Hazaras. The seeds of my interest in Hazara life stories, and the research project from which the interviews in this chapter are drawn, were sown.

---

1   Mary Bosworth and Blerina Kellezi, *Quality of Life in Detention: Results from the MQLD Questionnaire Data Collected in IRC Yarl's Wood, IRC Tinsley House and IRC Brook House, August 2010– June 2011* (Criminal Justice, Borders and Citizenship Research Paper No. 2448404, March 2012), available at: ssrn.com/abstract=2448404.

Dandenong: An emerging Hazara centre

In 2015, I knocked on the door of a comfortable house in suburban Dandenong. I had arranged to interview Salmi and Hassan, two Hazaras who had already expressed interest via email in taking part in my research on Hazara transitions from refugee to immigrant status. The interviewing stage of my research involved recording the life stories of Hazaras over 18 years of age, told in English, who had held a permanent visa in Australia for more than five years, as per the conditions agreed upon with my university's Human Research Ethics Committee.

It is worth describing Dandenong, since it is the site of the largest population of Hazaras living in Australia. Dandenong is a primarily working-class suburb with a deep-rooted Labor (centre-left) tradition. Located 30 kilometres south-east of Melbourne's central business hub, on the outskirts of the city, the region has a highly multicultural population comprising a mix of different ethnic groups, especially from China and the Middle East. The City of Greater Dandenong calls itself the 'City of Opportunity', and identifies as a refugee welcome zone. The city has implemented anti-racism policies, and welcoming policies and practices including programs for asylum seekers and survivors of torture, language learning, cultural centres and more. The local council cites its goal as 'building a sustainable future for the community', and highlights themes of progress and inclusivity in its acknowledgement of both Indigenous and new migrant histories.[2] In one interview I conducted, Dandenong was called 'the place to be' for new Hazara arrivals: when given the choice of resettlement areas, Hazaras selected it based solely on recommendations from their social networks.[3] In 2017, 2,000 of the 8,000 asylum-seeking refugees living in Victoria were located in Dandenong.[4] It was described to me as the fourth largest Hazara city-based centre in the world, after Kabul, Tehran and Quetta.

---

2   'Asylum Seekers and Refugees: Greater Dandenong's Role', Greater Dandenong: City of Opportunity, 2017. Copy in author's possession.

3   Laurel Mackenzie and Olivia Guntarik, 'Rites of Passage: Experiences of Transition for Forced Hazara Migrants and Refugees in Australia', *Crossings: Journal of Migration & Culture* 6, no. 1 (2015): 59–80, doi.org/10.1386/cjmc.6.1.59_1.

4   'Asylum Seekers and Refugees: Greater Dandenong's Role'.

One interview participant had described the Greater Dandenong region as home to approximately 10,000 Hazaras. This number is somewhat higher than the 2016 Australian census suggests, where Afghanistan was selected as 'country of birth' by just 4,799 people in the Dandenong region (or 3.2 per cent of the local population).[5] However, the census figure does not provide an accurate representation of the number of Hazaras living in Dandenong, for three reasons. Firstly, not all Hazaras would necessarily claim Afghanistan as their country of birth: Hazaras have been actively involved in fleeing persecution in Afghanistan since at least 1979, and members of the younger generations may have been born in Pakistan or Iran, or even in Australia. Secondly, people on temporary visas were excluded from taking part in the census, and the City of Dandenong proudly asserts that it is home to 2,000 asylum-seeking refugees. Any Hazaras within this category, living as members of the community while on temporary visas, would not have been counted in the census.[6] Finally, the form of data collection used in the 2016 census caused concerns to be raised around privacy, which potentially affected the accuracy of data collected from households where trust was already low.[7]

Although not all Hazaras would have identified Afghanistan as their birthplace, it still gives some indication of Hazara numbers to look at the numbers of people who gave their birthplace as Afghanistan, since no specific data was provided regarding people who identified as being of Hazara ethnicity. Compared with other regions in Australia, the number of Afghan-born residents in Dandenong was relatively high: across the state of Victoria 18,116 people (or 0.3 per cent of the population) identified Afghanistan as their country of birth. Overall, 46,799 people across Australia (or 0.2 per cent of the overall population) identified Afghanistan as their country of birth.[8] Linguistically, emerging scholar on Afghan languages Asya Pereltsvaig has noted that the number 'one thousand' in Hazaragi (the Hazara language in Afghanistan) is 'Hazaar', which also

5   '2016 Census Quickstats: Greater Dandenong', Australian Bureau of Statistics, 23 October 2017, available at: quickstats.censusdata.abs.gov.au/census_services/getproduct/census/2016/quickstat/ LGA22670.

6   'Microdata: Australian Census and Migrants Integrated Dataset, 2016', Australian Bureau of Statistics, 17 July 2018, available at: www.abs.gov.au/Ausstats/abs@.nsf/0/889792D645A7CC7FCA 2582CD0015C002?OpenDocument.

7   Senate Economics Reference Committee, *2016 Census: Issues of Trust* (Canberra: Commonwealth of Australia, 2016), available at: www.aph.gov.au/Parliamentary_Business/Committees/Senate/ Economics/2016Census/Report.

8   '2016 Census Quickstats'.

historically refers to a mountain tribal grouping in Afghanistan.[9] Further, the number 'ten thousand' appears to serve as a colloquial term for a larger population group comprising several tribes, and as a cultural referent for a large population group. Despite a lack of clarity around exact numbers, it is clear that the Dandenong region is an emerging cultural centre for Hazaras.

Meeting Salmi and Hassan

A young woman opened the door to my knock and introduced herself as Salmi's sister, followed by an older woman who Salmi later indicated was their (non–English speaking) grandmother. The younger women wore jeans, and headscarves in what I took to be a more modern style comprising a tube of stretchy fabric, rather than an artfully draped scarf. I followed the example set by the pile of shoes at the door and slipped mine off. Salmi offered me slippers to wear inside the house, and I followed her into a large room ringed with cushions.

Salmi introduced me to Hassan, her father's business partner. In my visits to detention centres and in community contacts beyond, I had grown used to meeting Hazara men with refugee experiences who had shifted away from more conservative traditions and would shake hands, even exchange hugs with women to whom they were not related. Hassan, however, was from a generation that still held to the older values. I had forgotten my habit of approaching with hands folded at my heart and waiting for the other person to make the first move. I reached to shake his hand, and he backed away slightly, apologising. It was a slightly awkward start to our first meeting. Salmi and I had corresponded via email after my research outline had been forwarded to her, but we had not met in person before.

In my interviews, I would strive to indicate via my professional demeanour that, as a representative of an academic institution, I understood and respected the seriousness of the stories I was about to hear. The academic props I carried (papers, recording device and consent forms) were part of the performance through which I demonstrated my credibility. The familiar flow of carefully chosen words as I talked through the process

---

9   Asya Pereltsvaig, 'Language of the "Mountain Tribe": A Closer Look at Hazaragi', *Languages of the World*, 12 December 2011, available at: www.languagesoftheworld.info/student-papers/language-of-the-mountain-tribe-a-closer-look-at-hazaragi.html.

describing the research aims and intended outcomes, the ethical guidelines that meant participants could withdraw from the research at any time, and my well-practised opening question that opened the unstructured interview into a space where the participant's stories took centre stage, all served to bolster the identities we were performing in that space. In every interview, both the interview participant and I shared a desire to record and publish their stories. My aim was to open the space I had access to as an early career researcher for more refugee stories to be told, bringing perspectives from my social justice activism to my academic work. The research participants desired to contribute to the narrative and media construction of Hazaras as desirable migrants in Australia. This shared goal gave us a common stake in the interviews being conducted and meant that social gaffes like my reaching to shake Hassan's hand were able to be overlooked, or reconstructed as an opportunity for education, in pursuit of our larger shared aim. Somewhat later in my interviewing process, another participant told me he always took part in research and surveys, as a way of helping the larger Hazara community, and of giving back to the wider Australian community. Similarly, Salmi and Hassan presented themselves as deeply invested in the future of the Hazara community in Australia.

Cultural and historical identity and persecution

We sat on the floor and Salmi placed a tray of wrapped chocolates and nuts and sweet tea between us. After I had asked my well-rehearsed introductory question, Hassan indicated my zoom recorder, which I had placed on the floor between us:

'It's going, is it?'

The gesture served to re-establish the context of our conversation and our roles as participant and interviewer with a shared aim. He introduced himself to the recording and proceeded to tell his story. 'In the name of God, I'm Hassan … I was born in 1969. I'm from Kabul, Afghanistan.'

Hassan's narrative encompassed not just events from his own experiences, but also described the wider political situation, demonstrating links with the greater Hazara community. He described how, even when he was eight or nine years old, he was aware of the widespread social discrimination against Hazaras. Hazaras were likened to a 'sewer', and the word 'Hazara' itself assumed derogatory meanings. Hazaras were not permitted to sit in buses or public cars and were excluded from political process. To become a politician or government minister was an unattainable dream for a Hazara.

This discrimination appeared as a cultural motif in other interviews I conducted, as a larger historical context also emerged, locating the Hazaras' vulnerability as stretching back generations. In Salmi's and other interviewees' analysis, Hazaras had been positioned as second-class citizens since the late 1800s, through events brought to a crux by the genocidal attacks on the Hazaras wrought by Emir Shah Abdur Rahman Khan in 1891, whose rise to power with the aid of British finances meant he was now acting with key authorities of the state at his disposal.[10]

> 65 per cent of the Hazara people were killed during the Abdur Rahman Khan's regime … he wanted to get rid of the Hazara people. (Salmi)

She described how Khan sent over 100,000 Pashtun fighters on a religious crusade into the Hazara lands in mountainous central Afghanistan, and destroyed the Hazara villages, subjugating their inhabitants.

This event was a common motif reflecting a shared history and cultural identity. The previous year I had interviewed Jahan, a Hazara community leader in Dandenong. Jahan had also located the massacre as significantly interwoven into Hazara cultural memory.

> People's lands was grabbed by force, and given it to the other tribe, which was Pashtun tribe. People were forced out from their region. Hazaras were pushed in towards the central region, and blocked, cut off all their supply lines. And Hazaras was economically, they were suppressed. (Jahan)

Jahan had explained that, in the century or so following the massacre of 1891, Hazaras were socially vilified in Afghanistan, given work as farm labourers or menials, prohibited from entering university, restricted from general education by the limited number of schools in the mountains, and more heavily taxed than their Pashtun neighbours.

---

10 Niamatullah Ibrahimi, *The Hazaras and the Afghan State: Rebellion, Exclusion and the Struggle for Recognition* (Oxford: Oxford University Press, 2017), 53–86.

> [Since then, Hazaras] may not be accepted in any form of government. They are not allowed to study higher education. They are not even allowed to enrol in a school. They are not allowed to be in a higher ranking, they are not allowed to join the military. (Jahan)

Hazara revolts were quashed, and Hazaras were socially cast as second-class citizens. Until the Communist invasion of 1978, Hazara people had been excluded from the education system. Illiteracy had contributed to social exclusion and oppression for over 100 years and confirmed in majority minds the fitness of Hazaras only for menial labour. The Soviet invasion was the beginning of bloody and destructive war in Afghanistan. But from 1979 the Communists imposed strict rules around access to schools, and Afghan Hazaras had the opportunity again to attend school past the fourth grade. Hazara scholar Niamatullah Ibrahimi has argued that the power vacuum within Afghanistan that made the invasion possible, as the central government lost control of the country, also gave Hazaras the first opportunity for autonomy they had had in decades – a chance for self-determination that only ended when the Taliban had firmly established themselves across the country in 1998.[11] The Communists were finally expunged in 1989, in a war in which many Hazaras participated, privileging national, ethnic and religious allegiance over identification with the Communist invaders. But the ensuing civil war in Afghanistan, and subsequent seizure of power by the Taliban (with its fundamentalist Pashtun roots), meant that Hazaras again were targeted for persecution. It was in the context of this persecution by the Taliban that the interview participants in this chapter fled Afghanistan.

Leaving Afghanistan

Born in 1993, Salmi was three years old when the Taliban took Kabul. Two years later the Taliban were reported moving throughout the rest of the country, circuitously approaching Mazar-i-Sharif as they gathered strength in south-eastern villages. By 1998 they had entered her province. She did not understand the significance of the news, but her father did, and loaded up a truck with provisions – flour, rice and oil – the essentials of living. Salmi remembers the day her father heard that the Taliban were approaching their village. He sent a message to her mother that the line

---

11 Ibrahimi, *The Hazaras and the Afghan State*, 119.

of defence had broken and asked her to pack up the things they would need to live on. Salmi remembers hurried movement and her confusion. 'I could not understand what was happening. I was asking but they were not answering, because they were upset.' She remembers taking things out of their house, and people running on foot from the village – 'snapshots of things'.

They left that day with their truck loaded up with provisions, counting themselves among the fortunate because they had a car. Salmi remembers sitting in the cabin of the truck and looking back into the body of the truck space to see it full of people. People travelling on foot would ride in the truck for a distance and get out at the next village. Others would replace them. Salmi remembers her mother imploring her father not to take any more people in – there were too many, they were overcrowding the space, slowing the truck down, making it unsafe. Salmi remembers her father's response, which she presented as a kind of family lore, revealing the esteem she holds him in:

> This is the only time you can show people who you really are. It's the hard times that you can show the true self of yours and show your humanity. We can't say anything to them. Just let them in and they will realise when it's too much and they'll stop coming in. (Salmi)

They reached Pakistan, but it became clear that her father was still in danger. In the most heartbreaking moment in her narrative, Salmi described her father's decision to try and make his way to Australia as a refugee. 'He decided that he'd come to Australia and he left us there in Pakistan.' At this point in her interview Salmi wept as she remembered the moment when her father left them behind. In Afghanistan, she had been a 'daddy's girl' – young and spoiled – he would do anything for her. In the evenings, he would tell her stories. Or there would be visitors, people talking late into the night, a feeling of community and life. 'In Pakistan, it was just too quiet for us. There was no Dad.' Her constructions of stability were based around him, and he had left them in Pakistan. Salmi remembered his absence keenly – she missed falling asleep to the safety of the sound of his voice when he was not there.

> We were left on our own, my mum, my older brother was eight at the time. My two sisters, one of them was five, my younger one was one. We were on our own in Pakistan and life was really hard there as well, because in there you know, you need a male person to live with you.

> The fact that my Dad wasn't with us was very hard for all of us.
> Now that I think of it, it would have been the hardest for my
> Mum, because she could understand everything. (Salmi)

The 'everything' encompassed the danger and fear that her mother worked to protect her children from, while Salmi's father made his way slowly to Australia, traversing a boat journey famous for its frequent fatalities, detention and other stages of the refugee determination process in Australia.

Jahan came from a small village in the mountains in Afghanistan where the villagers worked for seven or eight months of the year to store food for winter, and traded food with other villages – it was not so much a fiscal as a barter economy. Around 1995 the Taliban arrived in his area, bringing threats and violence.

> [The] Taliban came, I can't recall the dates, it's like 30 years, 25 years
> ago … But after '95, or during the '95 there was Talibans take most
> of regions, then they headed towards central region. (Jahan)

The urban centre of Kabul where Hassan was based was no safer than Jahan's small village in the mountains. By 1995 Hassan was married, with a family of his own. He feared for his and his family's safety, due to the ongoing persecution of the Hazara people in Kabul. Finally, he decided they would have to leave, and he sought out a people smuggler. With the assistance of the people smuggler, who provided documents and access to safe houses, Hassan and his family made their way overland to Pakistan, then via the people smugglers' routes to Indonesia.

Like Hassan, Jahan contacted a people smuggler – in our interview Jahan had explained, chuckling, that in Australia, in English, the term is 'people smuggler'; but in Pakistan it was just 'normal business'. Jahan and his father made their way to Indonesia on fake passports, travelling at night, waiting interminably for connections, not knowing where they were going. Finally, late at night, they were taken to a small boat that would bring them to Australia. About 36 people were crammed into the boat in complete darkness.

> I didn't know whether I was going to make a life from the Dead
> Sea, you know, sea journey. Because our boat was so small, it was
> sort of, you know, flying on the water, sort of as people so many.
> In the end water was finished, there was no rations there you
> know, there was … terrible, terrible condition. (Jahan)

In Indonesia, Hassan realised he did not have enough money to pay the passage for his family in the people smugglers' boats. He was forced to leave them in a refugee camp in Jakarta, where they lived for the next three years. He then endured a harrowing boat journey that he swore he would never repeat, not for half the land in Australia.

> If now the government takes me there, gives me half of Australia for me, I never come back there [the boat journey]. It's too hard. It's too hard. I know, I had a big storm there and all of us, 99.9 per cent, we thought we're going to go and by luck, we are alive. In that time, no water, no food and the captain lost the way.

> I don't know what they're using or they got navigation – I don't know actually. I was – under – down the stairs. Just the people talking like that and the captain says, yeah, they're lost. They went back to Indonesia and they took some more water and food and again came. It's all up, took us 14 days. (Hassan)

Reaching Australia: Curtin Detention Centre in 1999

On reaching Australia, Hassan and Jahan were both detained at Curtin Detention Centre. Jahan recalled how the guards seemed to delight in telling detainees stories of the dangers of the Australian outback, where crocodiles and carnivorous kangaroos abounded, and snakes whose bite would kill in two seconds. He related this to the policy changes at the time. He arrived in October 1999, when Temporary Protection Visas (TPVs) were being introduced to replace the Permanent Protection Visas (PPVs) that had previously been automatically granted once an applicant was identified legally as a refugee. TPVs provided far fewer rights – including work rights – than the older PPVs. They expired after three years, provoking criticisms of refoulement.[12] The shift exacerbated the already tense atmosphere inside Curtin. According to Jahan, the guards would try to scare the asylum seekers to deter escape if anyone was tempted to try their luck in the non-existent Australian underground instead of waiting for a limited and expiring visa.

---

12   Mary Crock, *Seeking Asylum Alone: A Study of Australian Law, Policy and Practice Regarding Unaccompanied and Separated Children* (Australia: Federation Press, 2006).

> [In 1999], law was changing, and that's why they told us to not go
> out, never escape, otherwise you will be dead in jungle, you can't
> make it, and kangaroo might eat you off, and crocodile might you
> know grab your leg, you know, or snake might bite you – and
> they're so deadly you will be dead in two seconds. (Jahan)

Issues at Curtin at that time included overcrowding, indefinite detention,
the extremely limited English classes that were offered to detainees,
children in detention, delays in processing, including communicating
the results of refugee determination hearings, and more. This had started
to attract the attention of human rights groups. Busloads of protestors
arrived from across the country to shout and wave placards outside the
gates. Conditions continued to worsen, and Jahan recalled tents being
used as a solution to overcrowding. In the Western Australian desert heat,
this solution was potentially fatal.

> I vividly remember ... in the start there was some 100 people ... And
> they were feeding us well, because we were few people. Then they
> reached to 500 and 1,000 people, and everything went badly.
> And there was hardly much food provided, there was hardly no
> utilities, it was very hard you know. And after that people were
> transferred to the tents, and that in the 44, 45-degree heat of
> Western Australia – it was hard to survive there. (Jahan)

Jahan had come from a different kind of desert. In his mountainous
village, rain was at least possible. Here he found himself in a place of red
earth, poisonous animals and almost unendurable heat.

> We were never exposed to this kind of heat, you know, this kind of
> country. I remember, when I was putting my feet first on the land,
> I remember that the land was very red. I've never seen such a red
> land, you know, I said what kind of land is that, you know, have
> I come in Mars or somewhere, you know. (Jahan)

In the year 2000 the Human Rights Commission conducted a review of
Immigration Detention Centre facilities across the country, which was
published the following year. Recommendations included the amendment
of the *Migration Act 1958* (Cth) to guarantee rights to detainees including:

> the right not to be arbitrarily detained, to have access to
> information and legal assistance, the right to humane treatment
> and the rights of children to special protection ... If detainees
> are deprived of their basic rights, a situation of distress, anxiety
> and grievance is created, which all too often results in the protests

and violence we have seen over the previous year ... I wish to emphasise that many of the problems in immigration detention facilities are significantly heightened by prolonged detention. The government must look seriously at a solution to long term detention as a matter of urgency.[13]

By the end of 1999 Jahan received the news that his refugee claim had been accepted, and he had been granted a TPV. At first, he didn't believe it – he had started to mistrust the system, as the guards at Curtin had enjoyed toying with the inmates, giving false information about, for instance, the dangers that waited outside:

> I remember Christmas '99. When I was given the news that I was accepted as a refugee. As asylum seeker, as a refugee. That I'd be going out. First I didn't believe, I said, they're lying, they're trying to punish us here, you know, I don't know, let us rot in here, you know. (Jahan)

Once he was able to accept the news it became a high point of his narrative – he had surmounted the obstacles, he had been recognised as a refugee, and he was on his way to freedom.

> And I was happy then! 25th, Christmas '99, it was good news for me. That's what sometimes I do. You know, like Christmas. It's lovely, you know. That was one of the good news, that my life was saved. (Jahan)

Policy in 1999: TPVs and family separation

In October 1999 immigration law changed to admit new classes of visas.[14] Until then, if applicants were identified as refugees, then they were automatically given permanent visas. In 1999 the Howard Government introduced TPVs, which removed access to social services and the guarantee of attaining permanent residency. According to political scientist Don McMaster, TPVs were clearly a response to a political issue, the

---

13   Australian Human Rights Commission, *A Report on Visits to Immigration Detention Facilities by the Human Rights Commissioner 2001* (Australian Human Rights Commission, 2001), available at: www.humanrights.gov.au/publications/report-visits-immigration-detention-facilities-human-rights-commissioner-2001#major.
14   Crock, *Seeking Asylum Alone.*

arrival of refugees by boat directly to Australia.[15] These arrivals, although numerically insignificant, were constructed as a problem, generating media hysteria and becoming a major electoral issue. People arriving in Australia by plane or people with expired visas were not subject to TPVs, but were usually granted Bridging Visas which included work rights and other benefits. TPVs granted their holders access to some medical and welfare services (not necessarily including English classes), no family reunification and no travel outside of Australia. TPV holders could work, however their immigration status excluded them from permanent jobs. TPV holders were eligible for a small Special Benefit from the Red Cross (an allowance later taken over and administered by social security benefits provider Centrelink), but not the slightly more substantive JobSeeker allowance. Despite the provision in the *1951 Refugee Convention* that explicitly prohibits refoulement, TPVs expired after three years and were not renewable: they could only be applied for afresh. This meant that TPV holders lived constantly in fear of their visas not being renewed and being sent back to the country they had fled. TPVs have thus been linked conclusively with mental illnesses such as stress and depression.[16]

Australia has a long tradition of enacting strictures on immigrants, based on its self-construction as white, which has bled into its restrictive refugee policies. Indigenous scholar and critical race theorist Aileen Moreton Robinson has written on the phenomenon of the 'white possessive' that is useful in unpacking this level of discrimination. Australia was classified as *Terra Nullius* on settlement; explicitly locating the assumption of white colonial ownership over the empty space – and, by implication, ownership over the Indigenous people already living there.[17] This assumption of white ownership of the land and the constructed identity of Australia later extended to migration policies as well. The Immigration Restriction Act was one of a suite of policies that aimed to promulgate a concept of a white Australia between Federation and the start of World War II.[18] As political scientist James Jupp has pointed out, non-British immigration

15   Don McMaster, 'Resettled Refugees: Temporary Protection Visas: Obstructing Refugee Livelihoods', *Refugee Survey Quarterly* 25, no. 2 (2006): 135–45, doi.org/10.1093/rsq/hdi0131.
16   Crock, *Seeking Asylum Alone.*
17   Aileen Moreton-Robinson, *The White Possessive: Property, Power, and Indigenous Sovereignty* (Minneapolis: University of Minnesota Press, 2015), 5, doi.org/10.5749/minnesota/97808166921 49.001.0001.
18   Ien Ang and Jon Stratton, 'Multiculturalism in Crisis: The New Politics of Race and National Identity in Australia', *TOPIA: Canadian Journal of Cultural Studies* 2 (1998): 22–41.

was strongly discouraged.[19] La Trobe University lecturer in politics Gwenda Tavan has argued that, rather than being controversial, this policy direction had strong popular support.[20] It was finally dismantled following World War II due to increasing international and domestic pressure, but this underlying worldview that positioned a white ownership of the land has persisted into current immigration policies.[21] These precedents can be seen to effect the political construction of non-white immigrants as a problem to be dealt with: local debates around whether immigrants should simply integrate or assimilate completely to Australian values are exacerbated in the case of undocumented migrants whose identity claims are tenuous to begin with.[22]

Jahan and Hassan were released into the community on TPVs. It could have been worse. By 2001 TPVs were refused if an applicant had spent more than seven days in another country on their way to Australia, in Pakistan, say, or Indonesia. The Human Rights Commission's investigation in 2001 had also found that TPVs contribute to stress and post-traumatic stress disorder (PTSD).[23] In 2008 TPVs were abolished, partly because of human rights objections, and partly because they were found to be administratively inefficient and expensive, requiring a complete reappraisal of the applicant refugee status at their expiration every three years. TPVs were reintroduced in 2014.[24]

Hassan was aware that the new class of visa did not guarantee him the security he had hoped for.

> In that time I was a TPV and I had a lot of problems … I stayed nine months in [detention] camp and when I was released I was working in a meat factory. (Hassan)

19   James Jupp, 'Politics, Public Policy and Multiculturalism', in *Multiculturalism and Integration: A Harmonious Relationship*, ed. Michael Clyne and James Jupp (Canberra: ANU E Press, 2011), 41–52, doi.org/10.22459/mi.07.2011.02.

20   Gwenda Tavan, 'The Dismantling of the White Australia Policy: Elite Conspiracy or Will of the Australian People?', *Australian Journal of Political Science* 39, no. 1 (2004): 109–25, doi.org/10.1080/1036114042000205678.

21   Moreton-Robinson, *The White Possessive*.

22   Jupp, 'Politics, Public Policy and Multiculturalism'.

23   Australian Human Rights Commission, *A Report on Visits to Immigration Detention Facilities*.

24   'Temporary Protection Visas', Asylum Seeker Resource Centre, 2018, available at: www.asrc.org.au/resources/fact-sheet/temporary-protection-visas/.

While Hassan worked through the three years of his TPV in an abattoir, his family in Jakarta were interviewed and identified as refugees, granted UNHCR refugee classification, and put on a waiting list to come to Australia. Hassan's TPV did not allow for family reunification, but his strategy was to earn enough to bring them to Australia – then, since they were already formally classified as refugees, his legal status would also change, under Australia's family reunification policy at the time. It was a good plan. It contained risks: his family's processing might take longer than he could stay in Australia on a TPV. His TPV might expire. He might fail the reapplication and get sent back to Afghanistan. But compared to what some individuals and families were able to organise, it was relatively secure.

> I was working there for three years. Since my family [were going to] come here, I thought I have to start some business because I was sure in that time, when my family come here the lawyer told us if one of us be a refugee, directly all family will be refugees. (Hassan)

This meant working 15-hour days in the abattoir to send money to his family, who still wanted more. The condition of his TPV that he found hardest was that it prevented him leaving Australia. He could not go to his family. While he was on a TPV he knew two men in similar visa situations who hanged themselves: it had become too hard, he explained, not having any power over their own lives, not being able to make decisions about the future, and not knowing if – or for how long – they would get to stay in Australia. With his family always on his mind, he sent money to Indonesia, as much as he could. His friends advised prudence, but he could not refuse his family.

> I remember my son messaged me from Indonesia. 'Dad, the money's finished.' As much I had, I send to them. Even Salmi's father – he's my best friend – like not friend, like brother – and he said, 'don't teach them like that'. I said, 'the only thing I can do for them is the money, nothing else. I can't go see them. I can't do anything. It doesn't matter, they will be happy, I will be happy'. (Hassan)

He worried about his family constantly. His own problems, uncertainty around his future, not knowing if he was going to get to stay in Australia or if he would be sent back to Afghanistan; if his visa would be refused, renewed or if he would attain permanent residency, all centred on his family, waiting in Indonesia. He phoned them every week. But time continued to pass, and after a while, his youngest daughter did not know who he was when he phoned. More than once he got in his car and drove to a quiet place where he could cry, without adding to the strain and tension he knew his roommates were also experiencing.

> My daughter was like five, six years old and when I was talking with her, it was hurt me, yeah. My wife, she crying at that time. I said, I can't do anything.

> [Years later] my daughter when she came here – one day I remember. I was driving and she said, 'Dad, when I …' she was in Jakarta and she thought she hasn't got any father. I told her, 'yeah, I was talking with you'. She said, 'yeah, I thought my Mum going to trick on me, give somebody else to talk like that'. It was very hard and I was crying that time. She said, 'why are you crying?' I said, 'don't say anything no more'. It hurt me seriously. (Hassan)

As in Salmi's story of being the daughter left behind, in Hassan's narrative the sadness came through clearly. The parallel narratives show both sides of the effects of the enforced family separation, as family members on both sides of the ocean waited hopefully for the TPV to expire, while dreading the other outcomes possible under the policy regulations.

On his release from Curtin, Jahan was put on a bus for a three-day journey across the country to Queensland. There he was able to take a 25-day English class donated to the newly arrived group of refugees by a private provider. The English teacher and his daughter found the refugees some paid work around their house, so they had some source of income. He stayed with a friend for a few months, and by March 2000 had found work in a factory as a process worker. Jahan was eager and excited for his life to begin – he could see so many possibilities, some of which were just about to become realities. He happily bought a Ford Festiva. He described his life as taking off. But his visa imposed limitations on him in terms of access to work and services – and the threatened penalties for breaching its conditions (being returned to detention) were very real.

> Um … here government as well says that you're not entitled to nothing. Because your visa is TPV, 788 or something. No … 785. Visa class. This is a piece of rubbish. You're not entitled to anything. So we might as well chuck it somewhere, somewhere in all the surf. (Jahan)

In 2003, Jahan ran into a legal quagmire. He had been on a TPV for three years and needed to submit an entirely new application. He had been given to believe that after three years his subclass 785 TPV would be automatically upgraded to a subclass 866 PPV – whether this was based on his arrival exactly coinciding with the shift from TPVs to PPVs is not clear. But the process dragged in time. He waited for his PPV to arrive – at first hopefully, since with it he would be able to live properly, which to him entailed enrolling in more English classes, finding longer-term employment and starting the family reunification process to bring his family over. The significance of these elements of a life properly lived came from the historical exclusion of Hazaras from education and work rights in Afghanistan. He had hoped that in Australia he would be able to live fully with the human rights of a recognised member of society. But time passed, and his visa did not appear. He waited more and more anxiously.

> 2003, I was very anxious. You know, waiting for that visa, you know, to come. It never came. Because, that 785 visa, it's preventing me from everything. I'm in Australia, but I'm sort of lost. I'm in Australia but I can't do anything. I'm in Australia but I can't study English. So that's everything is blocked here. I wanted to go to school to learn. Why I want to learn? Because in Afghanistan we've been suppressed, we've been depressed, we've been deprived of our rights, you know, to study higher education. (Jahan)

Finally, a letter arrived. Immigration had written to inform him that his entire claim for ongoing protection had been rejected, because he had missed an interview. He protested that he had never received the interview letter. Immigration insisted that it had been sent. Someone suggested that it may have been eaten by snails – which Jahan now, years later, has built into his story. Similar to the wild animals that had circled Curtin, this newest threat that might result in him being sent back to Afghanistan was represented by an animal force. The language in which he framed this threat locates it as a random, unpredictable event – even within the policy strictures that he had to follow, there was still room for the inexplicable and unexpected to happen.

> I don't know, [maybe] it's been eaten by a mouse, it's been eaten by snails, you know? (Jahan)

From here Jahan was required to lodge an appeal against the decision with the Refugee Review Tribunal (RRT). The complications facing asylum seekers lodging appeals with the RRT (and other versions of this tribunal in Europe and the UK) have been investigated and documented by numerous international scholars in refugee policy studies, including University of Geneva refugee specialist Michel-Acatl Monnier, Sri Lankan academic Professor E Valentine Daniel, John Knudsen at the University of Bergen and Professor Michael Welch in the Criminal Justice program at Rutgers University. Some of the issues facing refugees in these situations involve different cultural notions of credibility, where the different cultural meanings between looking someone in the eye and looking at the ground can have life and death implications.[25]

Jahan had a lawyer, who had helped him prepare a 25-page dossier documenting his protection claim. His documents were in order, his story checked out, and he won his case.

> Okay. When I went to RRT there was, a lawyer was representing my case as well. RRT generally – they say that they're impartial. But I can see that they're working straight under the hand of the government. Because that is another body set up from the government, by the government. They think that they are independent, but I don't think they are independent. Because all their words are so negative towards asylum seekers. Because many of the things they said is just people lying, you know. I don't know.
>
> And in fact there was a twenty-five page statement from my side, presented, sent on my behalf, to the RRT. Twenty-five pages. Am I here on murder trial on what? (Jahan)

The assumptions around credibility can be seen in the general disbelief towards refugee narratives that Jahan had felt in his tribunal hearing. He knew he was in the right, that he had come to Australia legally, his life in danger, and that it was a bureaucratic error that his claim had been rescinded. But there were mixed messages everywhere. The legal system declared first that he was a refugee and then that he was not. And the Australian Government's position around Afghanistan as a safe destination also changed. In 2003 the Australian Government had signed a memorandum of understanding with Afghanistan stating that Hazaras

---

25   E Valentine Daniel and John Chr Knudsen, *Mistrusting Refugees* (California: University of California Press Berkeley, 1995); Michel-Acatl Monnier, 'The Hidden Part of Asylum Seekers' Interviews in Geneva, Switzerland: Some Observations about the Socio-Political Construction of Interviews Between Gatekeepers and the Powerless', *Journal of Refugee Studies* 8, no. 3 (January 1, 1995): 305–25, doi.org/10.1093/jrs/8.3.305; Michael Welch, 'The Sonics of Crimmigration in Australia: Wall of Noise and Quiet Manoeuvring', *British Journal of Criminology* 52, no. 2 (2012): 324–44, doi.org/10.1093/bjc/azr068.

could now return safely to Afghanistan. But this formal agreement about Afghanistan's safety was not reflected in the reality that Jahan perceived. Thousands of Hazaras still held valid TPVs, which he saw as implicitly contradicting the government's position around Afghanistan's safety. And in this political context, where Hazaras were assured that they would be safe in Afghanistan, his case before the RRT was successful. His need for protection had been found to be legitimate. He was again classified as a refugee, which meant that he was – again – in the position of waiting for the PPV to arrive that would replace his TPV.

> And in fact the next day they sent me a letter that says, 'congratulations, you have been accepted as a refugee', you know? 'Your case is still valid.' (Jahan)

But by 2005 Jahan was still on a TPV. By now he had waited more than four years, and the prohibition on leaving Australia while on a TPV grew harder to bear as the years passed. He worried about his family left behind, and did what he could to send them money, and plan for their eventual reunion in Australia when he was granted a permanent visa. He had learned how Australian migration law worked – there was a time limit of five years in which he could apply for family reunification. But he could not apply for this while still on a TPV. He needed to wait until he was upgraded to a different visa. He had won his case at the RRT and should have been granted a PPV. His anxiety grew. The five years passed. It was too late.

> There is a migration clause that says that when you come here as refugee, within first five years you have to sponsor your family. After five years then you lose that privilege, you may no longer sponsor your family. So first five years you have the right to family reunion, after the first five years you forfeit that right. So from – I was initially told that within three years, you will be able to get your permanent visa. Then is stretched to four years, four and a half years.
>
> I did apply for family reunion, but under the TPV you got to understand, you don't have the right to apply for family reunion. It's only under the permanent 866 visa, that you have the right to apply for family reunion. So I lost the family reunion there. By the time when I become citizen it was already 2007. I got my citizenship, when I went to apply, they say, 'sorry, this no longer applies to you. Because you've forfeited that five years term'. And I could say nothing. But I think this is a discriminatory policy.

> Because whenever you make a policy, you make sure that the people who is being affected by that policy, it is fair, it is just, and it is catering to the people who is a minority in this society. (Jahan)

In 2007 he applied for citizenship and became an Australian citizen – but he had been unable to apply for family reunification. The snails and sharks of policy had got him. But he kept going. He could now work legally too, so he could send more money back to his family. His family were now living in Pakistan, since it hadn't been safe for them any longer back in the village. However, having his citizenship, which meant that he could both work and, now, study, was also the beginning of a time of exhaustion for Jahan. Working during the day and studying at night, his teachers would ask him, 'what's wrong with you?' He would show up exhausted, and sleep in lectures. But after two years he was awarded his diploma in business management.

Even though Jahan endured the five-year wait to bring his family over and was ultimately unable to, he presently locates himself as an immigrant success story. He has married in Australia, lives in Dandenong, owns a business and is involved in politics – he is happy and successful. But he also campaigns nonstop for the rights of refugees, particularly Hazaras. He has willingly shouldered the responsibilities of community advocacy that seem to accompany being a first-generation Hazara refugee migrant in Australia. His story, told with grace, humour and verve, illustrates the passion and intelligence he has brought to his own transition to an Australian Hazara identity. But underlying this is the responsibility, the Hazara need to give back, and the assumed responsibility for his people that characterises all the Hazara narratives in this piece. A communitarian sense of self prevents true happiness while other members of one's community are still suffering or in danger, which shows in Jahan's continual efforts on behalf of Hazara people.

Like Hassan's, Salmi's story ended more happily – after the five years of waiting in Pakistan, her family was reunited in Australia. This infused her construction of Australia as safe – both in terms of Australia itself, but also associated with the presence of her father:

> The feeling was really good and it was reassuring that we don't have to live away from my dad anymore and that we don't have to worry about anything else anymore. We are safe and everything is good and we're living with my dad. (Salmi)

Years later her father has continued to be a guiding presence in her life. He had always told her stories, a habit he had continued in their weekly phone conversations when she waited in Pakistan. When they were finally reunited, his stories spanned larger than his time in Australia, going back to the history of the Hazara people since the time of Abdur Khan; the social persecution and isolation of the Hazaras in Afghanistan, the exclusion of Hazaras from good schools, preventing their education; stories of Hazara women being sold for 20 paisa (less than one rupee); and other narratives that form part of modern Hazara political and cultural identity. In the context of her father's narrative, she was able to construct a political reading of her own forced abandonment by her father when she was six. This traumatic event, which scarred both father and daughter, would also become formative in Salmi's idea of herself as a force for change, influencing the choices she would make as she started to emerge as a community leader herself.

Hassan also described Australia as safe; though he longingly described Afghanistan as an absent mother. But it wasn't any longer a place where he could imagine raising a family. Hassan also framed his narrative as one of success, as he described the opportunities available to his children in Australia that there would not have been in Kabul.

> My country is like my mum. I can't change my mum with like a pretty girl because my mum is my mum. I know I love Australia for a lot of things. [There are] facilities here and it's safe here and I got a job here – everything is all right.

> I'm very happy, not only for myself, of course more for my family. My daughter, she is 18 years old now. She finished the school now. My son is around 25 and just last week he finished Uni and he studied as a civil engineer. If they had been in Afghanistan, no chance to study. (Hassan)

Conclusion: Lived effects of policy

Salmi, Hassan and Jahan all actively contribute to the creation of a popular understanding and social construction of Hazaras as one of Australia's newest migrant communities. This was a key motivation for all of them to speak with me – they are all invested in creating an image of Hazaras as desirable migrants in Australia. As part of this, and as part of their emergent migrant identity, they are also involved in the creation of a new migrant space within the Australian imaginary for Hazaras. This was demonstrated through their stories, but also through the embodied settings in which our interviews took place: the living room of Salmi's father's house, and in the various cafes around Dandenong where Jahan's social capital was demonstrated through his connections with his community. The embodied description of the interviewing process gives a sense of the relationships within the particular space of the interview: impelled by the shared motivation to communicate, their stories became a way of contributing to a more multicultural Australia as relationships and cultural differences were implicitly negotiated within the space of the interviews themselves.

All three interview participants described themselves as successful members of the Hazara community living in Dandenong. They all evinced a great deal of pride in Hazara culture in their narratives. But there was hardship in the narratives as well. Although both Hassan's and Salmi's fathers were able to reunite their families, they had to endure years of heartbreaking separation and backbreaking labour to do so. And Jahan was not able to achieve this goal. The limitations on his visa and the timeframe in which he was able to apply for family reunification clashed – and he was not able to reunite his family, which is a key desire that underscores many Hazara narratives.

These stories are also stories of the lived effects of policy. In all of these stories the Australian policy context provides an invisible structure that guides the course of their narratives. The trials the interview participants had to face were not just in the form of fleeing from their oppressors, negotiating with people smugglers and surviving the journeys over the sea. Australian immigration policy forms the context within which these narratives unfold. The progression of legal statuses attained by Hassan, Salmi's father, Salmi and Jahan describe the barriers and strictures that defined the choices available to them. In this way, the lived experiences described in this piece provide examples of the effects of policy on peoples' lives.

9

STEP BY STEP

The insidious evolution of Australia's asylum seeker regime since 1992

Savitri Taylor[1]

I have been thinking and writing about Australia's asylum seeker policies for over 25 years. When I started back in 1991, the asylum seeker policies now espoused by the major parties would have been inconceivable to most politicians on all sides – but here we are. Explaining how we got here requires me to start further back in time than 1991. It requires me to start, in fact, with the drafting of the founding document of the Australian political and legal system – the Constitution. From there, I consider two key features of contemporary asylum seeker policy – mandatory detention, which was introduced in 1992, and offshore processing, which was initially introduced in 2001. I end the chapter by reflecting on the lessons of our past for our future.

1   Associate Professor, Law School, La Trobe University. Part of this chapter is based on Savitri Taylor, 'How Did We Get Here? A Reflection on 25 Years of Australian Asylum Seeker Policy', *Law and Justice: La Trobe Law School Blog*, 25 February 2016, available at: law.blogs.latrobe.edu.au/2016/02/25/how-did-we-get-here-a-reflection-on-25-years-of-australian-asylum-seeker-policy/. Other parts of the chapter are based on earlier articles of mine as cited.

The original sin

The Australian obsession with immigration and border control pre-dates Federation, with a major motivator for Federation being the desire to achieve uniformity in such control across the Australian continent.[2] Constitutional enshrinement of parliament's unqualified power to legislate with respect to 'naturalization and aliens'[3] and 'immigration and emigration'[4] was taken as a matter of course through all the constitutional conventions from 1891.[5] By contrast, proposals made at those conventions to include due process and equal protection clauses in the Constitution were fervently and successfully opposed.[6] As Eve Lester explains in her excellent book, *Making Migration Law*, rejection of such clauses was:

> intended to ensure that the Commonwealth could discriminate on account of race and colour. This purpose is articulated by a number of delegates during the constitutional conventions, including Sir John Forrest and (most doggedly) Isaac Isaacs. Other delegates made clear their concerns that above all the provision should not prevent discrimination against non-Europeans.[7]

This was the original sin.

Mandatory detention

Julie Macken identifies the introduction of mandatory detention by the Labor Government as 'the stone that began the avalanche'.[8] Looking back over 25 plus years, I agree. What particularly struck me as I was reading Macken's piece was a quote from Neal Blewett's memoir, *A Cabinet Diary*. Neal Blewett, who was then minister for social security, had a meeting on

---

2   Mary Crock and Laurie Berg, *Immigration, Refugees and Forced Migration: Law, Policy and Practice in Australia* (Sydney: Federation Press, 2011), 24–26.
3   *Australian Constitution*, s 51(xix).
4   Ibid., s 51(xxvii).
5   Eve Lester, *Making Migration Law: The Foreigner, Sovereignty, and the Case of Australia* (Cambridge: Cambridge University Press, 2018), 115.
6   Ibid., 116.
7   Ibid.
8   Julie Macken, 'The Long Journey to Nauru', *New Matilda*, 12 January 2016, available at: newmatilda.com/2016/01/12/the-long-journey-to-nauru/.

30 March 1992 with Peter Staples, then the minister for aged, family and health services, and Gerry Hand, then the minister for immigration. In his diary entry about the meeting, Blewett said:

> A 9 pm meeting with Hand and Staples on the asylum-seekers' benefit. Hand wanted nothing to do with any ameliorative stance. He was for interning all who sought refugee status in camps, mostly at Port Hedland, where they would be fed and looked after. This is a nonsensical proposal – politically unsellable to the liberal constituency, impossible in practice (if any significant number of refugees took up the option his department would collapse) and financially irresponsible – if it worked it would cost more than the other options. It was obviously [Hand's] intention that if Staples provided an asylum-seekers' benefit, or I the charity option or a modified asylum-seekers' benefit, we would have to take responsibility for the measure. His left-wing mate Staples accused Hand of 'abdicating responsibility for his own shit'. So Staples and I decided to call his bluff and accept his lead as Immigration Minister. It will be interesting to see the cabinet response to his proposals.[9]

What Macken does not mention in her piece is that mandatory detention as we know it today was not introduced all at once; it was introduced bit by bit. In late 1989, Australia started experiencing its second wave of people arriving by boat (mostly Cambodian nationals). There were changes made to the *Migration Act 1958* (Cth) in 1989 that allowed immigration officials to detain 'illegal entrants' (as they were called at the time) until their immigration status was resolved and, as a matter of administrative policy, that is what happened. The next step was the one foreshadowed by Gerry Hand in his meeting with Blewett and Staples. In May 1992, the Labor Government, with the support of the Coalition, procured the passage of the *Migration Amendment Act 1992* (Cth). This legislation labelled the unauthorised boat arrivals as 'designated persons' and provided for their mandatory detention. In his second reading speech, Gerry Hand said that the legislation was 'only intended to be an interim measure' and was designed 'to address only the pressing requirements of the current situation'.[10] That original legislation also imposed a 273-day limit on the duration of detention, though there were circumstances in which the clock would stop ticking.

---

9   Neal Blewett, *A Cabinet Diary: A Personal Record of the First Keating Government* (Adelaide: Wakefield Press, 1999), 83.
10   Commonwealth, *Parliamentary Debates*, House of Representatives, 5 May 1992, 2370.

The most fateful step came with the passage of the *Migration Reform Act 1992* (Cth) in late 1992. The Act was passed with Coalition support and came into effect on 1 September 1994. It divided non-citizens into two categories: those with a visa (who were called 'lawful') and those without a visa (who were called 'unlawful'). It then provided that 'unlawful non-citizens' had to be detained until granted a visa or removed from the country. The 273-day time limit that applied to the previous version of mandatory detention was dropped. The legislation also introduced the bridging visa regime. Unlawful non-citizens who met certain criteria could be granted a bridging visa pending the granting of a substantive visa or departure from the country. The grant of a bridging visa made them lawful non-citizens and enabled their release from detention. The bridging visa criteria were such that if a person had become unlawful by overstaying they could get one with ease but if they had entered the country without a visa it was almost impossible to get one.

In 2004, the question of whether a person could be held in immigration detention indefinitely ended up before the High Court of Australia.[11] Mr Al-Kateb was a stateless Palestinian who was born and spent most of his life in Kuwait. He arrived in Australia without authorisation and thereby became an unlawful non-citizen subject to detention. After failing in his application for a protection visa, Mr Al-Kateb made a written request to be removed from Australia. However, the Department of Immigration[12] was unable to find any country prepared to allow him entry. The High Court majority (Justices Callinan, Hayne, Heydon and McHugh) held that the relevant provisions of the *Migration Act*, by providing that detention of an unlawful non-citizen must continue 'until' the occurrence of one of, at that time, three specified events (that is, grant of a visa, removal or deportation),[13] had the effect of unambiguously authorising the indefinite detention of unlawful non-citizens in the unfortunate position of neither qualifying for the grant of a visa nor, in practice, being removable/ deportable from Australia in the foreseeable future. Having decided the question of statutory interpretation, the majority judges had to consider whether the statutory provisions were, as argued by the appellant, constitutionally invalid. All four majority judges held that the provisions

---

11   *Al-Kateb v Godwin* [2004] HCA 37.

12   The Department of Immigration ceased to exist on 20 December 2017, with its functions being merged into the new Department of Home Affairs. The correct name at the time is used throughout this chapter.

13   A fourth specified event was added when the regional processing arrangements were introduced.

were constitutionally valid, being an exercise of the power conferred on the Australian Parliament by section 51(xix) of the Constitution to legislate with respect to aliens, which did not infringe the separation of powers between the parliament, the executive and the courts provided for by Chapter III of the Constitution.

Given that the minority judges (Chief Justice Gleeson and Justices Gummow and Kirby) were able to interpret the *Migration Act* provisions in favour of liberty for Mr Al-Kateb, the majority judges were, in fact, making an interpretive choice that hinged on their internalisation of the (white) nationalist ideology written into the Constitution itself. As Greta Bird points out, the language they used was telling.[14] For example, Justice Callinan (para. 301) referred to the undesirability of giving Mr Al-Kateb 'special advantages because he has managed illegally to penetrate the borders of this country over those who have sought to, but have been stopped before they could do so'. The majority judges were perfectly aware that the conclusion at which they had arrived was incompatible with human rights principles, but they insisted that any remedy lay elsewhere.

The mandatory detention regime was vigorously opposed from the outset by many civil society organisations. Increasing media scrutiny from 2000 also had an effect on public opinion.[15] In 2005, the then Coalition government introduced residence determinations (colloquially known as 'community detention') to appease members of its own backbench who had started rebelling against the harshness of mandatory detention.[16] The relevant *Migration Act* provisions – which are still in effect – give the minister for immigration a personal and non-compellable power exercisable 'in the public interest' to make a determination that a specified person is to reside in a specified place and comply with certain conditions instead of being detained in the manner usually required by the *Migration Act*.[17] The purpose of the power is to enable the de facto release[18] into

---

14 Greta Bird, 'An Unlawful Non-Citizen Is Being Detained or (White) Citizens Are Saving the Nation from (Non White) Non-Citizens', *University of Western Sydney Law Review* 9 (2005): 87–110.
15 Savitri Taylor, 'Achieving Reform of Australian Asylum Seeker Law and Policy', *Just Policy* 24 (2001): 41–54.
16 Savitri Taylor, 'Immigration Detention Reforms: A Small Gain in Human Rights', *Agenda: A Journal of Policy Analysis and Reform* 13 (2006): 49–62, doi.org/10.22459/AG.13.01.2006.04.
17 *Migration Act 1958* (Cth) pt 2 div 7 subdiv B ss 197AA–197AG.
18 As a matter of legal technicality, individuals subject to a residence determination are regarded as being nevertheless in 'immigration detention'.

the community of unaccompanied minors, families with children and particularly vulnerable adults. As at 26 April 2018, there were 457 people (including 180 children) in community detention in Australia.[19]

Another reform introduced in 2005 was the conferral on the minister for immigration of a personal and non-compellable power exercisable 'in the public interest' to grant any kind of visa the minister thinks appropriate to a person in immigration detention, even if the person does not fulfil the criteria for grant of a visa of that kind.[20] In November 2011, in the face of large numbers of so-called unauthorised maritime arrivals, the Labor Government started using this power to grant Bridging Visa Es to most of them[21] in order to relieve pressure on detention facilities. The Coalition Government continued the practice when it took office in September 2013. As at 26 April 2018, there were 18,027 unauthorised maritime arrivals (including 3,038 children) living in the Australian community on Bridging Visa Es.[22]

Despite the positive reforms made over time to law and policy, as at 26 April 2018, according to the Department of Home Affairs' statistics, there were 1,369 people (including seven children) in Australia's immigration detention facilities. They had been detained an average of 434 days with 264 people having been in detention for over 730 days.[23] As at 26 April 2018, the longest serving detainee had endured 3,970 days (i.e. over 10 years) in detention.[24] The fundamental problem remains the continued existence of the legal machinery of mandatory detention, with the non-compellable exercise of ministerial discretion being the only road out for many. Politicians, and the courts, have made it clear that this is a problem and a solution that remain within the purview of Australia's elected representatives.

19   Department of Home Affairs, *Immigration Detention and Community Statistics Summary* (Canberra: Australian Government Department of Home Affairs, 26 April 2018), available at: www.homeaffairs.gov.au/research-and-stats/files/immigration-detention-statistics-26-april-2018.pdf.

20   *Migration Act 1958* (Cth) s 195A.

21   Chris Bowen, 'Bridging Visas to be Issued for Boat Arrivals', media release, 25 November 2011, available at: pandora.nla.gov.au/pan/67564/20120320-0000/www.minister.immi.gov.au/media/cb/2011/cb180599.htm.

22   Department of Home Affairs, *Immigration Detention and Community Statistics Summary*.

23   Ibid.

24   Evidence to Senate Legal and Constitutional Affairs Legislation Committee (SLCALC), *Committee Hansard*, 21 May 2018 (evidence of Mr Outram, Australian Border Force Commissioner).

Offshore processing

From the legal device of 'excised offshore places' to the establishment of detention centres in other countries with which Australia has had colonial relationships, the history of offshore processing is vital to understand if we are to comprehend the fullness of successive Australian governments' approaches to managing the arrival of refugees.

Excision

In September 2001, in the wake of the *Tampa* incident[25] and in the shadow of the terrorist attacks in the United States, the Coalition Government with the support of Labor procured amendments to the *Migration Act* that defined Christmas Island, Ashmore and Cartier Islands and Cocos (Keeling) Islands to be 'excised offshore places' and allowed for the making of regulations designating other parts of Australia to be 'excised offshore places'. The 2001 amendments also specified that an unauthorised arrival who became an unlawful non-citizen by entering Australia at an 'excised offshore place' was an 'offshore entry person'. The amendments then went on to provide for two things. First, a purported visa application made by an offshore entry person who was an unlawful non-citizen in Australia was invalid unless the minister for immigration exercised a personal and non-compellable power to allow such an application to be made.[26] Second, an offshore entry person could be kept at an excised offshore place or taken to any 'place outside Australia', including a 'declared country'.[27]

In July 2005, regulations were adopted that effectively designated all parts of Australian territory with the exception of the mainland and Tasmania to be 'excised offshore places'.[28] In 2006, the Coalition Government tried to go a step further by extending the statutory bar on protection visa applications to all unauthorised maritime arrivals regardless of where they

---

25 In late August 2001, 433 asylum seekers were rescued from a sinking boat by the Norwegian freighter MV *Tampa*. The *Tampa* headed for Christmas Island, but was informed by Australian authorities that the rescued people would not be allowed to disembark there. The Pacific Solution was an outcome of the government's desperate attempts to resolve the ensuing standoff.

26 *Migration Act 1958* (Cth) s 46A.

27 These amendments were made by the *Migration Amendment (Excision from Migration Zone) Act 2001* (Cth) and the *Migration Amendment (Excision from Migration Zone) (Consequential Provisions) Act 2001* (Cth).

28 *Migration Regulations 1994* (Cth) reg 5.15C inserted by *Migration Amendment Regulations 2005 (No. 6)* (Cth).

first entered Australia. However, Australian civil society organisations mobilised successfully against the Bill intended to accomplish this purpose.[29] The Senate Legal and Constitutional Affairs Legislation Committee (SLCALC) inquiry into the Migration Amendment (Designated Unauthorised Arrivals) Bill 2006 received 137 submissions but only the Department of Immigration's submission supported the Bill.[30] The committee's majority report, written by government parliamentarians, recommended that the Bill should not proceed, or in the event that it did proceed, should be very significantly amended to respond to concerns raised during the inquiry and should include an 18-month sunset clause.[31] The minority and dissenting reports written by the non-government parliamentarians on the committee differed only in their refusal to contemplate an alternative to a complete abandonment of the Bill. The Bill passed the House of Representatives on 10 August 2006, but three government MPs crossed the floor and two abstained from voting.[32] Although the Coalition had a one-seat majority in the Senate, the prime minister was forced to withdraw the Bill when it became clear that at least one Liberal senator was willing to cross the floor to defeat it.[33]

The 'Pacific Solution'

By authorising the taking of 'offshore entry persons' to 'declared countries', the 2001 amendments to the *Migration Act* enabled the lawful implementation of the Pacific Strategy (colloquially known as the 'Pacific Solution') – or so it was thought at the time.[34] In the same year, Nauru and Papua New Guinea (PNG) were designated as declared countries after their governments had been persuaded to enter into Memoranda of Understanding (MoUs) allowing offshore entry persons to be taken to Australian-controlled facilities in their territory to have any protection

---

29   Savitri Taylor, 'Australia's Pacific Solution Mark II: The Lessons to be Learned', *UTS Law Review* 9 (2007): 106–24.

30   The Bill was introduced into the House of Representatives on 11 May 2006. On the same day, the Senate referred the Bill to the SLCALC for inquiry and report by 13 June 2006. The deadline for submissions was 22 May 2006. The submissions received by the inquiry are available at: www.aph. gov.au/Parliamentary_Business/Committees/Senate/Legal_and_Constitutional_Affairs/Completed_ inquiries/2004-07/migration_unauthorised_arrivals/submissions/sublist.

31   SLCALC, *Provisions of the Migration Amendment (Designated Unauthorised Arrivals) Bill 2006* (report, 2006), paras 3.208–3.217.

32   Ross Peake, 'Asylum Bill in Trouble as Senators Waver', *Canberra Times*, 12 August 2006, 3.

33   Ibid.

34   As explained in the next section, the lawfulness of the first iteration of the Pacific Solution was later cast into doubt by the High Court's decision in *Plaintiff M70/2011 v Minister for Immigration and Citizenship*.

claims considered by Australian Department of Immigration officers. It was Coalition Government policy that those found to be refugees would only be resettled in Australia as a last resort if no other country was willing to take them.[35]

The first iteration of the Pacific Solution remained in place from 2001 to 2008. During this period, 1,637 people were taken to Nauru or PNG.[36] One of them died and another 483 returned voluntarily to their country of origin.[37] The remaining 1,153 people were resettled in Australia (705), New Zealand (401), Sweden (21), Canada (16), Denmark (6) and Norway (4).[38]

The false spring

In February 2008 the newly elected Labor Government closed down the processing facilities in Nauru and PNG. In retrospect it seems to have done so only because the number of unauthorised boat arrivals had dwindled substantially since 2001,[39] leading Labor to believe that they were no longer a political problem. In 2009, unauthorised boat arrivals increased dramatically.[40] Most of those arriving on the boats fell into the definition of 'offshore entry persons' and therefore needed ministerial permission to make a visa application. The government took the boat arrivals to Christmas Island to have their protection claims determined there by the so-called Refugee Status Assessment/Independent Merits Review (RSA/IMR) process, which was a separate and inferior process to the protection visa application process. Only those found to be refugees were given ministerial permission to apply for a protection visa. In *Plaintiff M61/2010E & Others v the Commonwealth of Australia and Others*,[41] however, the High Court held that the RSA/IMR process was not lawful.

---

35 Savitri Taylor, 'The Pacific Solution or a Pacific Nightmare: The Difference between Burden Shifting and Responsibility Sharing', *Asian-Pacific Law and Policy Journal* 6 (2005): 1–43.

36 Janet Phillips, 'The "Pacific Solution" Revisited: A Statistical Guide to the Asylum Seeker Caseloads on Nauru and Manus Island' (Background Note, Parliamentary Library, Parliament of Australia, 4 September 2012), available at: www.aph.gov.au/About_Parliament/Parliamentary_Departments/Parliamentary_Library/pubs/BN/2012-2013/PacificSolution.

37 Ibid.

38 Ibid.

39 Janet Phillips, 'Boat Arrivals and Boat "Turnbacks" in Australia since 1976: A Quick Guide to the Statistics' (Research Papers 2016–17, Parliamentary Library, Parliament of Australia, updated 17 January 2017), available at: www.aph.gov.au/About_Parliament/Parliamentary_Departments/Parliamentary_Library/pubs/rp/rp1617/Quick_Guides/BoatTurnbacks.

40 Ibid.

41 [2010] HCA 41.

On 25 July 2011, Australia and Malaysia entered into a legally non-binding Arrangement on Transfer and Resettlement. The arrangement provided for the transfer to Malaysia of up to 800 persons arriving irregularly in Australia by boat after the date of signing. It also stated that, in exchange for Malaysia's assistance, Australia would resettle, over a period of four years, 4,000 UNHCR recognised refugees living in Malaysia at the time of signing. Minister for Immigration Chris Bowen then purported to make Malaysia a 'declared country' using the legal machinery created to implement the Pacific Solution.

Under *Migration Act* section 198A, 'offshore entry persons' could be taken to any country that the minister for immigration had declared, in writing, to meet three criteria: that it provided asylum seekers with access 'to effective procedures for assessing their need for protection' and protected them pending determination of their refugee status, that it provided protection to refugees pending their voluntary repatriation or resettlement, and that it met 'relevant human rights standards in providing that protection'. The orthodox interpretation of the provision at the time was that the minister's declaration did not have to be true as long as the minister believed it to be true. However, acting on behalf of a man who was to be transferred to Malaysia pursuant to the arrangement with that country, a team of pro bono lawyers coordinated by the Refugee and Immigration Legal Centre swung into action. The team, which had also been responsible for the successful *M61* litigation, challenged the orthodox interpretation of section 198A in the High Court and won.[42]

In *Plaintiff M70/2011 v Minister for Immigration and Citizenship*,[43] a High Court majority (Justice Heydon dissenting) held that section 198A required that a declared country, at a minimum, be bound under international law or their own national laws to provide the protections it specified to asylum seekers and refugees. Since Malaysia did not meet the minimum requirements of section 198A, the High Court's decision invalidated the declaration that the minister had purported to make in respect of it. The reasoning of the majority in *M70* cast retrospective doubt on the lawfulness of the Pacific Solution and prospective doubt on the government's ability to take asylum seekers to any country in which they would receive less protection than they would in Australia.

---

42 Caroline Counsel, 'M70 – The End of Offshore Processing?', *LIV President's Blog*, 2 September 2011, available at: www.liv.asn.au/LIVPresBlog/September-2011/M70-the-end-of-off-shore-processing.
43 [2011] HCA 32.

The decisions in *M61* and *M70* were read by some as a shift by a now differently composed High Court bench away from *Al-Kateb* and towards a more rights-oriented jurisprudence. And to some extent they were correct. However, because the shift was accomplished through the vehicle of statutory interpretation (i.e. purporting to give effect to the presumed intention of parliament), parliament was handed a trump card. Parliament could now continue to do the work of shaping legislation to circumvent the courts.

Back to the future

In March 2012, in the wake of its High Court losses in *M61* and *M70*, the Labor Government announced that it would no longer have a parallel processing system for unauthorised boat arrivals. Instead, it would lift the statutory bar on visa applications as a matter of course, enabling such individuals to apply for a protection visa from the outset.[44] However, Labor was not happy with the situation in which it found itself and, in June 2012, Prime Minister Gillard sought advice on how to 'stop the boats' from an Expert Panel.[45]

In its report released on 13 August 2012, the Expert Panel made 22 recommendations. One of its recommendations was that all unauthorised maritime arrivals, regardless of where they first entered Australia, should be prevented from applying for a protection visa. This was what the Coalition Government had unsuccessfully attempted to do in 2006. In response to the Expert Panel report, the Labor Government made the same attempt and succeeded. The *Migration Amendment (Unauthorised Maritime Arrivals and Other Measures) Act 2013* (Cth) entered into force on 1 June 2013.

The Expert Panel also recommended that the government should procure the passage of legislation overturning the High Court decision in *M70*. It promptly did so. The amendments made to the *Migration Act* by *Migration Legislation Amendment (Regional Processing and Other Measures) Act 2012* (Cth) give the minister for immigration the power to designate

---

44   Chris Bowen, 'New Single Protection Visa Process Set to Commence', media release, 19 March 2012, available at: web.archive.org/web/20120321130512/www.minister.immi.gov.au/media/cb/2012/cb184344.htm.
45   The panel consisted of a former chief of the Defence Forces, Angus Houston, a former secretary of the Department of Foreign Affairs and Trade, Michael L'Estrange, and an asylum seeker advocate, Paris Aristotle.

a country as a 'regional processing country'. *Migration Act* section 198AD provides that an unauthorised maritime arrival detained in the migration zone must be taken to a regional processing country unless the minister for immigration exercises a personal non-compellable power under section 198AE to exempt the person from being transferred.

Another two recommendations of the Expert Panel were to enter into new asylum seeker processing arrangements with Nauru and PNG.[46] The panel described the establishment of such arrangements as a 'necessary circuit breaker to the current surge in irregular migration to Australia'.[47] Again, the government implemented the recommendations with expedition and immediately thereafter the minister for immigration, acting under new *Migration Act* section 198AB, designated Nauru and PNG as regional processing countries in September and October 2012, respectively.

In the case of *Plaintiff S156/2013 v Minister for Immigration and Border Protection*,[48] the plaintiff tried to argue that *Migration Act* sections 198AB and 198AD were not supported by any constitutional head of power and were therefore invalid or, in the alternative, that the minister's designation of PNG as a regional processing country was not valid. The High Court held that sections 198AB and 198AD were supported by the 'aliens' head of power in section 51(xix) of the Constitution. It also held that the designation of PNG as a regional processing country was perfectly valid. This was just as well for the government, because it was clear that the standards of treatment received by the people transferred to Nauru and PNG had fallen egregiously short of human rights standards from the outset.[49] The decision in *S156* was an acknowledgement by the High Court that parliament had played the trump card handed to it in *M70*. It also underscored that, as intended by the drafters, the Constitution enabled parliament to deal with aliens exactly as it pleased.

---

46   The Expert Panel also recommended that the transfer provisions of the Malaysian Arrangement should be implemented, after the government had negotiated better human rights safeguards and accountability provisions with Malaysia. Theoretically, the minister for immigration could have done so after designating Malaysia as a regional processing country. However, any such designation would have been disallowed by the Senate because the Coalition opposed implementation of the arrangement for reasons that had more to do with political obstructionism than principle. By contrast, the Coalition had consistently advocated for a return to the Pacific Solution.

47   Expert Panel on Asylum Seekers, *Report of the Expert Panel on Asylum Seekers* (Canberra: Department of the Prime Minister and Cabinet, August 2012), para. 3.45.

48   [2014] HCA 22.

49   See Ken McPhail, Robert Nyamori and Savitri Taylor, 'Escaping Accountability: A Case of Australia's Asylum Seeker Policy,' *Accounting, Auditing & Accountability Journal* 29 (2016): 947–84, doi.org/10.1108/AAAJ-03-2014-1639 and sources cited therein.

On 19 July 2013, not long after replacing Julia Gillard as prime minister following an internal challenge, Kevin Rudd held a joint press conference with Peter O'Neill, the prime minister of PNG. At the press conference, it was announced that asylum seekers arriving in Australia by boat after that date would have 'have no chance of being settled in Australia as refugees'.[50] The MoUs with Nauru and PNG were subsequently updated to facilitate the implementation of what Rudd admitted was 'a very hard-line decision' intended to deter people smuggling.[51] I will return to this history of 'processing' in PNG and in Nauru below.

Operation Relex and Operation Sovereign Borders

In the aftermath of the *Tampa* incident, the Howard Coalition Government instituted Operation Relex to prevent unauthorised arrivals from entering Australian waters. Between October and December 2001, four vessels were intercepted at sea by the Australian navy and escorted back towards Indonesia.[52] The navy also attempted to turn back three other vessels in 2001. All sank at some point during the course of interception and were towed back towards Indonesia, though mercifully all but two of the passengers were successfully rescued. The fifth and final tow back of the Howard Government period took place in November 2003.[53]

The Abbott Coalition Government came into power in September 2013 on a platform that included a pledge to put an end to the resurgence of boat arrivals. Immediately upon taking office, the Coalition Government implemented the military-led Operation Sovereign Borders, which involved, among other things, the turn-back of unauthorised maritime arrivals to their most recent country of departure (usually Indonesia) or, in the case of those arriving directly from their country of origin, handing back to country of origin authorities. In theory, an exception is made for those found in a screening interview to have prima facie protection claims. Unauthorised maritime arrivals screened-in pursuant to this process are supposed to be taken to a regional processing country instead

50 Kevin Rudd, 'Transcript of Joint Press Conference', Press Office, Prime Minister of Australia, 19 July 2013, available at: webarchive.nla.gov.au/awa/20130730234007/pandora.nla.gov.au/pan/79983/20130731-0937/www.pm.gov.au/press-office/transcript-joint-press-conference-2.html.
51 Ibid.
52 Senate Select Committee on a Certain Maritime Incident, *Report of the Senate Select Committee on a Certain Maritime Incident* (Canberra: Parliament of Australia, 2002), para 2.74.
53 Savitri Taylor, 'Towing Back the Boats: Bad Policy Whatever Way You Look at It', *The Conversation*, 12 June 2013, available at: theconversation.com/towing-back-the-boats-bad-policy-whatever-way-you-look-at-it-15082.

of being turned back or handed back. Between the commencement of Operation Sovereign Borders and 21 May 2018, 800 people on 32 boats had been intercepted at sea.[54] Of those only two people had been screened-in – both in 2014.[55] In addition, 157 Sri Lankan passengers on a vessel departing from India, which was intercepted in late June 2014,[56] were transferred to Nauru on 2 August 2014 after a brief sojourn on the Australian mainland.[57] These individuals had not actually been screened-in; rather, Australia had tried but failed to convince Indian or Sri Lankan authorities to take them. In any event, the screen-in figures give rise to the strong inference that the screening process is, at best, unreliable or, at worst, cynical window-dressing.

The Nauru arrangement

As of August 2018, the arrangement with Nauru[58] means that 'unauthorised maritime arrivals' can be transferred to Nauru for processing of asylum claims by the Nauruan Government. As mentioned above, the most recent transfer took place in 2014. In theory, the processing centre in Nauru in which those transferred were detained until October 2015[59] and in which some still reside,[60] is run by the Nauruan Government. However,

---

54   Evidence to SLCALC, *Committee Hansard*, 21 May 2018 (evidence of Air Vice Marshal Osborne).
55   One passenger out of 41 arriving on a boat from Sri Lanka in late June 2014 was screened-in but elected to be repatriated with the others: Scott Morrison, 'Australian Government Returns Sri Lankan People Smuggling Venture', media release, 7 July 2014, available at: webarchive.nla.gov.au/gov/20140801014043/www.minister.immi.gov.au/media/sm/2014/sm216152.htm. Another passenger out of 38 arriving by boat from Sri Lanka in mid-November 2014 was also screened-in: Scott Morrison, 'People Smuggling Venture Returned to Sri Lanka', media release, 29 November 2014, available at: webarchive.nla.gov.au/gov/20141215053228/www.minister.immi.gov.au/media/sm/2014/sm219651. htm. Interestingly, Air Vice Marshal Osborne's evidence to the SLCALC on 21 May 2018 was that only one person had been screened-in during the period.
56   Department of Immigration, *Annual Report 2014–2015* (Australian Commonwealth Department of Immigration, 2015), 209.
57   Scott Morrison, 'Transfer of 157 IMAs from Curtin to Nauru for Offshore Processing', media release, 2 August 2014, available at: webarchive.nla.gov.au/gov/20141215053416/www.minister. immi.gov.au/media/sm/2014/sm216855.htm.
58   *Memorandum of Understanding between the Republic of Nauru and the Commonwealth of Australia, Relating to the Transfer to and Assessment of Persons in Nauru, and Related Issues*, signed 3 August 2013, available at: dfat.gov.au/geo/nauru/pages/memorandum-of-understanding-between-the-republic-of-nauru-and-the-commonwealth-of-australia-relating-to-the-transfer-to-and.aspx.
59   The processing centre in Nauru was made an open centre in October 2015: Joyce Chia and Asher Hirsch, 'Did "Ending" Detention on Nauru Also End the Constitutional Challenge to Offshore Processing?', *The Conversation*, 9 October2015, available at: theconversation.com/did-ending-detention-on-nauru-also-end-the-constitutional-challenge-to-offshore-processing-48667.
60   As at 21 May 2018, 253 people resided in the processing centre: evidence to SLCALC, *Committee Hansard*, 21 May 2018 (evidence of Ms Newton, Department of Home Affairs).

all the work is done by organisations contracted, instructed and paid by the Australian Government. These arrangements have been challenged by successive court cases. All, however, have failed, with the government changing the relevant legislation to deal with any breaches, or potential breaches, identified by the High Court.[61]

The PNG arrangement

Similarly, the current MoU with PNG[62] provides for the transfer of 'unauthorised maritime arrivals' to PNG for processing of asylum claims by the PNG Government. The most recent transfer to PNG took place in 2014.[63] As in the case of the processing centre in Nauru, the processing centre on Manus Island in PNG, which until recently was used to house those transferred, was run, in theory, by the PNG Government. However, as in the case of Nauru, all the work was done by organisations contracted, instructed and paid by the Australian Government.

On 26 April 2016, the PNG Supreme Court ruled that amendments to the PNG Constitution intended to enable the detention of those transferred at the processing centre were invalid and that such detention was therefore unconstitutional and illegal.[64] Following this, the PNG Government made the decision that the Manus Island processing centre would be closed. In April 2017, the two governments agreed to work towards a closing date of 31 October 2017. When this date came around, despite resistance by centre residents,[65] the foreshadowed closure of the Manus Island centre took place as planned.

---

61   See, for example, Nicole Hasham, 'High Court Finds Offshore Detention Lawful', *Sydney Morning Herald*, 3 February 2016, available at: www.smh.com.au/politics/federal/high-court-finds-offshore-detention-lawful-20160203-gmk5q6.html.

62   *Memorandum of Understanding between the Government of the Independent State of Papua New Guinea and the Government of Australia, Relating to the Transfer to, and Assessment and Settlement in, Papua New Guinea of Certain Persons, and Related Issues*, signed 6 August 2013, available at: dfat.gov.au/geo/papua-new-guinea/pages/memorandum-of-understanding-between-the-government-of-the-independent-state-of-papua-new-guinea-and-the-government-of-austr.aspx.

63   Evidence to SLCALC, *Committee Hansard*, 21 May 2018 (evidence of Air Vice Marshal Osborne).

64   *Namah v Pato* [2016] PGSC 13.

65   This resistance is described and its rationale explained in Behrouz Boochani, 'A Letter from Manus Island', *Saturday Paper*, 9 December 2017, available at: www.thesaturdaypaper.com.au/news/politics/2017/12/09/letter-manus-island/15127380005617.

Durable solutions?

The MoU with PNG provides that 'Transferees' recognised by it as refugees will be settled in PNG or elsewhere but not in Australia. As at 22 May 2017, only 38 recognised refugees had chosen to settle in PNG.[66] The MoU with Nauru also provides for the possibility that 'Transferees' recognised by it as refugees will be settled in that country, subject to the case-by-case agreement of the Nauruan Government. Thus far, however, the most that Nauru has been prepared to grant to those whom it has recognised as refugees is permission to remain in Nauru for 20 years.[67]

According to *The Guardian*:

> Over the past five years, Australia has approached dozens of countries – including Kyrgyzstan – offering millions of dollars and other inducements in exchange for resettling some refugees from Australia's camps.[68]

Thus far it has only had two successes.

On 26 September 2014, the Australian Government signed a four-year MoU with the Cambodian Government providing for the voluntary resettlement in Cambodia of people recognised as refugees by Nauru.[69] As at the time of writing, seven refugees had resettled in Cambodia[70] but four of them had subsequently returned to their countries of origin.[71]

On 13 November 2016, the Australian Government announced that unauthorised maritime arrivals, who had already been transferred to Nauru or PNG, would be considered for refugee resettlement in the

---

66   Evidence to SLCALC, *Committee Hansard*, 22 May 2017 (evidence of Ms Newton, Department of Immigration).

67   Department of Immigration, Answer to Question Taken on Notice AE17/213, Additional Estimates Hearing: 27 February 2017, available at: www.aph.gov.au/~/media/Committees/legcon_ctte/estimates/add_1617/DIBP/QoNs/AE17-213.pdf.

68   Ben Doherty, 'Australia's Refugee Deal "a Farce" after US Rejects All Iranian and Somali Asylum Seekers', *Guardian*, 8 May 2018, available at: www.theguardian.com/australia-news/2018/may/08/australias-refugee-deal-a-farce-after-us-rejects-all-iranian-and-somali-asylum-seekers.

69   *Memorandum of Understanding between the Government of the Kingdom of Cambodia and the Government of Australia, Relating to the Settlement of Refugees in Cambodia*, signed 26 September 2014, available at: www.refworld.org/docid/5436588e4.html.

70   Evidence to SLCALC, *Committee Hansard*, 21 May 2018 (evidence of Ms Geddes, Department of Home Affairs).

71   Erin Handley, 'Nauru Refugee Quietly Arrives', *Phnom Penh Post*, 25 May 2017, available at: www.phnompenhpost.com/national/nauru-refugee-quietly-arrives.

United States by officials of that country upon referral by UNHCR.[72] As at 21 May 2018, the United States had accepted 372 refugees for resettlement and actually resettled 249 of them (165 from Nauru and 84 from PNG).[73] However, it had also vetted and refused resettlement to a further 121 recognised refugees, including 70 Iranians.[74]

Since the recommencement of offshore processing, three refugees have managed to arrange resettlement for themselves in Canada.[75] Australia has so far resisted taking up a longstanding offer from New Zealand to resettle 150 refugees in case those resettled in New Zealand take advantage of the Trans-Tasman Travel Arrangement to relocate to Australia at a later date.[76] However, it has not entirely closed the door on the offer.[77]

As at 21 May 2018, 939 of the people, including women and children, transferred by Australia to Nauru were still in Nauru.[78] As at the same date, 716 of the people transferred by Australia to PNG were still in PNG.[79] A further 460 people, who had previously been transferred to Nauru or PNG, were in Australia after being brought there for the purpose of medical treatment.[80] Individuals in this last group are expected to return to Nauru or PNG as the case may be upon completion of treatment, though they often refuse to do so.

It is not clear exactly how many of the 2,115 people still subject to the offshore processing arrangements as at 21 May 2018 were recognised refugees. However, given the recognition rates of 87 per cent in Nauru

---

72   Peter Dutton, 'Joint Press Conference with the Prime Minister, Maritime Border Command, Canberra' [transcript], The Hon Peter Dutton MP Minister for Immigration and Border Protection, 13 November 2016, available at: web.archive.org/web/20170307202401/www.minister.border.gov. au/peterdutton/Pages/press-conference-with-the-minister-for-immigration-and-border-protection-maritime-border-command.aspx.

73   Evidence to SLCALC, *Committee Hansard*, 21 May 2018 (evidence of Ms Geddes, Department of Home Affairs).

74   Ibid.

75   Ibid. (evidence of Mr Pezzullo, Secretary, Department of Home Affairs).

76   Ibid.

77   Peter Dutton, 'Doorstop Interview, Parliament House' [transcript], The Hon Peter Dutton MP Minister for Home Affairs\Minister for Immigration and Border Protection, 24 May 2018, available at: web.archive.org/web/20180821025013/minister.homeaffairs.gov.au/peterdutton/Pages/Interview-Parliament-House.aspx.

78   Evidence to SLCALC, *Committee Hansard*, 21 May 2018 (evidence of Ms Newton, Department of Home Affairs).

79   Ibid. (evidence of Ms Geddes, Department of Home Affairs).

80   Ibid. (evidence of Ms Dunn, Department of Home Affairs).

and 74 per cent in PNG,[81] the majority would be. Even if the United States allocates the remainder of the 1,250 resettlement places it has put on the table, a large number of refugees will be left without the prospect of a durable solution in the foreseeable future.

A reflection

Australia did not get to where it currently is all at once but step by incremental step. Some of those steps were taken by Labor governments, others were taken by Coalition governments, but except for a period from 2004 to 2007 when the Coalition controlled both houses of parliament, the legislative steps at least could not have been taken without the support of non-government politicians. The most insidious thing about every step taken was that it became the new normal and brought the next step into the realm of conceivable. The upshot was that most politicians in the two major parties were able, at every crucial point along the 25-plus-year journey, to rationalise taking just that one step more for the sake of winning or at least not losing the ongoing struggle for political power.

It is possible through litigation to get Australian courts to adjudicate on the lawfulness of executive action and to award enforceable remedies for breaches of the law. As illustrated above, however, in the migration jurisdiction the usual reaction when the government of the day does not agree with a judicial decision is to seek passage of legislation overturning the decision as a precedent for the future. Usually, too, the government is able to muster the parliamentary numbers necessary to succeed in such attempts. The only scenario in which the courts have the upper hand is in the interpretation of the Australian Constitution. However, as interpreted by the courts, the Constitution does not place many limits on the executive government or the parliament. So far, just about everything that the government and parliament have done in relation to asylum seekers and refugees has passed the constitutionality test. My depressing conclusion is that the stain of Australia's original sin remains, tainting the present and future. Because of Australia's constitutional beginnings, Australians cannot rely on their existing legal and political structures to deliver them from evil.

---

81   Australian Border Force, 'Operation Sovereign Borders Monthly Update: October 2017', Australian Border Force Newsroom, 14 November 2017, available at: newsroom.abf.gov.au/channels/Operation-Sovereign-Borders/releases/a4e1949e-3a4b-4750-bc65-cda9b3a668d1. These percentages are from 31 October 2017, on which date the Australian Government stopped updating the statistics.

10

USES AND ABUSES OF REFUGEE HISTORIES

Klaus Neumann[1]

In recent years, scholars with an interest in the history of refugee policies have often noted the lack of historical analysis in discussions of current issues of forced displacement.[2] Such complaints are increasingly unfounded. In scholarly debates about displacement and protection, and in discussions about public policy, historians and their skills are now sought after rather than ignored. The discipline of history has become an essential part of what is variously called forced migration studies or refugee studies. This collection is but one of several recent edited books

---

1   The research for this paper was partially funded by the Australian Research Council (DP160101434). The research for and writing of this chapter was completed in 2018.
2   See, for example, Tony Kushner, *Remembering Refugees: Then and Now* (Manchester: Manchester University Press, 2006), 1; Philip Marfleet, 'Refugees and History: Why We Must Address the Past', *Refugee Survey Quarterly* 26, no. 3 (2007): 136–48, doi.org/10.1093/rsq/hdi0248; Peter Gatrell, 'Refugees – What's Wrong with History?' *Journal of Refugee Studies* 30, no. 2 (2017): 170–89. In 2006, Martin Jones analysed the profiles of staff and doctoral students of the four leading centres for refugee research at the time and found that only four out of 121 researchers self-identified as historians. See Martin Jones, 'Review of *Refuge Australia: Australia's Humanitarian Record*', *Refuge* 23, no. 1 (2006): 104 n. 21, doi.org/10.25071/1920-7336.21348. Many of those then writing about the silence of the historical profession, myself included, identified as historians and were busily contributing historical analyses to refugee studies; see, for example, Klaus Neumann, 'Refugees: The Silence of the Historians', *Age*, 11 June 2004, available at: www.theage.com.au/national/refugees-the-silence-of-the-historians-20040611-gdy0ic.html.

and special issues that attest to this trend.[3] Historians are also increasingly comparing and contrasting current and past responses to refugees. In 2018, for example, Pertti Ahonen and Tony Kushner compared British public responses to the 1938 German and Austrian refugee crisis with those to the mass arrival of refugees in Europe in 2015 and 2016.[4] While there is broad agreement that the origins of the current refugee regime lie in the early twentieth century, even historians specialising in earlier times have been able to convincingly relate their research to twenty-first-century questions. Elena Isayev, Benjamin Gray and Susanne Lachenicht, for example, have recently discussed practices up to two millennia apart, and highlighted the relevance of a study of responses to strangers in the ancient Greek and Roman worlds and in early modern Europe for a critical understanding of current issues.[5]

There are many reasons why historians investigate past responses to forced migration. Some do so because they expect their analyses to contribute to an understanding of topical issues or provide evidence in support of particular strategies for addressing these issues. Some believe that other historical developments need to be reinterpreted in the contemporary context of forced migrations. Others have identified refugee history as a field that thus far has attracted comparatively little academic research, and which therefore still offers plenty of opportunities for scholars to make their name. It is not my intention to deem some motivations worthier than others; rather, I wish to point out that there is a wide range of reasons that compel historians to be interested in refugee issues. By

---

3   Matthew Frank and Jessica Reinsch, eds, *Refugees in Europe, 1919–1959: A Forty Years' Crisis?* (London: Bloomsbury, 2017); Peter Gatrell and Liubov Zhvanko, eds, *Europe on the Move: Refugees in the Era of the Great War* (Manchester: Manchester University Press, 2017); Fernando Puell de la Villa and David García Hernán, eds, *War and Population Displacement: Lessons of History* (Brighton: Sussex Academic Press, 2018); J Olaf Kleist, ed., *History of Refugee Protection*, special issue, *Journal of Refugee Studies* 30, no. 2 (2017); Dan Stone, ed., *Refugees Then and Now: Memory, History and Politics in the Long Twentieth Century*, special issue, *Patterns of Prejudice* 52, no. 2–3 (2018).

4   Pertti Ahonen, 'Europe and Refugees: 1938 and 2015–16', *Patterns of Prejudice* 52, no. 2–3 (2018): 135–48, doi.org/10.1080/0031322x.2018.1433006; Tony Kushner, 'Truly, Madly, Deeply … Nostalgically? Britain's On–Off Love Affair with Refugees, Past and Present', *Patterns of Prejudice* 52, no. 2–3 (2018): 172–94, doi.org/10.1080/0031322x.2018.1433014.

5   Elena Isayev, 'Between Hospitality and Asylum: A Historical Perspective on Displaced Agency', *International Review of the Red Cross* 99, no. 1 (2017): 75–98, doi.org/10.1017/s1816383117000510; Benjamin Gray, 'Exile, Refuge and the Greek Polis: Between Justice and Humanity', *Journal of Refugee Studies* 30, no. 2 (2017): 190–219, doi.org/10.1093/jrs/few027; Benjamin Gray, 'Citizenship as Barrier and Opportunity for Ancient Greek and Modern Refugees', *Humanities* 7, no. 3 (2018): 72, doi.org/10.3390/h7030072; Susanne Lachenicht, 'Learning from Past Displacements? The History of Migrations between Historical Specificity, Presentism and Fractured Continuities', *Humanities* 7, no. 2 (2018): 36, doi.org/10.3390/h7020036.

comparison, *public* interest in the history of forced displacement tends to be prompted by the idea that history had either or both of two functions: to provide lessons and/or to make sense of the present.

Those looking for lessons expect historians to tell them about possible courses of action that ought to be avoided (because similar courses of action proved to be harmful or unsuccessful in the past), and others that should be pursued (because comparable approaches proved beneficial or were successful in earlier times). Such expectations are informed by the assumption that the past and the present are sufficiently similar to transfer insights gained by studying the former to the latter. Historians are partly to blame for this misconception. In order for their work to be considered socially useful, some of them refer to the past as if it were a repository of precedents.[6] The search for lessons is also guided by the illusion that human beings would be inclined to make rational decisions based on precedent if only they knew enough about the past. This is surprising because there is ample evidence to suggest that humankind has not been inclined to desist from repeating harmful courses of action.[7]

Many historians also claim that their discipline allows them to situate the present on a linear trajectory that reaches from the past to the future. Take, for example, the webpage of Monash University's History Program, which tells prospective students that 'historical studies tells us where we came from, who we are, and where we're heading'.[8] Or take the eminent social historian Peter Stearns, who, in a 1989 document published on the website of the American Historical Association, says: 'History helps us understand change and how the society we live in came to be … The past causes the present, and so the future'.[9]

***

6　For example, Jo Guldi and David Armitage, *The History Manifesto* (Cambridge: Cambridge University Press, 2014).

7　See, for example, Bill Fawcett, ed., *Doomed to Repeat: The Lessons of History We've Failed to Learn* (New York: William Morrow, 2013).

8　'History', School of Philosophical, Historical and International Studies, Monash University, available at: www.monash.edu/arts/philosophical-historical-international-studies/history.

9　Peter N Stearns, 'Why Study history?', *American Historical Association*, 1998, available at: www.historians.org/about-aha-and-membership/aha-history-and-archives/historical-archives/why-study-history-(1998). In the text published by the American Historical Association, the first sentence of this quote has been capitalised, but this appears to be a formatting error.

Narratives that supposedly tell us 'where we came from [and] who we are' are often used to underwrite particular policies and practices in the present. The more coherent and seamless the narratives are, the better they are suited for such a purpose. In Australia, the narrative that more than any other has been employed to shore up current responses to refugees and asylum seekers depicts Australia as a traditionally generous and compassionate society. Australian governments have repeatedly used this narrative domestically to suggest that current policies and practices ought to be seen as yet another instantiation of generosity and compassion, as if a break with a supposedly long-established tradition was inconceivable.[10]

The claim that Australia has *always* been generous and compassionate could also be used to dismiss criticism of specific instances in which Australia's approach is characterised by a lack of generosity and compassion. The following example illustrates this point. A report by the Special Rapporteur on Torture and Other Cruel, Inhuman or Degrading Treatment or Punishment, which was tabled at the 37th session of the United Nation's Human Rights Council (to which Australia had just been elected for three years) in February 2018, observed that, in response to the arrival of increasing numbers of irregular migrants:

> many States have initiated an escalating cycle of repression and deterrence to discourage new arrivals involving measures such as the criminalization and detention of irregular migrants, the separation of family members, inadequate reception conditions and medical care and the denial or excessive prolongation of status determination or habeas corpus proceedings, including expedited returns in the absence of such proceedings. Many States have even started to physically prevent arrivals, whether through border closures, fences, walls or other physical obstacles, through the externalization of their borders and procedures or extra-territorial 'pushback' and 'pullback' operations, often in cooperation with other States or even non-State actors.[11]

---

10   See, for example, in relation to Australian refugee and asylum seeker policies: Klaus Neumann, 'Oblivious to the Obvious? Australian Asylum-Seeker Policies and the Use of the Past', in *Does History Matter? Making and Debating Citizenship, Immigration and Refugee Policy in Australia and New Zealand*, ed. Klaus Neumann and Gwenda Tavan (Canberra: ANU E Press, 2009), 59–60, doi.org/10.22459/dhm.09.2009.03.

11   Nils Melzer, *Report of the Special Rapporteur on Torture and Other Cruel, Inhuman or Degrading Treatment or Punishment*, UN Doc A/HRC/37/50 (23 November 2018) para 7.

In conclusion, the report noted that the primary cause for the abuse suffered by migrants was neither migration itself nor organised crime, but rather states' growing tendency 'to base their official migration policies and practices on deterrence, criminalization and discrimination rather than on protection, human rights and non-discrimination'.[12]

It is common for the authors of such reports to be coy about the identity of state parties, and hence it is unsurprising that the report did not mention Australia. In fact, it did not name any of the 47 members of the Human Rights Council, which then included countries that have a human rights record far worse than Australia's, such as Kyrgyzstan and China. Yet Australia's foreign minister, Julie Bishop, felt sufficiently provoked by the report's veiled criticism to counter it by a reference to history:

> There are many who believe that what we have done in turning back the boats and imposing very strong border protection laws is the right thing to do … What we are doing is what every sovereign government should do – protect our borders and determine our immigration flows. Australia has one of the proudest records of bringing in refugees. Since the Second World War, 865,000 people have come to Australia on refugee and humanitarian visas. Every year we resettle 18,750 people on refugee visas. We've taken 12,000 additional refugees from Syria. It is a record that Australians should be proud of and it is certainly one that I am prepared to have scrutinised by the Human Rights Council and any other nation around the world.[13]

Bishop wielded history as a weapon, although she had not been called upon to respond to somebody else's interpretation of Australia's past. Her position is remarkably similar to that of some refugee advocates who have also suggested that Australia was traditionally generous. Rather than using a record of past generosity to gloss over current failings, or implying that strong border protection laws are a necessary corollary, some refugee advocates have characterised the present as an aberration, while otherwise agreeing with the kind of narrative offered by Bishop, and its patriotic premises.[14]

---

12 Ibid., para 66.
13 Julie Bishop, interview with Fran Kelly on *ABC RN Breakfast*, 27 February 2018, available at: www.foreignminister.gov.au/minister/julie-bishop/transcript-eoe/abc-rn-breakfast-interview-fran-kelly-0. Bishop responded to the report's advance unedited version.
14 For example, Klaus Neumann, 'Providing a "Home for the Oppressed"? Historical Perspectives on Australian Responses to Refugees', *Australian Journal of Human Rights* 9, no. 2 (2003): 1–2, doi.org/10.1080/1323238x.2003.11911103.

Elsewhere I have critiqued the idea that Australia has been traditionally generous when responding to refugees and asylum seekers, without, however, trying to suggest that the grand narrative about Australia's generosity needs to be replaced by one about Australian racism, fear of the other and lack of hospitality.[15] Here, I would like to take a different tack and briefly tell three stories that could disrupt grand narratives that tell us 'where we came from, who we are, and where we're heading'. They are also useless in that they don't provide ready-made lessons for the present.

***

As I began writing this chapter, newspapers around the world were drawing attention to the 80th anniversary of the Évian conference, which had been initiated by US President Franklin Roosevelt.[16] From 6 to 15 July 1938, the representatives of 32 countries – 10 from Europe, 20 from the Americas, and Australia and New Zealand – met in Évian-les-Bains on the shores of Lake Geneva to discuss the Jewish refugee crisis. The conference became notorious because it was spectacularly unsuccessful. The Dominican Republic, then led by the dictator and Hitler admirer Rafael Trujillo, was the only one of the countries represented at the French spa that offered to admit a contingent of Jewish refugees.[17] All other countries were determined to keep their borders closed, or at least not to increase their intake of refugees.

One statement more than any other has come to symbolise the supposed lack of compassion for refugees. The Australian delegate Thomas Walter White, the minister for trade and customs in the conservative Coalition Government of Joseph Lyons, said that: 'It will no doubt be appreciated also that as we have no real racial problem, we are not desirous of importing

---

15   Klaus Neumann, *Refuge Australia: Australia's Humanitarian Record* (Sydney: UNSW Press, 2004).

16   About the conference, see, most recently, Paul R Bartrop, *The Evian Conference of 1938 and the Jewish Refugee Crisis* (Cham: Palgrave Macmillan, 2018); Raphaël Delpard, *La conférence de la honte: Évian, juillet 1938* (Paris: Michalon, 2015); Jochen Thies, *Evian 1938: Als die Welt die Juden verriet* (Essen: Klartext, 2017). See also Wolfgang Benz, Claudio Curio and Heiko Kauffmann, eds, *Von Evian nach Brüssel: Menschenrechte und Flüchtlingsschutz 70 Jahre nach der Konferenz von Evian* (Karlsruhe: Loeper, 2008), which brings together a discussion of the Évian conference and a discussion of asylum in the early twenty-first century.

17   About the racism that informed Trujillo's decision, and the outcome of his offer, see Hans-Ulrich Dillmann and Susanne Heim, *Fluchtpunkt Karibik: Jüdische Emigranten in der Dominikanischen Republik* (Berlin: Ch. Links Verlag, 2009).

one by encouraging any scheme of large-scale foreign migration'.[18] These words are regularly quoted when the Évian conference is mentioned, particularly in the context of discussions about current responses to refugees and asylum seekers, not just in Australia. They are also prominently displayed at the Yad Vashem Holocaust memorial in Israel.

In Australia, at least, the position of the Australian Government at Évian was initially not widely perceived as problematic, not least because a critical account would have sat uneasily within a narrative emphasising 'traditional' Australian generosity. In 1976, New South Wales Liberal Senator Peter Baume said in the Senate:

> I cannot forget that in 1938 there was a conference at a town called Evian and that Australia was one of the few nations in the world willing to give entry permits to the refugees of those days ... We established then the kind of honourable tradition in matters of refugees of which I am very proud.[19]

More recently, however, embarrassment about White's words prompted Stuart Robert, a Liberal National Party politician who represents the Queensland seat of Fadden in Federal Parliament, to put forward a motion that condemned the indifference of White and the Lyons Government, and included an apology, although its addressee was not specified:

> Today this parliament, as representative of all political parties and the people of Australia, issues a profound apology and says sorry to the people for the indifference shown by the parliament in 1938 that worsened the impact of the Holocaust.[20]

The motion, which had bipartisan support, also suggested that a request be made to the Yad Vashem memorial authority to have the text of the parliamentary apology displayed next to White's words. The apology and the proposed plaque could be interpreted as an attempt to restore Australia's reputation as a caring nation, rather than as a form of symbolic reparation.

---

18   T W White, quoted in Intergovernmental Committee on Refugees, *Proceedings of the Intergovernmental Committee, Evian, July 6th to 15th, 1938: Verbatim Record of the Plenary Meetings of the Committee: Resolutions and Reports* (Chambéry: Imp. réunies de Chambéry, 1938), 20.

19   Commonwealth, *Parliamentary Debates* (hereafter: *CPD*), Senate, 19 October 1976, 1271 (Peter Baume). Baume made a similar claim four years later: *CPD*, Senate, 27 August 1980, 441 (Peter Baume).

20   *CPD*, Representatives, 26 March 2018, 2613 (Stuart Robert).

I would like to suggest that moral indignation about White's words, which are taken to be emblematic of Australian indifference towards the plight of German and Austrian Jewish refugees, usually thwarts a closer look at what happened at Évian and in its aftermath. What could such a look entail? For a start, it should be remembered that the delegates at Évian could not have known what we know today, namely that 6 million Jews were murdered in the Holocaust. Unlike most of today's public commentators writing about the Évian conference, contemporary observers did not believe that the situation of Jews in Germany was the only pressing issue. A preliminary report published by John Hope Simpson in July 1938 to inform international diplomatic discussions identified the 'imminent danger of new refugee movements'.[21] He did not only have Germany and Austria in mind but also countries in Eastern Europe, particularly Poland and Romania, whose governments were openly anti-Semitic, and Spain. Hope Simpson did not believe that large-scale international resettlement schemes were a realistic answer to the situation in Eastern and South-Eastern Europe.

White represented Australia at Évian not because he was responsible for Australia's immigration policy but because he happened to be in Europe at the time as part of a high-level delegation that tried to negotiate a new trade deal with the United Kingdom. While it is true that some of those responsible for Australian refugee policies and some key staff in the relevant government agency, the Department of the Interior (the immediate predecessor of the Department of Immigration), were anti-Semitic, the same could not be said of White. It is also true that the government of avowed pacifist Joseph Lyons supported an appeasement strategy towards the German Reich, but White himself was not in favour of appeasement.[22] He was also not a sympathiser of Nazi Germany. Before arriving in Évian, he toured Germany as a guest of the German Government 'to learn something of its present state under the Hitler regime', as he put it in his diary.[23] He admired the new Tempelhof airport and enjoyed a night at the opera, but otherwise was appalled by what he recognised as signs of a ruthless dictatorship. In a letter after his return to Australia, White

---

21 John Hope Simpson, *Refugees: Preliminary Report of a Survey* (London: Royal Institute of International Affairs, 1938), 190.
22 Christopher Waters, *Australia and Appeasement: Imperial Foreign Policy and the Origins of World War II* (London: I.B. Tauris, 2012), 94.
23 Thomas Walter White, '1938 Overseas Diary TWW', entry for 1 July 1938, Sir Thomas Walter White papers, National Library of Australia MS 9148, series 7, folder 41.

wrote that Germany was marked by 'regulations, restrictions, uniforms and hidden terrorism'.[24] His observations contrasted with those of his United Australia Party and Cabinet colleague Robert Menzies, whose views of the Nazi regime were ambivalent; he too had been a member of the Australian trade delegation in the United Kingdom and had visited Germany in July 1938.[25]

In his speech at the Évian conference, White said that Australia would not admit additional migrants from Europe, but as chair of the Sub-Committee on the Reception of Those Concerned with the Relief of Political Refugees from Germany including Austria, he sought the views of NGOs assisting refugees. The document that reports the findings of that sub-committee recognised that the situation of German and Austrian Jews was desperate.

White attended only the first four days of the 10-day diplomatic gathering at Évian and then returned to Australia; he had no direct say in the outcome of the conference. In any case, White was not the driving force behind Australia's eventual response to the persecution of German and Austrian Jews. The man who more than anybody else influenced that response was the former Australian prime minister and then high commissioner in London, Stanley Melbourne Bruce. He had represented Australia at the League of Nations and would have been a more obvious choice as leader of the Australian delegation. He too visited Évian in the second week of July 1938 – not in an official capacity but 'incognito', to consult with Alfred Stirling, a senior London-based diplomat who led the Australian delegation after White's departure. It is not known what Stirling and Bruce discussed.

Three months before the Évian conference, Bruce had warned the Australian Government to avoid gestures that might encourage mass expulsions of Jews from Eastern European countries.[26] However, in November 1938, a couple of weeks after the Reichskristallnacht pogroms in Germany and Austria, he convinced the Australian Government (which by then

---

24   White to Atchison, 10 October 1938, quoted in Christopher Waters, 'Understanding and Misunderstanding Nazi Germany: Four Australian Visitors to Germany in 1938', *Australian Historical Studies* 41, no. 3 (2010): 375, doi.org/10.1080/1031461x.2010.493950.

25   See Waters, 'Understanding and Misunderstanding Nazi Germany', 348–69; Rowan Cahill, 'A Forgotten Address', *Overland*, 15 June 2017, available at: overland.org.au/2017/06/a-forgotten-address/.

26   Stanley Melbourne Bruce to Prime Minister of Australia, 5 April 1938, National Archives of Australia (hereafter: NAA) A981, REF 4 PART 1.

no longer included White) to announce the establishment of a quota for refugees.[27] Bruce wanted a quota of 30,000 over three years; the Lyons Government agreed to half that number. While the government's instructions about the composition of that quota were problematic,[28] the quota itself was comparatively generous – not in relation to the overall need for resettlement places, but when compared with the number of German and Austrian refugees admitted in other non-European countries such as Canada and New Zealand. The decision of the Lyons Government in 1938 also compares favourably with the Australian response to other refugee crises, including the Syrian refugee crisis of 2015.[29]

A nuanced account that highlights the contradictory behaviour of historical actors, does not view the past through the telescope of the present and is attentive to the possibility that much of the past is unknowable, has little value for commentators who winnow the past for lessons or are primarily interested in genealogies. A simplistic narrative about the Évian conference allows the drawing of parallels between Western nations' responses to refugees in 1938, and the global North's response to refugees in the past few years. The Évian conference is interpreted as a precedent with catastrophic consequences, suggesting that the global North's current policies of containment and deterrence might have similar results. Such a narrative implies that those meeting at Évian were somehow responsible for the Holocaust. While the governments of some of the countries represented at Évian – for example, France and Hungary – later aided and abetted in the Jewish genocide, it was Germany, rather than the 32 countries that sent delegations to Évian, that was responsible for the Holocaust.

***

27   Stanley Melbourne Bruce to Prime Minister of Australia, 21 November 1938, NAA A433, 1943/2/46. White had resigned as minister on 8 November 1938, after learning that he had been demoted in a Cabinet reshuffle. See John Rickard, 'White, Sir Thomas Walter (1888–1957)', *Australian Dictionary of Biography*, 2002, available at: adb.anu.edu.au/biography/white-sir-thomas-walter-12013.

28   See Klaus Neumann, *Across the Seas: Australia's Response to Refugees: A History* (Melbourne: Black Inc., 2015), 38–39.

29   In 2015, the Abbott Government agreed to the resettlement of 12,000 refugees from Syria and Iraq – comparatively fewer than the 15,000 refugees over three years announced in 1938, both when considering the number of Syrians requiring resettlement (compared to the number of Austrians and Germans requiring resettlement in 1938), and when considering the size of the Australian population in 1938, compared to its size in 2015.

Countries in the global North have long tried to draw on colonies or former colonies to warehouse refugees. For example, since at least 2004, Italian governments have tried to reach agreements with their Libyan counterparts to prevent migrants in Libya from crossing the Mediterranean. As a result of the most recent agreement, signed between Italy and its former colony on 2 February 2017 and subsequently backed by the European Union, Italy has trained and funded Libyan militias to operate a so-called coastguard to intercept migrants at sea and return them to Libya, where they are kept in detention centres and exposed to human rights violations, including murder, rape and torture.[30] There are other examples. In 1940 the British deported Jewish refugees from Palestine to Mauritius.[31] In 1972 the Heath Government was hoping to be able to settle Indian Ugandan refugees in the Solomon Islands.[32] The US Government has used its Cuban possession Guantanamo Bay to detain Haitian and Cuban refugees.[33] The most infamous recent example is that of Australia, and its use of two former territories, Papua New Guinea and Nauru, to establish so-called regional processing centres to incarcerate asylum seekers and refugees.

Much like Thomas Walter White's much-quoted sentence about his government's decision not to invite large-scale immigration has been used to establish a genealogy reaching from 1938 via 1992 (the introduction of mandatory detention) and 2001 (the *Tampa* affair) to the present, a line might be drawn from the exploitation of formerly phosphate-rich Nauru under Australian colonial rule to the use of impoverished postcolonial Nauru as a kind of twenty-first-century penal colony.[34] In this genealogy,

---

30   Andrea de Guttry, Francesca Cappone and Emanuele Sommario, 'Dealing with Migrants in the Central Mediterranean Route: A Legal Analysis of Recent Bilateral Agreements Between Italy and Libya', *International Migration* 56, no. 3 (2018): 44–60, doi.org/10.1111/imig.12401. The Italian approach has to be seen within broader European attempts to prevent irregular migrants from reaching Europe and to set up facilities to hold, and possibly process, non-European asylum seekers in countries outside Europe. See David Scott FitzGerald, *Refuge Beyond Reach: How Rich Democracies Repel Asylum Seekers* (New York: Oxford University Press, 2019), Chapter 9, doi.org/10.1093/oso/9780190874155.001.0001.
31   Geneviève Pitot, *Le shekel mauricien: L'histoire des détenus juifs à l'île Maurice: 1940–1945* (Port Louis: Vizavi, 2014).
32   Klaus Neumann, '"Our Own Interests Must Come First": Australia's Response to the Expulsion of Asians from Uganda', *History Australia* 3, no. 1 (2006): 10.12, doi.org/10.2104/ha060010.
33   Azadeh Dastyari, *United States Migrant Interdiction and the Detention of Refugees in Guantánamo Bay* (Cambridge: Cambridge University Press, 2015), doi.org/10.1017/cbo9781316181584.
34   For a recent example, see Julia C Morris, 'Violence and Extraction of a Human Commodity: From Phosphate to Refugees in the Republic of Nauru', *The Extractive Industries and Society* 6, no. 4 (2019): 1122–33, doi.org/10.1016/j.exis.2019.07.001.

Nauruans feature only as extras: they are coerced into surrendering their island to allow the mining of phosphate, and have little choice but to agree to Australia's request to accommodate asylum seekers and refugees, now that Nauru's assets have been depleted. Here, I would like to disrupt this genealogy with a story featuring Nauruan agency and Australia's willingness to take responsibility for the displacement of the atoll's population.

In 1960, Dudley McCarthy, a senior Australian bureaucrat, visited Nauru to reassure Nauruans that Australia would find a new home for them once Nauru's phosphate had been exhausted (and the atoll had become uninhabitable as a result of the mining operations).[35] He told representatives of the then 2,600 indigenous Nauruans on behalf of the Australian Government:

> We ask you to live with us; to become part of us and to allow us to become part of you; to accept completely and absolutely without reservations of any kind all the privileges which we ourselves achieved with painful struggle for our own people; to share with us common responsibilities; to build your homes on our land without restriction as to how much of that land you can ultimately acquire for yourselves as individuals except the restrictions which are imposed by the system of justice which we will share and by the abilities of each individual; to make complete and unrestricted use of all our centres of learning and development; to accept the opportunity to gain for yourselves the highest offices in our country; to rest as securely under our protection as the most powerful and the most humble of our own people alike rest securely; to mix your blood with ours if you wish; to inherit with us everything of which we ourselves are the inheritors.[36]

He also assured his audience that 'You can preserve your traditions or national pride in any proper ways which seem fit to you'.[37] In his speech, he mentioned neither Australian citizenship and the means of acquiring it nor a values statement that immigrants would be required to sign. He did not refer to the protracted process that is designed to select only the most

35　The following draws on Neumann, *Across the Seas*, 182–87, and Gil Marvel Tabucanon and Brian Opeskin, 'The Resettlement of Nauruans in Australia', *Journal of Pacific History* 46, no. 3 (2011): 337–56, doi.org/10.1080/00223344.2011.632992.
36　'Minutes of a special meeting of the Nauru Local Government Council with the Acting Administrator and D. McCarthy … on Monday, 5th December, 1960', NAA A452, 1961/3157 PART 1, p. 6.
37　Ibid., p. 7.

suitable among the refugees who want to settle in Australia. Instead he said: 'We ask you … to become part of us *and to allow us to become part of you*'.

The Nauruans were then considered to be prospective environmental refugees (although that term was not yet being used). In more recent times, the Australian Government has rejected suggestions that it would be responsible for resettling Pacific Islanders – such as the inhabitants of the island nations of Nauru, Tuvalu and Kiribati – if they were to become displaced due to rising sea levels. Back in 1962, however, Australian Prime Minister Robert Menzies told Queensland Premier Frank Nicklin:

> The availability of a source of cheap rock phosphate at Nauru has been of very great importance to the primary industries of Australia, the United Kingdom and New Zealand and there is a clear obligation on the Governments of these countries to provide a satisfactory future for the Nauruans.[38]

In 1963 the Menzies Government offered to resettle the Nauruans on Curtis Island, whose land area is well in excess of that of Nauru and which is within easy reach of the Queensland town of Gladstone. The government was not deterred by opposition to its plans from both Australians then living on Curtis Island and the Queensland Government. It was not swayed either by the prospect of breaching the then still sacrosanct White Australia policy. The following year, Cabinet authorised the purchase of Curtis Island, and agreed that the Commonwealth's powers under sections 51 and 52 of the Constitution be used to acquire the land if the Queensland Government was not willing to sell it. The Nauruans, however, wanted more than the resettlement Dudley McCarthy had offered them: they also insisted on political sovereignty. This was not something the Menzies Government was willing to countenance, and therefore, much to its surprise, the deal fell through.

***

In 2004, the Melbourne *Age* published a feature article by writer and filmmaker Paul Berczeller that promised to tell 'the real story behind Steven Spielberg's *The Terminal*'.[39] In that film, Tom Hanks plays Viktor

---

38   Menzies to Nicklin, 22 January 1962, NAA A452, 1961/3157 PART 1.
39   Paul Berczeller, 'A Man in Limbo', *Age*, 13 September 2004, A3, 1 and 4–5. The *Age* feature was first published in the *Guardian* (Paul Berczeller, 'The Man who Lost his Past', *Guardian*, 6 September 2004, available at: www.theguardian.com/film/2004/sep/06/features.features11).

Navorski, a citizen of the fictive Eastern European Republic of Krakhozia, who arrives at John F. Kennedy Airport in New York only to find that events in his home country have rendered him stateless, and prevent him from either returning home or entering the United States.[40] Navorski is then forced to spend nine months in the airport's transit area. The *Age* article revealed that the film was based on a real story, that of Iranian man Merhan Karimi Nasseri, who spent 18 years in the transit area of Charles De Gaulle Airport near Paris.[41]

Nasseri's story had been told many times before, in feature films, documentaries and magazine articles, including in Berczeller's own film *From Here to Where*.[42] The *Age* editor responsible for placing Berczeller's article may not have remembered Nasseri's case; he obviously did not recall either that 13 years earlier another man had spent several months in the transit lounges of airports in Asia, Europe and South America because of a botched Australian attempt to deport him.

On 18 February 1991, the Australian authorities deported a Cuban national by the name of Francisco Vazquez, who, four years earlier, had been sentenced to two years in prison for assault.[43] In one sense, the case – the criminal deportation of a non-citizen – is hardly noteworthy. But there were several complicating factors. First, Vazquez had been resettled in Australia as a refugee. Second, the Cuban authorities were unwilling to take him back. And third, Vazquez was fearful of being deported to Cuba. The immigration department, however, was not troubled by these complications. 'He was deported as a criminal and he has to take his chances', a spokesman for the department told a journalist. 'Deporting someone doesn't necessarily mean we deport them to another country. We put them on an aircraft and having left, the book is closed.'[44]

---

40   *The Terminal* [film], directed by Steven Spielberg (United States of America: 2004).

41   The story has been told in: Sir Alfred Mehran and Andrew Donkin, *The Terminal Man* (London: Corgi, 2004).

42   *From Here to Where* [film], directed by Paul Berczeller (Netherlands, 2002). The first feature film about Nasseri appeared in 1993 (*Tombés du ciel* [film], directed by Philippe Lioret (France, 1993)).

43   The following draws on Klaus Neumann and Savitri Taylor, '"He has to Take his Chances": The Resettlement of a Refugee in Australia and his Deportation to the Country he had Fled, 1980–1992', *History Australia* 16, no. 3 (2019): 459–79, doi.org/10.1080/14490854.2019.1636672.

44   Quoted in Janet Fife-Yeomans, 'Deportee Faces Life of Endless Airports', *Sydney Morning Herald*, 7 March 1991.

Vazquez was booked to fly from Sydney to Havana via Singapore and Moscow. In Moscow, the authorities refused to let Vazquez board a plane to Cuba, and returned him to Singapore. The Australians then booked him on another flight to Havana, this time via Rome and Madrid. He got as far as Madrid, and then returned to Rome, where he was issued with a new ticket to Cuba, this time via Caracas. When that attempt also failed, the Italian authorities compelled Singapore Airlines to return Vazquez to Singapore, where he arrived on 2 March. He was not allowed to leave the airport, as the Singaporean immigration authorities did not deem him to possess the required travel document.

For the next four months, the Singaporean and Australian governments argued over whose responsibility Vazquez was. On 22 May, Singapore's immigration department instructed Singapore Airlines to return Vazquez to Australia. As the Australian Department of Immigration served notice on the airline 'not to move the aircraft unless Mr Vazquez "is on that plane for the purposes of his removal out of Australia"', Singapore Airlines flew Vazquez back to Singapore on the same day.[45]

On 7 June, Singapore gazetted regulations that made it possible to ground a plane at Singapore Airport, if its captain refused to take on board a passenger whom the airline in question had previously brought to Singapore without authorisation. In Australia, both sides of politics were alarmed by the prospect that these regulations would be used to procure the return of Vazquez to Australia on a Qantas flight. On 13 June 1991, Shadow Minister for Immigration Philip Ruddock released a media statement in which he said:

> This action by the Singaporean Government puts Australia's deportation laws at grave risk. There is a provision in our law for criminal deportation for those who are found guilty of serious offences committed here in Australia. If we are forced, by other countries, to accept them back into Australia, our whole system of control is jeopardised.[46]

At the time of passage of the Singaporean regulations, the Migration Amendment Bill 1991 was before the Senate, awaiting resumption of the second reading debate. According to Gerry Hand, the immigration

---

45   High Commission of the Republic of Singapore to Department of Foreign Affairs and Trade Canberra, 29 May 1991, Annex, NAA A9737, 1991/1765 PART 1.
46   Philip Ruddock, 'Double Jeopardy', media statement, 13 June 1991, available at: parlinfo.aph. gov.au/parlInfo/download/media/pressrel/HPR02004731/upload_binary/HPR02004731.pdf.

minister in the Hawke Government, the new legislation was part of a 'continuing process of fine tuning the major and far-reaching reforms' made by the *Migration Legislation Amendment Act 1989*.[47] The 1989 Act had replaced a system of largely discretionary decision-making to minimise the scope for judicial intervention.

The immigration department, after being made aware of Singapore's intention to return Vazquez, saw the opportunity to amend the Migration Amendment Bill then before parliament to have legislation in place designed to ensure his detention upon arrival in Australia. On 21 June, the second reading debate on the Migration Amendment Bill 1991 resumed in the Senate, with the government moving amendments in anticipation of Vazquez's return. The Explanatory Memorandum tabled with the Senate amendments justified them as follows:

> The Government is ... concerned about certain persons who have been deported from Australia under the Act and who may be returned by the authorities of another country to Australia ... It is intended that these persons should not be capable of using judicial review to secure their release and entry into the Australian community.[48]

In the House of Representatives, Philip Ruddock announced that the federal opposition 'enthusiastically endorse[d]' the Senate amendments and the 'Government's intention to send a clear signal that Australia has control over its own borders'.[49] He also offered the opposition's support for further amendments 'to limit the capacity of the courts to make decisions in that area'.[50] For the Australian Democrats, its leader Janet Powell also supported the amendments 'in recognition of the need for the Government to be in control of the question of who does or does not enter this country'.[51] The Bill was amended as proposed, and passed on 21 June.

When Singapore returned Vazquez to Australia on 9 July 1991, the new legislation allowed for Vazquez's detention until his departure from Australia. 'Technically, Mr Vazquez has not re-entered Australia',

---

47   *CPD*, Representatives, 17 April 1991, 2846 (Gerry Hand).
48   Supplementary Explanatory Memorandum, Migration Amendment Bill 1991.
49   *CPD*, Representatives, 21 June 1991, 5269 (Philip Ruddock).
50   Ibid., 5270.
51   *CPD*, Senate, 21 June 1991, 5294 (Janet Powell).

a representative of the immigration department was quoted as saying.[52] The government lobbied Spain, the United States and Venezuela to accommodate Vazquez, but its requests were knocked back. Vazquez himself unsuccessfully applied to be admitted for residence to Spain, Argentina, Uruguay, Costa Rica, Colombia and Ecuador. In September 1991 he went on hunger strike. He sent a note to his solicitor saying: 'I cry for help, can you save me?'[53] She could not. In early 1992, the government was eventually successful in persuading Cuba to agree to the return of its citizen. On 21 February 1992, Vazquez flew out of Sydney on travel documents provided by Cuba, reaching Havana two days later.

There had been no public outcry when Vazquez was kept in prison for more than two years after serving his sentence, while the government was trying to secure his deportation, nor when he was deported in February 1991, and then returned to Long Bay Gaol in July 1991. His deportation in February 1992 was barely noted. His status as somebody who had come to Australia as a refugee seemed to amount to little, at least in public debate.

The story of Francisco Vazquez draws attention to an aspect of the prerogative that the government ought to decide whether a non-citizen may enter the country or remain in it, that has been comparatively uncontroversial. Vazquez's story would not easily lend itself to be turned into a Hollywood movie – or an ABC miniseries, for that matter. Yet from today's vantage point, the response to Vazquez is still surprising. He came to Australia as a refugee, and was to be returned to a communist country at a time when the Cold War was not yet just a distant memory. Is it not surprising that his case – and, in particular, the amendment of legislation specifically to ensure that he could be detained indefinitely and that his detention could not be challenged in the courts – did not attract more attention at the time? Is it not equally surprising that Australians may know about Merhan Nasseri, but have never heard about Vazquez?

From today's vantage point, the single-mindedness with which the Hawke Government prosecuted the Vazquez case may also come as a surprise, given that the dictum 'we decide who comes to this country and the circumstances under which they come' is nowadays mostly traced back to

---

52 Jennie Curtin, 'Jail is the Only Place that will take Deportee', *Sydney Morning Herald*, 10 July 1991.

53 Janet Fife-Yeomans, 'Globetrotter Deportee on Food Strike', *Sydney Morning Herald*, 11 September 1991.

John Howard's pitch to voters during the 2001 federal election campaign, and the origins of Australia's current border control policies tend to be associated with Hawke's successor Paul Keating, if not, once again, with the Howard Government's response to the arrival of the *Tampa* off Christmas Island. Vazquez's story makes it more difficult to think of current Australian Government policies as an anomaly that began in 2001.

***

All three stories have the potential to unsettle views of the past and the present that are indebted to a notion of history whereby past, present and future are on a linear trajectory, and which assume that there is an inexorable progression along that trajectory.

The past-becomes-the-present-becomes-the-future variety of history privileges pasts that can be seen to form the nucleus of the present. Not only does such history pay scant attention to presumed cul-de-sacs, it is also often content with truncated genealogies that ostensibly suffice to establish how the present came into being. At the end of the day, a history that does *only* that risks becoming an apology of the present. A history that does *only* that makes it harder for us to envisage futures that are not already contained in the present. Some pasts are ostensibly inconsequential in that they did not turn into the present. But these 'dead ends', once rendered as history, might retain some currency. In my previous work about postcolonial histories in Papua New Guinea, I termed accounts of such pasts 'the trash of history'.[54] Such trash can be unwieldy, awkward, even subversive.

In grand narratives that chart Australian history from the *Immigration Restriction Act 1901* via the *Tampa* affair to the creation of the Department of Home Affairs in 2017, or from the arrival of 843 Displaced Persons aboard the *Heintzelman* in 1947 via the resettlement of Indochinese refugees in the late 1970s and early 1980s to the Abbott Government's decision in 2015 to admit an additional 12,000 Syrian and Iraqi refugees,

---

54   Klaus Neumann, 'Starting from Trash', in *Remembrance of Pacific Pasts: An Invitation to Remake Histories*, ed. Robert Borofsky (Honolulu: University of Hawai'i Press, 2000), 62–77, doi.org/10.1515/9780824864163-006.

the Menzies Government's invitation to the Nauruans to settle in Australia, as a group, preserving their 'national pride', with all the rights and privileges of Australian citizens, constitutes precious trash.

The three stories I told could be interpreted as attempts to set the record straight. They could be seen as attempts to point out that in order to understand Australia's response to the refugee crisis in 1938 we ought to focus on Bruce's politicking behind the scenes, rather than White's infamous line; that we ought to be wary of accounts that don't accord agency to the Nauruans; and that deportation policies and practices in the late 1980s and early 1990s may tell us as much about border protection as the introduction of mandatory detention and the *Tampa* affair.

Yet this is not simply an argument for more nuanced accounts. Not least Australia's history wars taught me that a dispute over what happened, based on an interpretation of 'historical evidence', may well be counterproductive – unless it is accompanied by a discussion about what history is, how it produces truth effects, what it is for, who benefits from it and why it is done.[55] When contributing to such a discussion, historians may want to reflect on how they respond to public expectations about the usefulness of their craft. Are they perhaps too readily drawing lessons, explaining the present or writing accounts that could easily be slotted into patriotic narratives of the nation?

Personally, I wish that disputes over what happened – for example, over the precise number of Indigenous people killed by European settlers in Van Diemen's Land – were accompanied by the search for a historical practice that does not shore up the present but that produces histories that are unsettling, disrupting notions of a seamless progression from the status quo ante to the status quo. Such histories may even allow for futures to be imagined that are not yet contained in the present, and which are attentive to pasts that did not culminate in the present.

---

55 This is not the place to revisit the issue of the history wars, during which many of Keith Windschuttle's opponents too readily accepted his premises about how historical truth is produced. See Klaus Neumann, 'Among Historians', *Cultural Studies Review* 9, no. 2 (2003): 177–91.

EPILOGUE

Rachel Stevens and Jordana Silverstein[1]

According to recent United Nations High Commissioner for Refugees (UNHCR) figures, there are currently 70.8 million forcibly displaced people worldwide, a statistic that includes 41.3 million internally displaced people, 25.9 million refugees and 3.5 million asylum seekers.[2] If such people were a country of their own, the nation of the forcibly displaced would be the twenty-first largest country in the world by population size. To put this ranking into context, this nation would be larger than the United Kingdom or France, and just a smidge behind Thailand. Despite the sheer number of refugees in the modern world, discourse and debates surrounding their existence and experiences remains strikingly restricted. The stated purpose of this collection of essays is to open a space for thinking about the histories, presents and futures for refugees and asylum seekers. Through rigorous and accessible analyses, the authors in this volume hope that readers will come away with an appreciation of the multiplicity of refugee stories, which proscribes any simplistic narrative of refugee journeys.

This collection is deliberately designed to bring together the writings of practitioners and academics from different disciplinary backgrounds. The scope of the book is broad, covering the sweep of twentieth and early twenty-first century refugee history, and while focused on Australia, is mindful of international trends and the inherent transnational nature of refugee journeys across national borders. The methodologies and

1   This chapter was written with funding provided by the Australian Research Council Laureate Research Fellowship Project FL140100049, 'Child Refugees and Australian Internationalism from 1920 to the Present'.
2   'Figures at a Glance', UNHCR.org, as at 18 June 2020, available at: www.unhcr.org/en-au/figures-at-a-glance.html.

backgrounds of the authors also vary and include legal scholars, historians, sociologists, journalists and former refugees who have since resettled in Australia. What we have, then, is a collection of diverse accounts tied together by a shared interest in promoting rigorous and accurate public discussions on, with and by refugees. With distinct chapters all telling a specific story, how then can we make sense of this collection? What should readers take away from the essays?

Legal scholars and practitioners Eve Lester (Chapter 1) and Savitri Taylor (Chapter 9) provide us with the complex and essential legal backdrop for understanding the approach of the Australian Government to the resettlement, or exclusion, of refugees and asylum seekers. By outlining the modern refugee protection framework, Lester astutely notes that Australia's approach to refugee resettlement has long been situation specific and highly differentiated. Both the *1951 Refugee Convention* and the *1967 Protocol* were born out of the Cold War and in the shadow of the Holocaust. These historical factors influenced who was defined as a refugee, how they were resettled and on what basis. Lester also observes that the notion that receiving states resettle refugees for purely humanitarian reasons is overly simplistic. Indeed, state actions are mostly guided by utilitarian factors (such as the need for labour or the desire to entrench colonial settlement of Aboriginal land) and geopolitical interests, with the refugee appearing as a 'secondary consideration'. Savitri Taylor, meanwhile, draws our attention to the long legal roots of the mandatory detention regime. With anxieties about migration dating back to the mid-nineteenth century, Australia's colonial founding fathers devised a national constitution that bestowed on the Federal Government absolute authority over matters relating to naturalisation and aliens, and by extension, emigration and immigration. With what Taylor has dubbed the nation's 'original sin', the Constitution has allowed politicians from both major parties to withstand some juridical challenges to the legality of detaining asylum seekers. Some may wonder: how on earth is the indefinite offshore detention of people seeking asylum *legal*? Well, in this case, domestic constitutional law overrides international law (and moral expectations), granting the nation's political leaders a legal defence to imprison indefinitely refugees on Pacific islands.

One of the important contributions this collection makes is that the experiences of former refugees are provided space. As we mentioned in the introduction, so much ink is used writing *about* refugees; it is vitally important that academic works allow room for refugees to speak for themselves. In this volume we work towards that, often going partway with a researcher as intermediary. Melanie Baak (Chapter 2) explores what it means in Australia to be labelled a refugee and if one can ever shed this descriptor. While some refugees of European backgrounds can potentially vanish into whiteness, and thus maybe enjoy all the privileges this entails, refugees who are visibly different often remain haunted by the label and stereotyped as someone in deficit and in need of assistance. Baak argues that we should 'rehumanise' refugees by hearing their stories in all their complexity, and through this, repair broken dignity. In Chapter 7, *Behind the Wire* journalist André Dao joins narrator Jamila Jafari to reflect on the unique benefits and challenges of creating a multi-platform oral history project for public consumption. Rather than being relegated to an object to be analysed, the *Behind the Wire* team explicitly maintain the subjectivity and agency of their narrators. In this 'behind the scenes' examination of the processes involved in creating refugee stories, Jafari acknowledges the tension between wanting to share her story but not wanting to share *too much*. Laurel Mackenzie (Chapter 8) continues this exploration by discussing the narratives of three Hazara refugees, living in Dandenong, south-east of Melbourne. The Hazaras represent one of the country's newest migrant communities, but beyond community circles, little is known of their experiences of fleeing Afghanistan. Mackenzie demonstrates that Salmi, Hassan and Jahan understand their journey through the prism of their family. Rather than focusing on individual perspectives, these Hazaras stress the importance of securing safety for all family members and the devastation that is felt when families remain separated.

The flipside to any discussion about the experiences of refugees is an examination of perceptions of refugees. Two chapters in this book unpack how refugees are portrayed and, importantly, who benefits from such depictions. Ann-Kathrin Bartels (Chapter 4) examines media portrayals of asylum seekers in West Germany during the 1980s. With the dissolution of Yugoslavia and collapse of communism throughout Eastern Europe, West Germany rapidly became a major recipient country of immigrants, ushering in a period of heightened tensions surrounding national identity and xenophobia. Bartels argues that public debates around asylum seekers are driven by the politics of fear and (racially defined) notions of nationhood. These drivers help create a perception of threat, whether that be over jobs, standards of living, values or culture. These forces are presently at play throughout Western Europe and even

Scandinavian countries, once considered the bedrock of liberalism and tolerance of marginalised others. Kathleen Blair (Chapter 6) also considers the political and electoral gains politicians seek by scapegoating asylum seekers in Australia. Looking at three federal election campaigns in 1977, 2001 and 2013, Blair documents the remarkable consistency in the derogatory language employed to describe asylum seekers. While terms such as 'queue jumper' and 'bogus asylum seeker' have been in the political discourse for over 40 years, what is new is the effectiveness such rhetoric has on shaping electoral outcomes.

Lastly, three chapters in this collection seek to challenge existing orthodoxies in refugee histories. Jordana Silverstein's chapter on Australian imaginings of Vietnamese and Timorese child refugees in the 1970s and 1980s draws our attention to the ways in which categorisation itself is a problematic process (Chapter 3). When so much public discourse has been focused on releasing children from detention, Silverstein's chapter presents a sharp reminder of how bureaucracies seek to control children and silence them as well. Her reflections on the ethics of accessing sensitive welfare case notes on children – who by now would only be in middle age – is an important reminder to historians that even declassified government archives contain material that may cause harm. In Chapter 5, Rachel Stevens considers Australian responses to the East Pakistani refugee crisis in 1971, an event largely forgotten by those outside of South Asian communities. Although it is widely acknowledged that history writing is a highly selective process, Stevens asks: Why is it that some atrocities (and the ensuing exodus of people) are remembered and memorialised while others are forgotten? Do we only write about and remember the migrations in which the refugees resettled in the West? Does the refugee need to have some impact on *us* if we are to acknowledge them? In the final chapter, Klaus Neumann (Chapter 10) extends this reflection on historical practice, challenging us to avoid the temptation of trying to make lessons out of the past or forcibly create a linear narrative to understand our current world. Instead, Neumann argues, we should produce histories that are unsettling, and even unwieldy, as this is how we can imagine futures not yet contained in the present.

The 10 chapters in this collection cover much ground but they are connected by a single theme: resistance. In terms of the representations of refugees, we encourage readers to challenge stereotypes and ways of categorising groups of people. With refugee policies, we hope readers find in this volume a nuanced understanding of the legal apparatus that enable policies of mandatory detention to continue, and with this knowledge, be empowered to challenge the legal foundations of the refugee detention regime. We also encourage readers to resist the dehumanisation of refugees and provide ample space for refugees and former refugees to tell their stories, in all of their messy complexity. There needs to be an appreciation that their refugee journey is just one part of their lived experience.

What we have, then, is a collection of essays that provoke thought, challenge assumptions and defy neat narratives. We are also left wondering, almost inevitably, what is next? It is here that we find ourselves often stuck. If many of the origins of refugee movements are caused by state actions, how can the solution also lie with state actors? If mobility is a human reality, why do states remain in perpetual opposition to the refugee journey? We don't pretend to offer the answers, but we do hope to prompt more questions and engage in more conversation.

SELECT BIBLIOGRAPHY

Adichie, Chimamanda Ngozi. 'The Danger of a Single Story'. Talk presented at TEDGlobal 2009. Available at: www.ted.com/talks/chimamanda_adichie_the _danger_of_a_single_story/transcript.

Ahluwalia, Pal. 'When Does a Settler Become a Native? Citizenship and Identity in a Settler Society'. *Pretexts: Literary and Cultural Studies* 10, no. 1 (2001): 63–73. doi.org/10.1080/713692599.

Ang, Ien and Jon Stratton. 'Multiculturalism in Crisis: The New Politics of Race and National Identity in Australia'. *TOPIA: Canadian Journal of Cultural Studies* 2 (1998): 22–41. doi.org/10.3138/topia.2.22.

Arendt, Hannah. 'We Refugees'. In *Altogether Elsewhere: Writers on Exile*, edited by M Robinson. Boston: Faber and Faber, 1994.

Baak, Melanie. 'Murder, Community Talk and Belonging: An Exploration of Sudanese Community Responses to Murder in Australia'. *African Identities* 9, no. 4 (2011): 417–34. doi.org/10.1080/14725843.2011.614415.

Baak, Melanie. *Negotiating Belongings: Stories of Forced Migration of Dinka Women from South Sudan.* Rotterdam: Sense Publishers, 2016. doi.org/10.1007/978-94-6300-588-3.

Baak, Melanie, Emily Miller, A Sullivan and Kathleen Heugh. 'Improving Educational Outcomes for Students from Refugee Backgrounds in the South Australian Certificate of Education Project: A Case Study of Two Catholic Schools'. University of South Australia, 2018. Available at: apo.org.au/node/136916.

Bakewell, Oliver. 'Research Beyond the Categories: The Importance of Policy Irrelevant Research into Forced Migration'. *Journal of Refugee Studies* 21, no. 4 (2008): 432–53. doi.org/10.1093/jrs/fen042.

Banivanua Mar, Tracey. *Decolonisation and the Pacific: Indigenous Globalisation and the Ends of Empire.* Cambridge: Cambridge University Press, 2016. doi.org/10.1017/cbo9781139794688.

Bartrop, Paul R. *The Evian Conference of 1938 and the Jewish Refugee Crisis.* Cham, Switzerland: Palgrave Macmillan, 2018.

Bashir, Bashir and Amos Goldberg. 'Deliberating the Holocaust and the Nakba: Disruptive Empathy and Binationalism in Israel/Palestine'. *Journal of Genocide Research* 16, no. 1 (2014): 77–99. doi.org/10.1080/14623528.2014.878114.

Bates, Laura, Diane Baird, Deborah J Johnson, Robert E Lee, Tom Luster and Christine Rehagen. 'Sudanese Refugee Youth in Foster Care: The "Lost Boys" in America'. *Child Welfare Journal* 84, no. 5 (2005): 631–48.

Bauman, Zygmunt. *Wasted Lives: Modernity and its Outcasts.* John Wiley & Sons, 2013.

Bird, Greta. 'An Unlawful Non-Citizen Is Being Detained or (White) Citizens Are Saving the Nation from (Non White) Non-Citizens'. *University of Western Sydney Law Review* 9 (2005): 87–110.

Bleiker, Roland, David Campbell, Emma Hutchison and Xzarina Nicholson. 'The Visual Dehumanisation of Refugees'. *Australian Journal of Political Science* 48, no. 4 (2013): 398–416. doi.org/10.1080/10361146.2013.840769.

Bloch, Alice and Shirin Hirsch. '"Second Generation" Refugees and Multilingualism: Identity, Race and Language Transmission'. *Ethnic and Racial Studies* 40, no. 14 (2017): 2444–62. doi.org/10.1080/01419870.2016. 1252461.

Boochani, Behrouz. 'A Letter from Manus Island'. *Saturday Paper.* 9 December 2017. Available at: www.thesaturdaypaper.com.au/news/politics/2017/12/09/ letter-manus-island/15127380005617.

Boochani, Behrouz. *No Friend but the Mountains: Writing from Manus Prison.* Translated by Omid Tofighian. Sydney: Picador, 2018.

Bose, Sarmila. *Dead Reckoning: Memories of the 1971 Bangladesh War.* London: Hurst Publishers, 2011.

Brough, Mark, Don Gorman, Elvia Ramirez and Peter Westoby. 'Young Refugees Talk About Well-Being: A Qualitative Analysis of Refugee Mental Health from Three States'. *Australian Journal of Social Issues* 38, no. 2 (2003): 193–208. doi.org/10.1002/j.1839-4655.2003.tb01142.x.

Butler, Judith. *Frames of War: When Is Life Grievable?* 2nd ed. London: Verso, 2010.

Chimni, B S. 'The Birth of a "Discipline": From Refugee to Forced Migration Studies'. *Journal of Refugee Studies* 22, no. 1 (2009): 11–29. doi.org/10.1093/ jrs/fen051.

Colic-Peisker, Val. '"At Least You're the Right Colour": Identity and Social Inclusion of Bosnian Refugees in Australia'. *Journal of Ethnic and Migration Studies* 31, no. 4 (2005): 615–38. doi.org/10.1080/13691830500109720.

Colic-Peisker, Val. 'The "Visibly Different" Refugees in the Australian Labour Market: Settlement Policies and Employment Realities'. In *Refugees, Recent Migrants and Employment: Challenging Barriers and Exploring Pathways*, edited by S McKay. New York: Routledge, 2009. doi.org/10.4324/9780203890745.

Crock, Mary. *Seeking Asylum Alone: A Study of Australian Law, Policy and Practice Regarding Unaccompanied and Separated Children*. Sydney: Federation Press, 2006.

Crock, Mary and Laurie Berg. *Immigration, Refugees and Forced Migration: Law, Policy and Practice in Australia*. Sydney: Federation Press, 2011.

Damousi, Joy. 'The Campaign for Japanese-Australian Children to enter Australia, 1957–1968: A History of Post-War Humanitarianism'. *Australian Journal of Politics and History* 64, no. 2 (2018): 211–26. doi.org/10.1111/ajph.12461.

Dellios, Alexandra. *Histories of Controversy: The Bonegilla Migrant Centre*. Melbourne: Melbourne University Press, 2017.

Dhanji, Surjeet. 'Welcome of Unwelcome? Integration Issues and the Resettlement of Former Refugees from the Horn of Africa and Sudan in Metropolitan Melbourne'. *The Australasian Review of African Studies* 30, no. 2 (2009): 152–78.

Due, Clemence. '"Who Are Strangers?": "Absorbing" Sudanese Refugees into a White Australia'. *ACRAWSA E-Journal* 4, no. 1. (2008). Available at: acrawsa. org.au/wp-content/uploads/2017/12/CRAWS-Vol-4-No-1-2008-1.pdf.

Fawcett, Bill, ed. *Doomed to Repeat: The Lessons of History We've Failed to Learn*. New York: William Morrow, 2013.

Gatrell, Peter. 'Refugees – What's Wrong with History?' *Journal of Refugee Studies* 30, no. 2 (2017): 170–89. doi.org/10.1093/jrs/few013.

Gatrell, Peter and Liubov Zhvanko, eds. *Europe on the Move: Refugees in the Era of the Great War*. Manchester: Manchester University Press, 2017.

Gordon, Avery F. *Ghostly Matters: Hauntings and the Sociological Imagination*. Minneapolis: University of Minnesota Press, 2008.

Gray, Benjamin. 'Citizenship as Barrier and Opportunity for Ancient Greek and Modern Refugees'. *Humanities* 7, no. 3 (2018): 72. doi.org/10.3390/h7030072.

Gray, Benjamin. 'Exile, Refuge and the Greek Polis: Between Justice and Humanity'. *Journal of Refugee Studies* 30, no. 2 (2017): 190–219. doi.org/10.1093/jrs/few027.

Green, Michael and André Dao, eds. *They Cannot Take the Sky: Stories from Detention*. Crows Nest, NSW: Allen & Unwin, 2017.

Guldi, Jo and David Armitage. *The History Manifesto*. Cambridge: Cambridge University Press, 2014.

Hahn, Hans Henning and Eva Hahn. 'Nationale Stereotypen. Plädoyer für eine historische Stereotypenforschung'. In *Stereotyp, Identität und Geschichte. Die Funktion von Stereotypen in gesellschaftlichen Diskursen*, edited by Hans Henning Hahn, 17–56. Frankfurt: Peter Lang, 2002.

Halpern, Jodi and Harvey M Weinstein. 'Rehumanizing the Other: Empathy and Reconciliation'. *Human Rights Quarterly* 26, no. 3 (2004): 561–83. doi.org/10.1353/hrq.2004.0036.

Higgins, Claire. *Asylum by Boat: Origins of Australia's Refugee Policy*. Sydney: NewSouth Publishing, 2017.

Hyndman, Jennifer. *Managing Displacement: Refugees and the Politics of Humanitarianism*. Minneapolis: University of Minnesota Press, 2000.

Ignatieff, Michael. 'The Refugee as Invasive Other'. *Social Research: An International Quarterly* 84, no. 1 (2017): 223–31.

Jupp, James. 'From "White Australia" to "Part of Asia": Recent Shifts in Australian Immigration Policy Towards the Region'. *International Migration Review* 29, no. 1 (1995): 207–28. doi.org/10.2307/2547002.

Jupp, James. *From White Australia to Woomera: The Story of Australian Immigration*. Melbourne: Cambridge University Press, 2002. doi.org/10.1017/cbo9781139195034.

Jupp, James. *Immigration*. 2nd ed. Melbourne: Oxford University Press, 1998.

Kevin, Catherine and Karen Agutter. 'The "Unwanteds" and "Non-Compliants": "Unsupported Mothers" as "Failures" and Agents in Australia's Migrant Holding Centres'. *The History of the Family* 22, no. 4 (2017): 554–74. doi.org/10.1080/1081602X.2017.1302891.

Kremp, Herbert. 'Preußische Tugenden', *Welt*, 2001. Available at: www.welt.de/print-welt/article431886/Preussische-Tugenden.html.

Kumsa, Martha Kuwee. '"No! I'm Not a Refugee!" The Poetics of Be-Longing among Young Oromos in Toronto'. *Journal of Refugee Studies* 19, no. 2 (2006): 230–55. doi.org/10.1093/jrs/fel001.

Kushner, Tony. *Remembering Refugees: Then and Now*. Manchester: Manchester University Press, 2006.

Lester, Eve. *Making Migration Law: The Foreigner, Sovereignty, and the Case of Australia*. Cambridge: Cambridge University Press, 2018.

Limbu, Bishupal. 'Illegible Humanity: The Refugee, Human Rights and the Question of Representation'. *Journal of Refugee Studies* 22, no. 3 (2009): 257–82. doi.org/10.1093/jrs/fep021.

Ludwig, Bernadette. '"Wiping the Refugee Dust from My Feet": Advantages and Burdens of Refugee Status and the Refugee Label'. *International Migration* 54, no. 1 (2016): 5–18. doi.org/10.1111/imig.12111.

Lueck, Kerstin, Clemence Due and Martha Augoustinos. 'Neoliberalism and Nationalism: Representations of Asylum Seekers in the Australian Mainstream News Media'. *Discourse & Society* 26, no. 5 (2015): 608–29. doi.org/10.1177/0957926515581159.

Mackenzie, Laurel and Olivia Guntarik. 'Rites of Passage: Experiences of Transition for Forced Hazara Migrants and Refugees in Australia'. *Crossings: Journal of Migration & Culture* 6, no. 1 (2015): 59–80. doi.org/10.1386/cjmc.6.1.59_1.

Malkki, Liisa H. 'National Geographic: The Rooting of Peoples and the Territorialization of National Identity among Scholars and Refugees'. In *Culture, Power Place: Explorations in Critical Anthropology*, edited by Akhil Gupta and James Ferguson, 52–74. Durham, NC: Duke University Press, 1997. doi.org/10.1215/9780822382089-002.

Malkki, Liisa H. *Purity and Exile: Violence, Memory, and National Cosmology among Hutu Refugees in Tanzania*. Chicago: The University of Chicago Press, 1995. doi.org/10.7208/chicago/9780226190969.001.0001.

Malkki, Liisa H. 'Refugees and Exile: From "Refugee Studies" to the National Order of Things'. *Annual Review of Anthropology* 24 (1995): 495–523. doi.org/10.1146/annurev.an.24.100195.002431.

Malkki, Liisa H. 'Speechless Emissaries: Refugees, Humanitarianism, and Dehistoricization'. *Cultural Anthropology* 11, no. 3 (1996): 377–404. doi.org/10.1525/can.1996.11.3.02a00050.

Mares, Peter. *Not Quite Australian: How Temporary Migration is Changing the Nation*. Melbourne: Text Publishing, 2016.

Marlowe, Jay M. 'Beyond the Discourse of Trauma: Shifting the Focus on Sudanese Refugees'. *Journal of Refugee Studies* 23, no. 2 (2010): 183–98. doi.org/10.1093/jrs/feq013.

McBrien, J Lynn. 'Educational Needs and Barriers for Refugee Students in the United States: A Review of the Literature'. *Review of Educational Research* 75, no. 3 (2005): 329–64. doi.org/10.3102/00346543075003329.

McKinnon, Sara L. 'Unsettling Resettlement: Promblematizing "Lost Boys of Sudan" Resettlement and Identity'. *Western Journal of Communication* 72, no. 4 (2008): 397–414. doi.org/10.1080/10570310802446056.

McMaster, Don. 'Resettled Refugees: Temporary Protection Visas: Obstructing Refugee Livelihoods'. *Refugee Survey Quarterly* 25, no. 2 (2006): 135–45. doi.org/10.1093/rsq/hdi0131.

McPhail, Ken, Robert Nyamori and Savitri Taylor. 'Escaping Accountability: A Case of Australia's Asylum Seeker Policy'. *Accounting, Auditing & Accountability Journal* 29 (2016): 947–84. dx.doi.org/10.1108/AAAJ-03-2014-1639.

Miller, Emily, Tahereh Ziaian and Adrian Esterman. 'Australian School Practices and the Education Experiences of Students with a Refugee Background: A Review of the Literature'. *International Journal of Inclusive Education* (2017): 1–21. doi.org/10.1080/13603116.2017.1365955.

Moreton-Robinson, Aileen. *The White Possessive: Property, Power, and Indigenous Sovereignty*. Minneapolis: University of Minnesota Press, 2015. doi.org/10.5749/minnesota/9780816692149.001.0001.

Neumann, Klaus. *Across the Seas: Australia's Response to Refugees: A History*. Collingwood: Black Inc., 2015.

Neumann, Klaus. 'Among Historians'. *Cultural Studies Review* 9, no. 2 (2003): 177–91. doi.org/10.5130/csr.v9i2.3571.

Neumann, Klaus. 'Oblivious to the Obvious? Australian Asylum-Seeker Policies and the Use of the Past'. In *Does History Matter? Making and Debating Citizenship, Immigration and Refugee Policy in Australia and New Zealand*, edited by Klaus Neumann and Gwenda Tavan, 47–64. Canberra: ANU E Press, 2009. doi.org/10.22459/dhm.09.2009.03.

Neumann, Klaus. '"Our Own Interests Must Come First": Australia's Response to the Expulsion of Asians from Uganda'. *History Australia* 3, no. 1 (2006): 10.1–10.17. doi.org/10.2104/ha060010.

Neumann, Klaus. 'Providing a "Home for the Oppressed"? Historical Perspectives on Australian Responses to Refugees'. *Australian Journal of Human Rights* 9, no. 2 (2003): 1–25. doi.org/10.1080/1323238X.2003.11911103.

Neumann, Klaus. *Refuge Australia: Australia's Humanitarian Record*. Sydney: UNSW Press, 2004.

Neumann, Klaus. 'Starting from Trash'. In *Remembrance of Pacific Pasts: An Invitation to Remake Histories*, edited by Robert Borofsky, 62–77. Honolulu: University of Hawai'i Press, 2000. doi.org/10.1515/9780824864163-006.

Neumann, Klaus and Sandra M Gifford. 'Producing Knowledge About Refugee Settlement in Australia'. In *Critical Reflections on Migration, 'Race' and Multiculturalism*, edited by Martina Boese and Vince Marotta, 120–36. London: Routledge, 2017. doi.org/10.4324/9781315645124-7.

Neumann, Klaus and Savitri Taylor. '"He has to Take his Chances": The Resettlement of a Refugee in Australia and his Deportation to the Country he had Fled, 1980–1992'. *History Australia* 16, no. 3 (2019): 459–79. doi.org/10.1080/14490854.2019.1636672.

O'Hanlon, Seamus and Rachel Stevens. 'A Nation of Immigrants or a Nation of Immigrant Cities? The Urban Context of Australian Multiculturalism'. *Australian Journal of Politics and History* 63, no. 4 (2017): 556–71. doi.org/10.1111/ajph.12403.

Ong, Aihwa. *Buddha is Hiding: Refugees, Citizenship, the New America*. Berkeley: University of California Press, 2003.

Persian, Jayne. *Beautiful Balts: From Displaced Persons to New Australians*. Sydney: NewSouth Publishing, 2017.

Phillips, Melissa. 'Convenient Labels, Inaccurate Representations: Turning Southern Sudanese Refugees Into "African-Australians"'. *Australasian Review of African Studies* 32, no. 2 (2011): 57–79.

Rajaram, Prem Kumar. 'Humanitarianism and Representations of the Refugee'. *Journal of Refugee Studies* 15, no. 3 (2002): 247–64. doi.org/10.1093/jrs/15.3.247.

Ramsay, Georgina. 'Central African Refugee Women Resettled in Australia: Colonial Legacies and the Civilising Process'. *Journal of Intercultural Studies* 38, no. 2 (2017): 170–88. doi.org/10.1080/07256868.2017.1289904.

Ryu, Minjung and Mavreen Rose S Tuvilla. 'Resettled Refugee Youths' Stories of Migration, Schooling, and Future: Challenging Dominant Narratives About Refugees'. *The Urban Review* (2018): 1–20. doi.org/10.1007/s11256-018-0455-z.

Saxton, Alison. '"I Certainly Don't Want People Like That Here": The Discursive Construction of "Asylum Seekers"'. *Media International Australia* 109, no. 1 (2003): 109–20. doi.org/10.1177/1329878X0310900111.

Schrover, Marlou and Willem Schinkel. 'Introduction: The Language of Inclusion and Exclusion in the Context of Immigration and Integration'. *Ethnic and Racial Studies* 36, no. 7 (2013): 1123–41. doi.org/10.1080/01419870.2013.783711.

Silverstein, Jordana. '"The Beneficent and Legal Godfather": A History of the Guardianship of Unaccompanied Immigrant and Refugee Children in Australia, 1946–1975'. *The History of the Family* 22, no. 4 (2017): 446–65. doi.org/10.1080/1081602X.2016.1265572.

Silverstein, Jordana. '"I Am Responsible": Histories of the Intersection of the Guardianship of Unaccompanied Child Refugees and the Australian Border'. *Cultural Studies Review* 22, no. 2 (September 2016): 65–89. doi.org/10.5130/csr.v22i2.4772.

Soguk, Nevzat. *States and Strangers: Refugees and Displacements of Statecraft.* Minneapolis: University of Minnesota Press, 1999.

Stevens, Rachel. *Immigration Policy from 1970 to the Present.* New York: Routledge, 2016.

Stevens, Rachel. 'Political Debates on Asylum Seekers during the Fraser Government, 1977–1982'. *Australian Journal of Politics and History* 58, no. 4 (2012): 526–41. doi.org/10.1111/j.1467-8497.2012.01651.x.

Strang, Alison and Alastair Ager. 'Refugee Integration: Emerging Trends and Remaining Agendas'. *Journal of Refugee Studies* 23, no. 4 (2010): 589–607. doi.org/10.1093/jrs/feq046.

Swain, Shurlee. 'Beyond Child Migration: Inquiries, Apologies and the Implications for the Writing of a Transnational Child Welfare History'. *History Australia* 13, no. 1 (2016): 139–52. doi.org/10.1080/14490854.2016.1156212.

Tavan, Gwenda. 'The Dismantling of the White Australia Policy: Elite Conspiracy or Will of the Australian People?' *Australian Journal of Political Science* 39, no. 1 (2004): 109–25. doi.org/10.1080/1036114042000205678.

Taylor, Savitri. 'Achieving Reform of Australian Asylum Seeker Law and Policy'. *Just Policy* 24 (2001): 41–54.

Taylor, Savitri. 'Australia's Pacific Solution Mark II: The Lessons to be Learned'. *UTS Law Review* 9 (2007): 106–24.

Taylor, Savitri. 'Immigration Detention Reforms: A Small Gain in Human Rights'. *Agenda: A Journal of Policy Analysis and Reform* 13 (2006): 49–62. doi.org/10.22459/AG.13.01.2006.04.

Taylor, Savitri. 'The Pacific Solution or a Pacific Nightmare: The Difference between Burden Shifting and Responsibility Sharing'. *Asian-Pacific Law and Policy Journal* 6 (2005): 1–43.

Taylor, Savitri. 'Towing Back the Boats: Bad Policy Whatever Way You Look at It'. *The Conversation*. 12 June 2013. Available at: theconversation.com/towing-back-the-boats-bad-policy-whatever-way-you-look-at-it-15082.

Wills, Sara. 'Between the Hostel and the Detention Centre: Possible Trajectories of Migrant Pain and Shame in Australia'. In *Places of Pain and Shame: Dealing with 'Difficult Heritage'*, edited by William Logan and Keir Reeves, 263–80. Florence: Taylor and Francis, 2008. doi.org/10.4324/9780203885031.

Zetter, Roger. 'Labelling Refugees: Forming and Transforming a Bureaucratic Identity'. *Journal of Refugee Studies* 4, no. 1 (1991): 39–62. doi.org/10.1093/jrs/4.1.39.

Zetter, Roger. 'More Labels, Fewer Refugees: Remaking the Refugee Label in an Era of Globalization'. *Journal of Refugee Studies* 20, no. 2 (2007): 172–92. doi.org/10.1093/jrs/fem011.

Zetter, Roger. 'Refugees and Refugee Studies – A Label and an Agenda'. *Journal of Refugee Studies* 1, no. 1 (1988): 1–6. doi.org/10.1093/jrs/1.1.1.

www.ingramcontent.com/pod-product-compliance
Lightning Source LLC
Chambersburg PA
CBHW040820280326
41926CB00093B/4628